ASSERT YOURSELF!

Harnessing the Power of Assertiveness in Your Career

RAE A. STONEHOUSE

Live For Excellence Productions

COPYRIGHT

ISBN - E-book: 978-1-998813-39-1

ISBN – Paperback: 978-1-998813-38-4

ISBN – Audiobook: 978-1-998813-37-7

INTRODUCTION

Are you looking to enhance your interpersonal skills, build stronger relationships, and gain the respect you deserve? Look no further than Assert Yourself!, Harnessing the Power of Assertiveness in Your Career a transformative book designed to empower you with the tools and techniques of responsible assertive behavior.

Respect is at the heart of assertiveness, and this training focuses on two crucial parts: respecting yourself and honoring the needs and rights of others. By mastering assertiveness, you can establish meaningful connections, protect yourself from being taken advantage of, and make confident decisions that align with your values.

My goal is to help you achieve anxiety reduction and develop essential social skills. With assertiveness, you can express a wide range of thoughts and emotions, both positive and negative, without guilt or excessive anxiety. This training not only builds on your existing abilities, but also equips you with new verbal and nonverbal communication skills, expanding your repertoire for effective interpersonal interactions.

Responsible assertive behavior promotes direct, honest communication and mutual respect. It creates a foundation for fair play, equal exchange, and compromise when conflicting needs and rights arise. Worried about hurting others' feelings? The content of this book reduces this risk, as those who feel hurt may be overly sensitive or trying to manipulate you. It's time to focus on your own needs and rights while maintaining compassion for others.

By embracing responsible assertion, you unlock a world of personal growth and enriched relationships. You gain self-respect and earn the respect of others as you stand up for yourself and make your voice heard. No longer will you sacrifice your rights or let others take advantage of you. Instead, you'll assertively express how their behavior affects you, granting them the opportunity to make positive changes.

I wish this book had been available when I was in the formative years of my career. I had to learn about assertiveness the hard way. Some may call it the School of Hard Knocks. There is a saying in psychology "if the only tool you have in your toolbox is a hammer... Then every problem is a nail."

My hammers were aggression and passive aggression. They worked for me until they didn't.

My first career was in dietary. I wanted to be a chef. My lack of interpersonal skills and communication skills resulted in downward promotions. I went from preparing food, to the dishwasher and finally to the pot washer. As a 19-year-old I was working with coworkers and supervisors 30 and 40 years my superior. And many were jaded and cynical.

Emulating their behaviors and performance was not a good career enhancing practice.

After two years in a community college, I qualified as a registered nurse. I started off working in medical nursing and after three years transitioned into mental health/psychiatry.

When it came to thinking and behaving assertively, this is where a big "aha" moment came for me. I was now working in a field that was predominantly women. Some 98% of healthcare workers are female.

My aggressive and passive-aggressive behaviour no longer worked. Now to clarify this point, those behaviours of mine didn't work because many of my fellow nurses were using the same behaviours.

I recall one workplace where two nurses had a disagreement ten years ago. The incident was still fresh in both of their minds. Neither of them would work with each other. If they were scheduled to work with the other, one would book off sick rather than do so. It seemed like a race sometimes to see who would be the first to book off sick. It was a strained work setting for their coworkers when neither of these two nurses would communicate with each other.

As a token male in a female profession I often held different perspectives to situations than my female counterparts did. I was held to their standards. One example being if I didn't cry over a particular sad situation, I was considered insensitive and non-caring. I had crying knocked out of me before I was four years old. "Big boys don't cry!"

I was several years into my career as a mental health nurse and undertook a postgraduate course in psychiatric nursing. This exposed me to different modalities to aid me in being an effective mental health therapist. Assertive skill development was one of them.

When working as a therapist with my patients I often found that lack of assertiveness was at the root of their interpersonal relationships, often causing increased stress and anxiety and often leading to a psychiatric hospital admission. Laypeople may call this having a nervous breakdown. In reality there is no such thing. Your nerves don't break down.

Even the few assertive skills I taught them in the short time we were together proved beneficial for many.

I wrote this book because I still believe there is a great need for the development of assertive skills, whether you are developing and advancing through your career or in non-work related situations.

Remember, self-care and self-respect are essential parts of a fulfilling life. By focusing on your well-being and understanding your own needs, you become better equipped to nourish and support others. It's time to embrace your true self, appreciating your strengths and weaknesses, and cultivating a deep sense of self-liking and comfort.

Take the first step toward personal and professional empowerment. Join me on a journey toward self-discovery, enhanced communication, and fulfilling relationships helped with through the pages of this book. Invest in yourself and watch as your newfound assertiveness transforms every part of your life.

As I have with my other self-help, personal/professional development books I have taken an iterative approach. The content often takes material previously presented and takes it in a different direction. This helps to build your understanding of assertiveness.

Throughout this book you will be presented with practical exercises. You can't learn to be assertive by osmosis. You must try the exercises, assess your results and adapt them for the next time. Self-confidence is built incrementally. Small successes can lead to big successes.

Assertiveness is standing up for personal rights and expressing thoughts, feelings and beliefs in direct and honest ways, without denying the rights of others. It involves getting across a message such as:

- This is what I think
- This is how I feel, or
- This is how I see the situation.

Are you ready to be assertive in your career and in your personal life?

Rae A. Stonehouse Author

July 2023

ASSERTIVENESS IN THE BUSINESS WORLD

E ffective communication is a fundamental skill in the business world, crucial to achieving success and accomplishing organizational goals. Among different communication styles, assertiveness stands out as a powerful approach that enables individuals to express their thoughts, needs, and concerns while considering the perspectives of others. In this chapter, we will delve into the definition and idea of assertiveness, highlighting its distinction from aggression and passivity. We will explore the significance of assertive communication in achieving business goals.

Understanding Assertiveness:

Assertiveness is a communication style characterized by expressing oneself confidently, directly, and respectfully, without violating the rights of others. It involves striking a fair balance between self-advocacy and consideration for others, ensuring both parties feel heard and respected. Assertive individuals skillfully communicate their ideas, opinions, and desires while acknowledging and valuing alternative viewpoints.

. . .

Differentiating Assertiveness, Aggression, and Passivity:

To comprehend the true essence of assertiveness, it is essential to contrast it with aggression and passivity. Aggression often involves forceful, hostile behavior aimed at overpowering others' opinions or needs. It disregards the rights and perspectives of others, leading to conflicts and strained relationships. But passivity refers to a communication style where individuals fail to express their thoughts, needs, or desires effectively. Passivity often stems from fear of confrontation and leads to missed opportunities and unmet goals. Assertiveness, however, emphasizes open and honest communication while fostering mutual understanding and collaboration.

The Importance of Assertive Communication in Achieving Business Goals:

Assertive communication plays a vital role in the business world and significantly contributes to achieving organizational goals. Below are key reasons why assertiveness is crucial:

Building Strong Relationships:

Assertive communication fosters trust, respect, and transparency within business relationships. By clearly expressing thoughts and expectations, individuals can create open lines of communication, paving the way for effective collaboration and problem-solving.

Enhancing Decision-Making:

In an assertive communication environment, individuals are encouraged to voice divergent opinions and perspectives. This helps with a more comprehensive evaluation of ideas, leading to informed decision-making and innovative solutions.

Conflict Resolution:

Conflict is inevitable in any business setting. However, an assertive communication style helps to manage conflicts constructively. By addressing concerns directly and respectfully, assertive individuals can seek resolutions that satisfy all parties involved, reducing the negative impact of conflicts.

Strengthening Leadership:

Effective leaders exemplify assertive communication, inspiring those around them to adopt a similar approach. By modeling assertiveness, leaders encourage their teams to express ideas and concerns, fostering a culture of openness, trust, and continuous improvement.

Negotiation and Influence:

In business, negotiation is a frequent occurrence. Assertiveness equips individuals with the ability to clearly articulate their interests without undermining or dominating others. Such skillful negotiation leads to win-win outcomes and strengthens one's ability to influence stakeholders positively.

Assertiveness manifests as a powerful communication style in the business world and sets the stage for individual and organizational success. By understanding the distinction between assertiveness, aggression, and passivity, professionals can harness the power of assertive communication to build strong relationships, enhance decision-making, resolve conflicts, strengthen leadership skills, and excel in negotiations. Adopting assertiveness as a guiding principle is pivotal in achieving business goals, fostering a culture of open dialogue, and propelling organizations toward growth and prosperity.

THE BENEFITS OF ASSERTIVENESS IN THE WORKPLACE:

In the fast-paced and competitive world of the workplace, assertiveness is a key skill that can bring many benefits to both individuals and teams. Assertiveness involves expressing one's thoughts, feelings, and needs in a confident and respectful manner. By adopting an assertive approach, individuals can contribute to effective teamwork, conflict resolution, and decision-making, thus improving productivity, establishing respect, and fostering a positive work environment.

First, assertiveness plays a crucial role in effective teamwork. By communicating openly and honestly, assertive individuals can express their ideas and suggestions, leading to more robust discussions and a broader range of perspectives. This diversity of thought enables teams to explore creative solutions and make informed decisions. Additionally, assertiveness helps team members to address any conflicts or concerns promptly and constructively, making sure they do not linger and hinder the team's progress. Assertive individuals are more likely to listen actively and respectfully to their teammates' opinions, fostering an environment of trust and collaboration.

Assertiveness contributes to efficient conflict resolution. In any workplace, conflicts are inevitable, and how they are managed can determine the productivity and morale of the team. Assertive individuals confidently and directly address conflicts, without resorting to aggressive or passive-aggressive behaviors. By expressing their concerns and emotions, they enable others to understand their perspectives and work toward a mutually beneficial resolution. This assertive approach avoids any lingering resentment or animosity and paves the way for healthier relationships among team members.

Additionally, assertiveness enhances decision-making processes. When individuals feel comfortable expressing their opinions and contributing to discussions, they offer valuable insights and suggestions. An assertive approach encourages active participation in decision-making, encourages critical thinking, and enables individuals to make informed choices. By speaking up assertively, employees can make sure their input is considered, ultimately leading to better decision outcomes.

Another significant benefit of assertiveness is its impact on productivity. By expressing their needs, boundaries, and concerns assertively, individuals can maintain a healthy work-life balance. Assertiveness lets employees manage their workload effectively, set realistic deadlines, and say no when necessary, reducing stress and preventing burnout. Assertive individuals are more likely to seek clarification or assistance when facing challenges, leading to quicker problem-solving and efficient task completion.

Adopting an assertive approach creates a culture of respect within the workplace. When individuals confidently express their thoughts and needs, they command the attention and respect of their colleagues and superiors. Assertiveness fosters an atmosphere where ideas are heard and valued, despite hierarchical positions. In such an environment, employees feel empowered and appreciated, leading to increased job satisfaction, motivation, and loyalty.

Last, assertiveness contributes to establishing a positive work environment. By communicating assertively, individuals encourage open and honest dialogue. They create a safe space for discussion and constructive feedback, allowing for continuous improvement and personal growth. This positive work environment fosters effective teamwork, boosts morale, and encourages creativity and innovation.

Assertiveness in the workplace has numerous benefits that contribute to effective teamwork, conflict resolution, and decision-making. By adopting an assertive approach, individuals can improve productivity, establish respect, and foster a positive work environment. Encouraging assertiveness within organizations can lead to enhanced communication, collaboration, and overall success.

Overcoming barriers to assertiveness:

Overcoming barriers to assertiveness in the business world can be a challenging task. Many individuals struggle to assert themselves due to various reasons, including fear of conflict, lack of confidence, or societal expectations. However, developing assertiveness skills is crucial for success in the professional realm. In this chapter, we will identify common obstacles that individuals may face and provide strategies and practical tips to help readers overcome these barriers.

Fear of conflict: One of the most significant barriers to assertiveness is the fear of conflict. Many people avoid assertiveness because they fear negative consequences or damaging relationships. To overcome this barrier:

- **Adopt a positive mindset:** Remind yourself that assertiveness is not about creating conflicts, but about expressing your thoughts and needs respectfully.
- **Focus on win-win solutions:** Emphasize finding solutions that benefit both parties by actively listening and seeking common ground.
- **Practice assertiveness techniques:** Role-play different scenarios with a trusted friend or colleague to build confidence in handling potential conflicts.

Lack of confidence: Low self-esteem or lack of self-assurance can hinder assertiveness. To overcome this barrier:

- **Set realistic goals:** Start with small, achievable assertiveness goals and gradually work your way up to more significant challenges.
- **Enhance self-awareness:** Identify your strengths, weaknesses, and areas for improvement to build confidence based on a realistic understanding of your skills.
- **Celebrate successes:** Acknowledge and celebrate your assertive achievements, despite their size, to boost your confidence and reinforce positive behavior.

Societal expectations: Social norms and expectations can discourage assertiveness, particularly for certain genders or cultural backgrounds. To overcome this barrier:

- **Challenge assumptions:** Recognize that everyone has the right to express their opinions and needs, despite social expectations.
- **Seek support:** Find a mentor or coach who can provide guidance and encouragement to help you navigate societal barriers.
- **Educate others:** Raise awareness about the importance of assertiveness and challenge stereotypes by modeling assertive behavior and explaining its benefits.

Lack of communication skills: Inadequate or ineffective communication skills can impede assertiveness. To overcome this barrier:

- **Enhance active listening skills:** Practice attentive listening to understand others' perspectives better and respond appropriately.
- **Learn assertive communication techniques:** Develop skills such as using "I" statements and expressing needs directly and clearly.
- **Seek feedback:** ask for feedback from colleagues or supervisors about your communication style to identify areas for improvement.

Fear of rejection or negative feedback: The fear of being judged, criticized, or rejected can deter individuals from asserting themselves. To overcome this barrier:

- **Embrace vulnerability:** Recognize it is natural to feel vulnerable when asserting yourself and view it as an opportunity for growth.
- **Focus on self-validation**: Develop a sense of self-worth that is not dependent on others' approval. Remember that everyone has different opinions, and not all feedback should be taken personally.
- **Practice self-care:** Engage in activities that boost your self-esteem and resilience, such as exercise, meditation, or personal hobbies.

Assertiveness is a vital skill in the business world, and overcoming barriers to assertiveness is essential for professional growth. By identifying common obstacles and implementing strategies and practical tips, individuals can develop their assertiveness skills and enhance their effectiveness in the workplace. Remember that assertiveness is a journey, and consistent practice and perseverance will lead to significant improvements.

Techniques For Assertive Communication:

Assertive communication is a valuable skill that individuals can develop to express themselves effectively, stand up for their rights, and maintain positive relationships. Using certain techniques, people can communicate assertively without being aggressive or passive. Here are effective techniques for assertive communication:

"I" Statements: Using "I" statements lets individuals express their thoughts, feelings, and needs in a non-confrontational way. Instead of blaming or accusing, focus on explaining how a certain situation affects you personally. For example, instead of saying, "You never consider my ideas," try saying, "I feel frustrated when my ideas are not considered."

Active Listening: Active listening involves paying full attention to the speaker, understanding their message, and responding appropriately. It includes maintaining eye contact, nodding, summarizing, and asking clarifying questions. By actively listening, you show respect and create an open dialogue, fostering a more assertive communication style.

Positive Body Language: Non-verbal cues play a crucial role in assertive communication. Project confidence with an upright posture, open gestures, and facial expressions. Maintain a proper personal space and make eye contact without staring. These actions communicate attentiveness, confidence, and openness.

Clear and Concise Communication: Being clear and concise helps ensure your message is understood and reduces the chance of misunderstandings. Use simple and straightforward language, avoid excessive jargon or technical terms, and organize your thoughts before speaking. Practicing clarity lets you express your thoughts assertively and confidently.

Now, let's explore some workplace scenarios and see how assertive communication can be applied.

Scenario 1: During a team meeting, a colleague keeps interrupting you and disregarding your opinions.

Assertive response: "I understand that we may have different perspectives, but I would appreciate it if you let me finish speaking before sharing your thoughts. I believe it's important to consider everyone's viewpoints for a more comprehensive discussion."

Scenario 2: Your workload keeps increasing, and you're struggling to manage it all.

Assertive request: "I'm feeling overwhelmed with my current workload. I think it would be helpful if we could discuss redistributing some tasks or find a way to prioritize more effectively. Is there any way we can work together to alleviate some of the pressure?"

Scenario 3: Your boss consistently gives you more tasks at the last minute, causing you to stay late.

Assertive boundary-setting: "I understand that additional tasks arise unexpectedly. However, I need to balance my workload and personal commitments effectively. Is it possible for us to discuss these tasks in advance so I can plan accordingly and avoid staying late too often?"

By incorporating assertive communication techniques like "I" statements, active listening, positive body language, and clear communication, individuals can establish their needs, express their opinions respectfully, and build better workplace relationships. Practice these techniques consistently to become a confident and assertive communicator.

THE ROLE OF ASSERTIVENESS IN NEGOTIATION AND PROBLEM-SOLVING:

Assertiveness plays a crucial role in both negotiation and problem-solving situations as it empowers individuals to express their needs and concerns clearly, while also being receptive to others' perspectives. It involves effectively communicating one's own ideas, desires, and boundaries while respecting and understanding the viewpoints of others. This balanced approach not only fosters better understanding and collaboration, but also leads to mutually beneficial resolutions.

In negotiation, assertiveness is essential because it lets individuals advocate for their own interests without being overly aggressive or excessively passive. By clearly expressing their needs and concerns, negotiators can make sure their views are heard and considered. This helps in creating an open and honest dialogue between parties, leading to a constructive exchange of ideas and, ultimately, to a resolution that satisfies the interests of all involved.

Assertiveness in negotiation helps build trust and credibility. It conveys confidence, professionalism, and a firm belief in one's own stance. This can enhance one's position in the negotiation and increase the likelihood of a positive outcome. By openly communicating their goals and priorities, assertive negotiators set a framework for cooperation and show their commitment to reaching a mutually beneficial agreement.

In problem-solving situations, assertiveness is equally valuable. Expressing needs and concerns clearly enables individuals to identify and address the root causes of a problem efficiently. By clearly articulating their perspectives, stakeholders create an environment where different viewpoints are acknowledged and respected. This inclusive approach helps with the exploration of various potential solutions and encourages creative thinking.

Assertiveness in problem-solving makes sure all parties contribute to the process and feel heard. By actively listening to others, an assertive individual shows their willingness to understand alternative perspectives. This mutual respect and receptiveness to diverse viewpoints are essential for fostering collaboration and overcoming challenges effectively. It builds stronger relationships among individuals involved, leading to more sustainable and mutually acceptable solutions.

However, while assertiveness is valuable, it is crucial to strike a balance and avoid becoming overly dominant or dismissive of others' views. Being receptive to others' perspectives demonstrates openness and an understanding that every party has valuable contributions to make. It allows for the extraction of vital information, increased creativity, and the potential for innovative problem-solving approaches. By considering alternative viewpoints, individuals can uncover new insights and find unexpected win-win solutions that may not have been apparent.

Assertiveness is a valuable asset in negotiation and problem-solving situations. It lets individuals express their needs and concerns clearly while remaining open to others' perspectives. This balance fosters effective communication, collaboration, and the exploration of innovative solutions. By embracing assertiveness in these contexts, individuals can achieve mutually satisfactory outcomes and build stronger relationships based on trust and understanding.

ASSERTIVENESS ACROSS HIERARCHICAL LEVELS:

Assertiveness across hierarchical levels is crucial for creating a healthy and productive work environment within an organization. It involves individuals at different levels having the confidence and ability to express their thoughts, ideas, concerns, and feedback openly and respectfully. This communication dynamic is not limited to just the bottom-up approach where subordinates express themselves effectively to their superiors, but it also encompasses the top-down approach where leaders encourage and welcome open communication from their subordinates.

At every level, assertiveness plays a significant role in fostering collaboration, fostering innovation, ensuring transparency, improving decision-making, and ultimately influencing the overall success of an organization. Therefore, examine how assertiveness can be practiced by individuals at various levels within an organization.

Upward Assertion: Upward assertion is when employees feel comfortable expressing themselves to their superiors. This form of assertiveness is critical in creating an inclusive work environment where employees can voice their opinions, concerns, and suggestions without fear of retribution or dismissal.

To promote upward assertion:

- **Encourage an open-door policy:** Leaders should actively promote an environment where employees feel comfortable approaching them with their concerns or ideas, without fear of judgment or repercussions.
- **Active listening:** Leaders need to actively listen to their subordinates, giving them their undivided attention, and providing constructive feedback or guidance.
- **Solicit feedback:** Leaders need to proactively seek feedback from their subordinates through surveys, one-on-one meetings, or team discussions, emphasizing that their input is valuable and will be genuinely considered.
- **Recognize and reward assertiveness:** When employees show assertiveness by expressing their ideas or concerns, leaders should recognize and reward their efforts, highlighting the importance of open communication.

Downward Assertion: Downward assertion is when leaders encourage open communication from their subordinates. Leaders must create an environment where employees feel empowered to express their thoughts, provide feedback, or challenge ideas. To promote downward assertion:

- **Actively seek input:** Leaders should proactively seek input from their subordinates, encouraging their perspectives, and creating opportunities for participation in decision-making processes.
- **Foster psychological safety:** Leaders need to create a safe and supportive environment where employees are encouraged to share their thoughts or dissenting opinions without fear of negative consequences.
- **Lead by example:** Leaders should model assertive behavior by being open to feedback and showing active listening skills. This will encourage employees to follow suit and feel more comfortable expressing themselves.
- **Provide recognition and opportunities:** Recognizing assertive behavior by employees, publicizing their

contribution, and providing opportunities for growth and development will motivate them to continue being assertive.

Assertiveness across hierarchical levels is essential for effective communication and collaboration within an organization. Encouraging upward assertion lets employees express themselves freely to their superiors, while promoting downward assertion empowers leaders to welcome open communication from their subordinates. By valuing and practicing assertiveness, organizations can create a culture of transparency, trust, and collaboration, which ultimately leads to improved performance and success.

DEVELOPING ASSERTIVENESS SKILLS:

To help you develop and enhance your assertiveness skills, here are some practical exercises and strategies you can implement:

Self-reflection: Take some time to reflect on your communication style and identify areas where you need improvement. Assess your strengths and weaknesses in terms of being assertive.

Set clear boundaries: Clearly define your personal and professional boundaries. This will help you show what is acceptable and what is not and make it easier for you to assertively communicate these boundaries to others.

Practice active listening: Assertive communication involves listening to others attentively. Practice active listening skills by maintaining eye contact, nodding to show understanding, and paraphrasing to ensure clarity.

Use "I" statements: When expressing your needs or concerns, use "I" statements to avoid sounding accusatory or confrontational. For example, instead of saying, "You always interrupt me during meetings," say, "I feel unheard when I get interrupted during meetings."

Express your thoughts and feelings: Be honest and open about your thoughts and feelings, rather than suppressing them. Practice expressing yourself assertively, without being aggressive or passive.

Role play scenarios: Create various professional scenarios and practice assertive communication with a friend or colleague. This will help you become more comfortable and confident in expressing yourself assertively in real-life situations.

Seek feedback: Ask trusted colleagues or mentors for feedback on your assertive communication skills. They may provide valuable insights and suggestions for improvement.

Take small steps: Start by implementing assertive communication in less challenging situations, gradually working your way up to more difficult conversations. This will let you build confidence and knowledge.

Developing assertiveness skills is an ongoing process. It takes time and practice to become more comfortable and confident in expressing yourself assertively. By applying these exercises and strategies to various professional contexts, you can enhance your assertiveness skills and ultimately improve your overall communication effectiveness.

CHAPTER 1 SUMMARY: ASSERTIVENESS IN THE BUSINESS WORLD

Chapter 1 explores the importance of assertiveness in the business world and provides an understanding of assertive communication. Assertiveness is defined as a communication style that lets individuals express their thoughts, needs, and concerns while considering the perspectives of others. The chapter emphasizes the distinction between assertiveness, aggression, and passivity.

Assertiveness is highlighted as a crucial skill in achieving business goals for several reasons. It helps in building strong relationships by fostering trust and transparency. It enhances decision-making by encouraging diverse opinions and perspectives. Assertiveness also plays a significant role in conflict resolution and strengthens leadership capabilities. It enables effective negotiation and influence in the business environment.

Overcoming barriers to assertiveness is addressed, providing strategies to tackle common obstacles, such as fear of conflict, lack of confidence, societal expectations, lack of communication skills, and fear of rejection or negative feedback. Practical tips are given to help individuals develop their assertiveness skills, such as adopting a positive mindset, practicing assertiveness techniques, setting realistic goals, challenging assumptions, seeking support, and enhancing self-awareness.

The chapter concludes by emphasizing the benefits of assertiveness in the workplace, including improved teamwork, efficient conflict resolution, enhanced decision-making, increased productivity, establishment of respect, and fostering a positive work environment. It highlights the transformative impact of assertiveness on individuals and teams, leading to personal and professional growth.

Overall, Chapter 1 serves as a comprehensive introduction to the idea of assertiveness in the business world, providing readers with a solid foundation and understanding of the role and benefits of assertive communication.

CHAPTER 2

THE KEY TRAITS AND BEHAVIORS OF ASSERTIVE PROFESSIONALS

DEFINITION AND EXPLANATION OF ASSERTIVENESS IN A PROFESSIONAL CONTEXT:

I n the professional world, assertiveness plays a vital role in effective communication, collaborative problem-solving, and fostering a positive work environment.

Assertiveness refers to the ability to communicate needs, thoughts, and ideas confidently in a professional setting while respecting others' rights and opinions.

It is essential for navigating the dynamic nature of the business world.

Characteristics of Assertiveness:

- It differs from aggression, which involves forcing views onto others or using intimidation.
- Assertiveness focuses on open and honest expression while maintaining respect and cooperation.
- It balances passivity and aggression.

Key Elements of Assertiveness:

· · ·

- Articulating viewpoints, expressing needs, and setting boundaries in a diplomatic and courteous manner.
- Listening, acknowledging different opinions, and seeking collaborative solutions.
- Perceiving disagreements as opportunities for growth and engaging in constructive dialogue for resolution.

Importance of Assertiveness in a Professional Context:

- Crucial for effective teamwork, negotiation, and leadership.
- Enables individuals to advocate for their ideas, assert their rights, and handle difficult situations professionally.
- Helps in giving feedback, addressing conflicts, and managing competing priorities.

Benefits of Assertiveness:

- Builds trust and establishes healthy working relationships.
- Helps with open communication within the team.
- Fosters a harmonious and productive work environment.

Overall Impact of Assertiveness:

- Empowers individuals to express themselves confidently.
- Contributes to successful goal achievement in the professional setting.

In the realm of assertiveness, there are various examples of behaviors that demonstrate effective communication and confident self-expression.

Clear Communication: Assertive professionals actively communicate their thoughts, feelings, and ideas clearly and directly. They express themselves in a concise way, while respecting others' perspectives. For example, when providing feedback, they share specific examples and address both positive and negative aspects without being aggressive or passive.

Expressing Needs and Opinions Confidently: Assertive individuals confidently express their needs and opinions, believing that their thoughts and feelings are valid. They are not afraid to voice different perspectives and contribute to discussions, even if their viewpoint differs from others. For example, in a team meeting, an assertive professional would confidently share their ideas, offer suggestions, and actively engage in problem-solving.

Setting Boundaries: Assertive individuals establish and maintain boundaries regarding their personal space, time, and workload. They clearly communicate their limits and expectations to others. For example, when someone approaches an assertive professional for help with an excessive workload, they respond by respectfully declining or negotiating a manageable timeframe to complete the task.

Active Listening: Assertive professionals actively listen to others, acknowledging their thoughts and feelings. They give their full attention, maintain eye contact, and avoid interrupting. They create an environment of open communication and respect. For example, an assertive team leader listens attentively during a team member's presentation, asks relevant questions, and acknowledges their contribution.

Constructive Conflict Resolution: Assertive professionals are confident in addressing conflicts in a healthy and respectful manner. They engage in open and honest discussions, focusing on the issue at hand and seeking a mutually beneficial solution. For example, in a disagreement, an assertive individual approaches the other party calmly, expresses their concerns, and actively listens to the other person's viewpoint to find common ground.

Positive Self-Assertion: Assertive individuals focus on their own needs and well-being without neglecting the needs of others. They engage in self-care practices and confidently advocate for themselves. For example, if an assertive professional feels overwhelmed with their workload, they may request help or negotiate deadlines to maintain a healthy work-life balance.

Refusing Unreasonable Requests: Assertive professionals are comfortable refusing unreasonable requests without feeling guilty or apologizing excessively. They assertively explain their reasons for declining and suggest alternative solutions. For example, when pressured to take on more responsibilities that go beyond their job description, an assertive employee would firmly decline, highlighting their current workload and suggesting a possible redistribution of tasks.

Overall, assertive behavior involves clear communication, expressing one's needs and opinions confidently, setting and maintaining boundaries, active listening, constructive conflict resolution, positive self-assertion, and refusing unreasonable requests while remaining respectful and professional.

BENEFITS OF ASSERTIVENESS IN THE BUSINESS WORLD:

Developing assertiveness skills has numerous benefits in the business world, ranging from improved communication to increased personal fulfillment.

Improved Communication: Being assertive in the business world allows individuals to clearly and effectively express their thoughts, ideas, and concerns. This leads to effective communication with colleagues, clients, and superiors, making sure messages are understood and tasks are performed efficiently.

Increased Confidence and Self-esteem: Assertiveness helps individuals feel more confident in their abilities and helps them develop a positive self-image. By expressing their opinions and needs in a clear and respectful manner, assertive individuals can gain respect and recognition, which further boosts their confidence and self-esteem.

Enhanced Problem-solving Abilities: Assertive individuals are more likely to speak up and express their viewpoints during team discussions, contributing to a diverse range of ideas and perspectives.

This allows for more creative problem-solving and decision-making within the organization. By actively participating in discussions and offering suggestions without fear of rejection, assertive individuals can help find innovative solutions to challenges.

Effective Boundary-Setting: Assertiveness helps individuals establish and maintain clear boundaries in the workplace. By clearly communicating their limits, assertive individuals can prevent others from taking advantage of their time, skills, or resources. This ensures a healthy work-life balance and prevents burnout, leading to improved overall productivity and job satisfaction.

Career Advancement: Assertive individuals are often perceived as confident, capable, and proactive. These features are highly valued in the business world and can lead to increased opportunities for career advancement. By expressing their ambitions, showcasing their skills, and effectively promoting their achievements, assertive individuals are more likely to be recognized for their talents and considered for promotions or more responsibilities.

Improved Conflict Resolution: In the professional setting, conflicts are inevitable. Being assertive lets individuals address conflicts directly and openly, rather than avoiding or escalating them. Assertive individuals can express their concerns, identify common ground, and work toward mutually beneficial resolutions. This helps to have positive working relationships, foster a harmonious work environment, and reduce misunderstandings or animosities.

Increased Personal Fulfillment: By being assertive, individuals have a greater sense of control over their work environment and relationships. They can actively pursue their goals, advocate for their needs, and make meaningful contributions. This sense of personal agency and fulfillment leads to higher job satisfaction and overall happiness in the business world.

The Role of Assertiveness in Effective Leadership:

The role of assertiveness in effective leadership cannot be overstated. Assertiveness is a necessary trait that enables leaders to make critical decisions, delegate tasks effectively, and motivate and inspire team members. It sets the foundation for strong leadership skills and helped to achieve success in various organizational settings.

Decisiveness is a key aspect of assertive leadership. Leaders who have assertiveness show clear and prompt decision-making abilities. They analyze available information and quickly arrive at well-informed choices, even in challenging situations. Their assertiveness lets them project confidence, instilling trust in their subordinates and ensuring a sense of direction within the team. Decisiveness also enables leaders to overcome obstacles swiftly and efficiently, as they can swiftly identify and address issues before they escalate.

Effective delegation is another area where assertiveness plays a vital role. Assertive leaders can delegate tasks based on their understanding of individual strengths and weaknesses within the team. Their assertiveness makes sure expectations, deadlines, and responsibilities are clearly communicated, thus empowering team members to contribute their best work. By assigning tasks appropriately, assertive leaders not only lighten their workload but also create opportunities for growth and skill development among their team members.

Assertive leaders have exceptional communication skills, letting them motivate and inspire their subordinates. Their ability to communicate assertively creates an environment where ideas are freely exchanged, and constructive feedback is encouraged. Through effective communication, assertive leaders express their vision and goals, garnering support and commitment from their team. By motivating and energizing individuals, assertive leaders can drive successful outcomes and create a positive work culture.

Additionally, assertiveness helps leaders handle conflicts and provides feedback in a constructive way. Assertive leaders are not afraid to address contentious issues, making sure conflicts are resolved promptly and fairly. They provide honest feedback, both positive and constructive, enabling their team members to grow and improve. Their assertiveness in delivering feedback is balanced with empathy and respect, fostering open communication, and maintaining healthy working relationships.

Assertiveness is indispensable for effective leadership. The ability to be decisive, delegate tasks effectively, and motivate and inspire others are all vital traits that assertive leaders have. By leveraging assertiveness, leaders can provide guidance, create a positive work environment, and propel their teams toward achieving organizational goals. Assertiveness, when combined with other leadership qualities, forms the cornerstone for effective leadership, fostering growth and success in various organizational settings.

STRATEGIES FOR DEVELOPING ASSERTIVENESS:

To cultivate assertiveness is a valuable skill, it is important to begin with a positive mindset and adopt specific strategies that promote confident communication and self-advocacy.

- Begin by understanding and cultivating a positive mindset. Recognize that assertiveness is a valuable skill that can benefit you in various parts of your life.
- Practice assertive communication by expressing your thoughts, feelings, and needs directly, while being respectful toward others. Use "I" statements to convey your perspective and avoid blaming or criticizing others.
- Focus on maintaining confident and assertive body language. Stand or sit up straight, maintain eye contact, and use appropriate gestures to support your assertive communication.
- Develop active listening skills to show you genuinely value others' opinions and are attentive to their input. This will also help you respond effectively to any potential objections or disagreements.
- Build your self-confidence by challenging negative self-talk and embracing positive affirmations. Recognize your worth and believe in your abilities to achieve what you desire.

- Set specific goals for yourself, both short-term and long-term, and practice assertiveness in various situations. Start with low-stakes situations and gradually progress to more challenging ones.
- Role-play different scenarios or seek assertiveness training programs to gain practical experience and feedback on your assertive behaviors.
- Practice self-advocacy by standing up for yourself and your rights in professional and personal settings. This involves defining boundaries, saying "no" when necessary, and asserting your needs and wants without guilt or fear.
- Seek support from friends, family, or a therapist who can provide guidance and encouragement throughout your journey toward developing assertiveness.
- Reflect on your assertive experiences and learn from them. Analyze what worked well and what could be improved and make adjustments accordingly. Remember that assertiveness is a lifelong skill that can be continually developed and refined.

OVERCOMING BARRIERS TO ASSERTIVENESS:

Assertiveness is a crucial skill that lets individuals effectively communicate their needs, desires, and boundaries while respecting the rights and feelings of others. However, many people struggle to be assertive due to various barriers that prevent them from expressing their thoughts and opinions confidently. This section will delve into common barriers to assertiveness, including fear of conflict or rejection, and provide strategies to overcome them.

Fear of conflict:

One significant barrier to assertiveness is the fear of conflict. Many individuals avoid expressing themselves assertively because they expect disagreements or confrontations that may arise. They prefer to keep the peace, even at the cost of their own needs and wants.

Strategies for overcoming the fear of conflict:

a) **Shift your mindset:** Recognize that conflict is a natural part of any relationship or interaction. Instead of viewing conflict as inherently negative, reframe it as an opportunity for growth and understanding.

b) **Practice assertiveness skills:** Cultivate the ability to express your thoughts and feelings assertively, using "I" statements, active listening, and maintaining a calm and respectful tone. This will help you navigate conflicts more effectively.

c) **Choose appropriate timing:** Select the right moment to address concerns or share your ideas. Waiting for a calm and suitable time can reduce the potential for conflict and increase the likelihood of a productive conversation.

Fear of rejection:

The fear of rejection is another common barrier to assertiveness. People may worry that speaking up for themselves will lead to the disapproval or rejection of others. This fear often stems from a desire to be liked and accepted, even if it means sacrificing personal needs.

Strategies for overcoming the fear of rejection:

a) **Build self-confidence:** Work on developing a healthy sense of self-worth and recognizing that your needs and opinions are as valid as anyone else's. Engaging in self-affirmations and practicing self-care can boost self-confidence.

b) **Focus on positive outcomes:** Remind yourself that assertiveness can lead to positive outcomes, such as improved relationships, increased self-respect, and enhanced personal fulfillment. By focusing on these potential benefits, the fear of rejection can be diminished.

c) **Start with small steps:** Begin by practicing assertiveness in low-stakes situations and gradually work your way up. Starting with close friends or family members more likely to be understanding and supportive can offer a safe environment for practicing assertiveness.

Lack of assertiveness skills:

Some individuals struggle with assertiveness simply because they lack the necessary skills. They may not know how to communicate their needs effectively or find it challenging to express themselves with clarity and confidence.

Strategies for developing assertiveness skills:

a) Seek education and resources: Utilize self-help books, online resources, or workshops that focus on assertiveness training. These tools can provide guidance on communication techniques and help build assertiveness skills.

b) Role play and practice: Engage in role-playing exercises or seek opportunities to practice assertiveness in real-life scenarios. This can help you become more comfortable and proficient in expressing your thoughts and feelings assertively.

c) Seek support: Consider seeking support from a therapist or joining assertiveness training groups where you can learn from others also working on developing their assertiveness skills. Their insights and experiences can be invaluable.

Overcoming barriers to assertiveness requires recognizing and addressing fears and beliefs that hinder open and direct communication. By understanding common barriers such as fear of conflict or rejection, individuals can use strategies like shifting mindsets, building self-confidence, and developing assertiveness skills to break free from these constraints. With practice and patience, anyone can overcome these barriers and embrace assertiveness as an empowering tool in all parts of life.

ETHICAL CONSIDERATIONS IN ASSERTIVENESS:

When practicing assertiveness, it is crucial to uphold ethical considerations that prioritize respect, empathy, diverse perspectives, honesty, consistency, and confidentiality.

- **Respect and professionalism:** One of the key ethical considerations in assertiveness is the importance of maintaining respect and professionalism when expressing one's needs, desires, or opinions. It is crucial to remember that assertiveness should not involve manipulating or disrespecting others. Instead, it should focus on clearly and confidently communicating one's stance while still respecting the rights and feelings of others.

- **Balancing assertiveness with empathy:** Being assertive does not mean disregarding the perspectives or feelings of others. It is essential to balance being firm and understanding. When asserting oneself, it is important to consider the potential impact on others and to show empathy toward their beliefs, values, and emotions. Empathy can help create an environment of mutual respect and understanding, leading to more effective communication and problem-solving.

- **Understanding diverse perspectives:** Ethical assertiveness involves recognizing the diversity of opinions and experiences among individuals. It is crucial to acknowledge and respect different viewpoints, even if they differ from our own. By seeking to understand alternative perspectives, we can avoid becoming overly aggressive or dismissive when expressing ourselves assertively. This consideration helps maintain a fair and inclusive approach that values diversity and encourages open dialogue.

- **Honesty and transparency:** Ethical assertiveness demands honesty and transparency in communication. It is essential to be truthful and straightforward when expressing needs, concerns, or disagreements. Dishonesty or manipulation undermines the trust and integrity of assertiveness, leading to potential ethical issues. By speaking honestly and transparently, individuals are more likely to be respected and taken seriously, fostering an environment that values ethical assertiveness.

- **Consistency and fairness:** Ethical assertiveness requires individuals to be consistent and fair in their approach. It implies treating everyone equally, despite their position or status. Being consistent and fair prevents favoritism, discrimination, or unfair treatment and encourages ethical behavior within interpersonal interactions. It also makes sure assertiveness is exercised with integrity and without creating conflicts or biases.

- **Confidentiality and privacy:** In certain situations, assertiveness may involve discussing sensitive or confidential matters. Ethical considerations demand that individuals respect the privacy and confidentiality of others when asserting themselves. Sharing personal information or private conversations without consent not only breaches trust, but also raises ethical concerns. Respecting boundaries and maintaining confidentiality are essential to ethical assertiveness and fostering a safe and respectful environment.

CHAPTER TWO SUMMARY: THE KEY TRAITS AND BEHAVIORS OF ASSERTIVE PROFESSIONALS

Chapter Two delves into the key traits and behaviors of assertive professionals in a professional context. It begins by defining assertiveness as the ability to confidently communicate needs, thoughts, and ideas while respecting others' rights and opinions. The chapter emphasizes that assertiveness is distinct from aggression, as it focuses on open and honest expression while maintaining respect and cooperation.

The chapter highlights the features of assertiveness, such as its balance between passivity and aggression, and its role in navigating the dynamic nature of the business world. It explores the key elements of assertiveness, including articulating viewpoints, expressing needs, setting boundaries, active listening, perceiving disagreements as growth opportunities, and engaging in constructive dialogue.

The importance of assertiveness in a professional context is discussed, emphasizing its role in effective teamwork, negotiation, and leadership. It enables individuals to advocate for their ideas, assert their rights, and handle difficult situations professionally. The chapter also explores the benefits of assertiveness, such as building trust, fostering open communication, and creating a harmonious and productive work environment. Overall, assertiveness empowers individuals to express themselves confidently and contributes to successful goal achievement.

The chapter provides examples of assertive behaviors, including clear communication, expressing needs and opinions confidently, setting boundaries, active listening, constructive conflict resolution, positive self-assertion, and refusing unreasonable requests while remaining respectful and professional.

The chapter explores the benefits of assertiveness in the business world, including improved communication, increased confidence and self-esteem, enhanced problem-solving abilities, effective boundary-setting, career advancement opportunities, improved conflict resolution, and increased personal fulfillment.

The role of assertiveness in effective leadership is discussed, emphasizing its importance in decision-making, task delegation, motivation, and conflict resolution. Assertiveness sets the foundation for strong leadership skills and contributes to success in various organizational settings.

Strategies for developing assertiveness are provided, including cultivating a positive mindset, practicing assertive communication and body language, developing active listening skills, building self-confidence, setting goals, role-playing, seeking support, and continual reflection and learning.

The chapter also addresses common barriers to assertiveness, such as the fear of conflict or rejection and lack of assertiveness skills. Strategies for overcoming these barriers are presented, including shifting mindsets, building self-confidence, practicing assertiveness skills, choosing timing, and starting with small steps.

Ethical considerations in assertiveness are discussed, emphasizing the importance of respect, empathy, diverse perspectives, honesty, consistency, and confidentiality. Ethical assertiveness involves maintaining professionalism, balancing assertiveness with empathy, understanding diverse perspectives, being honest and transparent, ensuring consistency and fairness, and respecting confidentiality and privacy.

Chapter Two comprehensively explores the key traits and behaviors of assertive professionals. It emphasizes the importance of assertiveness in effective communication, collaboration, and leadership, while providing practical strategies for developing assertiveness and overcoming barriers. The chapter also highlights the ethical considerations that should be upheld when practicing assertiveness in a professional context.

CHAPTER 3

BUILDING CONFIDENCE: OVERCOMING FEAR OF ASSERTIVENESS

UNDERSTANDING THE ROOTS OF FEAR:

Fear is a powerful emotion that can affect various parts of our lives, including how we express ourselves assertively. Fear of assertiveness can stem from experiences and societal expectations that shape our beliefs about how we should behave. By exploring these roots, we can gain a deeper understanding of why this fear exists and learn how to identify and challenge the underlying beliefs that contribute to it. In this chapter, we will delve into the origins of fear of assertiveness, discuss its connection to experiences and societal expectations, and provide strategies to overcome it.

1. Past experiences and the fear of assertiveness:

a. Traumatic events: Negative experiences, such as being humiliated or rejected when expressing ourselves assertively in the past, can create a fear that hinders our ability to be assertive again. These experiences can leave lasting imprints on our self-esteem and confidence.

b. Conditioning and reinforcement: If we were consistently discouraged or punished for being assertive, we may have internalized the belief that assertiveness is wrong or unacceptable. This conditioning can lead to a fear of facing similar negative consequences in the future.

2. Societal expectations and the fear of assertiveness:

a. Gender roles and expectations: Cultural and societal norms often dictate different expectations for men and women regarding assertiveness. Men are often expected to be more assertive, while women may be judged negatively for displaying assertive behavior. This societal pressure can lead to fear and anxiety about deviating from these norms.

b. Power dynamics: Hierarchical structures in society and workplaces may discourage individuals from being assertive if they fear reprisal or consequences. Fear of challenging those in positions of authority can contribute to the fear of assertiveness.

3. Identifying and challenging underlying beliefs:

a. Self-reflection: Take time to reflect on your experiences with assertiveness and identify any negative beliefs or fears associated with it. Consider how past events or societal expectations may have influenced your perception of assertiveness.

b. Question the beliefs: Once identified, challenge these beliefs by questioning their validity and exploring alternative perspectives. Recognize that assertiveness is a valuable skill for effective communication and self-advocacy.

c. Positive affirmations and visualization: Use positive affirmations to counteract negative beliefs and visualize yourself successfully engaging in assertive behavior. This can help rewire your thinking patterns and build confidence.

Understanding the roots of fear of assertiveness is essential for personal growth and development. By recognizing how experiences and societal expectations contribute to this fear, individuals can begin to challenge and overcome these limiting beliefs. Through self-reflection, questioning negative beliefs, and practicing positive affirmations, individuals can empower themselves to express their needs and opinions assertively. Overcoming the fear of assertiveness opens doors to meaningful interactions, personal growth, and improved self-esteem.

RECOGNIZING THE IMPORTANCE OF ASSERTIVENESS: UNLOCKING A WORLD OF BENEFITS

Assertiveness is an invaluable quality that empowers individuals to effectively express their thoughts, feelings, and needs while also respecting others. By recognizing the significance of assertiveness, we can understand its remarkable benefits, including improved self-esteem, stronger relationships, and increased personal satisfaction. This chapter aims to shed light on the advantages of assertiveness, highlighting why overcoming the fear associated with it is truly worth the effort.

Improved Self-esteem:

Assertiveness plays a crucial role in developing and enhancing one's self-esteem. When individuals assertively express themselves, they show self-respect and confidence in their own opinions and ideas. This leads to a sense of pride and satisfaction, contributing to heightened self-assurance and a positive self-image. By standing up for themselves, assertive individuals bolster their belief in their abilities and increase their overall self-worth.

Stronger Relationships:

Assertiveness greatly influences the quality of our interpersonal connections. By effectively communicating our needs and boundaries, we establish healthier and more authentic relationships. Assertive individuals can express their feelings, preferences, and concerns, which encourages open and honest communication with others. This fosters mutual respect, trust, and understanding, allowing for stronger connections built on genuine interactions. Assertiveness empowers individuals to address conflicts constructively and collaboratively, resulting in healthier and more fulfilling relationships.

Increased Personal Satisfaction:

When we assert ourselves and strive to fulfill our needs and desires, we experience personal satisfaction. By expressing our preferences and asserting our rights, we actively shape our lives according to our values and goals. Assertiveness lets us take ownership of our choices, leading to a more fulfilling and meaningful existence. As we live in alignment with our authentic selves, we experience a sense of personal fulfillment, knowing that our actions and decisions are true reflections of who we are.

Enhanced Emotional Well-being:

Assertiveness positively affects our emotional well-being, aiding in stress reduction and the prevention of pent-up emotions. By assertively communicating our thoughts and feelings, we prevent resentment and frustration from building up. This promotes emotional clarity and stability, reducing anxious thoughts and alleviating the mental burden of suppressed emotions. The ability to express oneself assertively is a powerful tool for managing emotional health, fostering resilience, and promoting a balanced state of mind.

Recognizing and embracing the importance of assertiveness lets individuals unlock a multitude of benefits that positively influence their lives. Improved self-esteem, stronger relationships, increased personal satisfaction, and enhanced emotional well-being are just some advantages associated with assertiveness. While overcoming the fear of asserting oneself may challenge, the rewards far outweigh the discomfort. With practice and determination, individuals can develop assertiveness skills, empowering themselves to live a more fulfilling and authentic life.

DEVELOPING SELF-AWARENESS:

Developing self-awareness is a crucial step in understanding and overcoming fears and insecurities related to assertiveness. By examining our thoughts, beliefs, and emotions in a safe and non-judgmental way, we can gain clarity and take steps toward assertiveness. Here are exercises and techniques to help in this process:

Mindfulness and Meditation:

- Take a few minutes each day to practice mindfulness meditation. Observe your thoughts, emotions, and bodily sensations without judgment. Notice thoughts or fears that arise regarding assertiveness.
- Use guided meditation apps or videos that focus on self-awareness and self-compassion.

Journaling:

- Set aside dedicated time to journal about your fears and insecurities related to assertiveness. Write without judgment, letting your thoughts and emotions flow freely onto the pages.
- Reflect where you have felt less assertive. Identify any patterns or underlying beliefs that may be contributing to your fears or insecurities.

Identifying Core Beliefs:

- Consider the core beliefs you hold about yourself and assertiveness. Are there underlying beliefs such as "I'm not good enough" or "Conflict is bad" that are influencing your fears?
- Challenge and reframe these beliefs by finding evidence to the contrary. For example, if you believe that assertiveness will lead to conflict, search for instances where assertiveness has resulted in positive outcomes.

Emotional Awareness:

- Pay attention to your emotions during interactions where assertiveness is required. Notice any discomfort, anxiety, or fear that arises. Label and acknowledge these emotions without judgment.

- Take a moment to explore the underlying reasons for your emotions. Are they based on past experiences, negative self-perceptions, or assumptions about how others may react?

Role-Playing and Visualization:

- Practice assertiveness by role-playing scenarios that make you uncomfortable. Enlist the help of a friend or therapist to play different roles.
- Use visualization techniques to imagine yourself being assertive and handling conflicts confidently. Picture successful outcomes and positive responses from others.

Seeking Feedback:

- Ask trusted friends, family members, or mentors for their perspective on your assertiveness. Ask for honest feedback about areas where you could improve and areas where you already excel.
- Reflect on their feedback and use it as a starting point for self-exploration and growth.

Developing self-awareness is a continuous journey. Be patient and kind with yourself as you navigate your fears and insecurities related to assertiveness. Progress may take time, but by observing, reflecting, and challenging your thoughts and beliefs, you can cultivate a sense of self-awareness that supports your journey toward assertiveness.

STRATEGIES FOR BUILDING CONFIDENCE:

To cultivate greater self-confidence, it's important to implement specific strategies that promote personal growth and empowerment. By setting achievable goals, practicing assertive communication, cultivating self-compassion, challenging negative self-talk, visualizing success, embracing failure as a learning opportunity, surrounding yourself with positive support, practicing self-care, and celebrating achievements, you can steadily build your confidence and face new challenges with a strong sense of self-assurance.

Set achievable goals: Start by setting small, realistic goals you can accomplish easily. As you meet these goals, your confidence will naturally grow. Gradually increase the difficulty level of your goals as your confidence strengthens.

Practice assertive communication: Assertiveness involves expressing your thoughts, feelings, and needs in a respectful way. Practice speaking up for yourself in a calm and confident way. Remember to maintain eye contact, use clear and concise language, and stand or sit with good posture.

Cultivate self-compassion: Treat yourself with kindness and understanding when facing setbacks or mistakes. Instead of criticizing yourself, practice self-compassion by acknowledging that everyone makes mistakes and that failures are opportunities for growth. Offer yourself words of encouragement and remember that you are doing your best.

Challenge negative self-talk: Identify negative thoughts and beliefs that undermine your confidence, such as "I'm not good enough" or "I can't do this." Replace those thoughts with positive and affirming statements like "I am capable" or "I have the skills and knowledge to succeed." By challenging negative self-talk, you can shift your mindset toward more positive and empowering thoughts.

Visualize success: Use visualization techniques to mentally rehearse successful outcomes. Imagine yourself confidently meeting your goals and feeling proud of your accomplishments. Visualization helps train your brain to believe in your abilities, boosting your self-confidence.

Embrace failure as a learning opportunity: Failure is a normal part of life, and even successful individuals face setbacks. Instead of being discouraged by failures, use them as learning experiences. Analyze what went wrong, make necessary changes, and keep trying. Embracing failure as a steppingstone to success will help you maintain confidence during difficult times.

Surround yourself with positive and supportive people: Building confidence becomes easier when you have a strong support network. Surround yourself with friends, family, and mentors who believe in you and provide encouragement. Avoid spending time with those who bring you down or undermine your confidence.

Practice self-care: Take care of your physical, mental, and emotional well-being. Engage in regular exercise, eat a balanced diet, and get enough sleep. Additionally, engage in activities that bring you joy and relaxation. When you focus on self-care, you increase your overall resilience and confidence.

Celebrate your achievements: Acknowledge and celebrate your accomplishments, no matter how small they may seem. Reflect on your progress and give yourself credit for the steps you've taken toward building your confidence. Celebrating your achievements helps reinforce positive feelings and encourages you to keep striving for success.

Building confidence takes time and practice. By implementing these strategies into your daily life, you can gradually enhance your confidence and ultimately embrace new challenges with a sense of self-assurance.

OVERCOMING COMMON OBSTACLES:

Fear of conflict or rejection is a common obstacle that individuals may face when trying to overcome the fear of assertiveness. Here are strategies to navigate these obstacles effectively:

Recognize the underlying fears: Understanding that fear of conflict or rejection is natural is the first step toward overcoming it. Acknowledge that everyone faces these fears at some point, and it is a part of personal growth.

Build self-confidence: Developing self-confidence is crucial regarding assertiveness. Practice positive self-talk and focus on your strengths. Remind yourself of past successes and situations where you handled conflict or rejection effectively.

Start small: Begin by asserting yourself in low-pressure situations. Practice with close friends or family members who are supportive. Gradually move on to more challenging situations and build your assertiveness skills.

Learn effective communication techniques: Learning how to communicate assertively can help you express your needs and opinions without being aggressive or overly passive. Techniques such as using "I" statements, active listening, and showing empathy can be valuable in navigating conflicts and reducing the fear of rejection.

Prepare and plan: Before entering a potentially challenging situation, take some time to prepare and plan your approach. Set clear goals for the conversation, expect possible objections or conflicts, and think about how you will respond in different scenarios.

Focus on the outcome: When facing the fear of conflict or rejection, it's helpful to focus on the potential positive outcomes rather than the negative ones. Visualize the benefits of assertiveness, such as improved relationships, increased self-esteem, and personal growth.

Seek support: Overcoming fear of conflict or rejection can be challenging, so it's important to seek support from trusted friends, family, or mentors. They can provide encouragement, offer advice, and help you navigate difficult situations.

Practice resilience: Rejection or conflict rarely means the end of a relationship or opportunity. Embrace rejection as a learning experience, and view conflict as an opportunity for growth and understanding. Develop a resilient mindset that lets you bounce back and stay motivated even when facing setbacks.

Celebrate successes: As you navigate these obstacles successfully, take time to celebrate your accomplishments. Acknowledge your growth and progress, no matter how small it may seem. Positive reinforcement can boost your confidence and motivate you to continue overcoming fear.

Overcoming the fear of assertiveness takes time and practice. Be patient with yourself, and don't be discouraged by occasional setbacks.

By starting these strategies and continuing to challenge yourself, you can gradually overcome the barriers that prevent you from being assertive.

BUILDING A SUPPORT NETWORK:

Building a support network is crucial for personal growth and development, especially when working toward assertiveness. Surrounding oneself with supportive individuals who can provide encouragement, guidance, and reassurance can make the journey toward assertiveness easier and more fulfilling. Here are a few reasons building a support network is important and how it can help in one's journey toward assertiveness:

Encouragement: When working on becoming more assertive, one may encounter obstacles and self-doubt. Having a support network of individuals who believe in your abilities can provide the necessary support and encouragement to keep going. They can offer words of motivation and remind you of your strengths, helping you push through difficulties.

Guidance: Building a support network gives you access to a wide variety of experiences and perspectives. This diversity lets you seek guidance from people who have developed assertiveness skills. They can share their experiences, offer advice, and provide valuable insights on how to handle different situations. Their guidance can help you navigate challenges and make informed decisions regarding assertiveness.

Reassurance: Stepping out of your comfort zone and asserting yourself can be intimidating. In such moments, having a support network can offer reassurance and remind you that what you're doing is important and valuable. They can provide a safe space for you to express your thoughts and feelings and assure you that taking assertive actions is acceptable and necessary.

Accountability: Building a support network creates a sense of accountability. When you share your goals with supportive individuals, they can help hold you accountable for taking consistent steps toward assertiveness. They can offer constructive feedback, celebrate your achievements, and gently push you to keep progressing even when faced with setbacks or self-doubt.

Emotional support: Developing assertiveness skills can be emotionally challenging. In moments when you feel overwhelmed, having a support network can provide the emotional support you need. They can be a sounding board for your frustrations and fears, offering empathy and understanding. Their presence can help nurture your self-confidence and belief in your ability to become more assertive.

To build a support network, start by identifying individuals who exhibit supportive features such as empathy, understanding, and open-mindedness. Look within your existing social circle, seek mentors or join assertiveness-focused groups or communities. Remember that building a support network is a reciprocal process, and you must provide support to others in return.

Building a support network plays a vital role in developing assertiveness skills. Supportive individuals who can provide encouragement, guidance, and reassurance can make the journey toward assertiveness more manageable and rewarding. Surround yourself with those who believe in your abilities and will uplift you throughout your assertiveness journey.

CULTIVATING SELF-ACCEPTANCE:

Cultivating self-acceptance is an essential step toward building confidence and overcoming fear. Accepting yourself for who you are, with all your strengths and imperfections, lets you embrace your uniqueness and feel comfortable in your own skin. It is through self-acceptance that you can foster a positive self-image and increase assertiveness in various areas of your life.

One of the first things to understand is that self-acceptance is not about self-improvement or trying to meet societal expectations. It is about acknowledging that you are a work in progress and that it is okay to have flaws and make mistakes. By accepting yourself as a constantly evolving individual, you create a space for self-growth and learning.

Mindfulness is a powerful practice that can aid in developing self-acceptance. By being present in the current moment and non-judgmentally observing your thoughts and emotions, you can detach from negative self-perceptions. Mindfulness lets you acknowledge your insecurities without being consumed by them. Through regular mindfulness practice, you can develop a compassionate attitude toward yourself, recognizing that everyone experiences doubts and struggles.

Self-care is another critical part of cultivating self-acceptance. Taking care of your physical, emotional, and mental well-being sends a message to yourself that you are deserving of love and care. Engaging in activities that bring you joy, whether it's practicing a hobby, spending time in nature, or connecting with loved ones, helps to strengthen your self-worth and reinforce a positive self-image.

In addition to mindfulness and self-care, challenging negative self-talk is vital for promoting self-acceptance. Learn of the critical inner voice that often undermines your confidence and replaces it with more empowering thoughts. Instead of focusing on perceived flaws or mistakes, remind yourself of your unique qualities, accomplishments, and personal growth. Affirmations, positive self-talk, and keeping a gratitude journal can all be helpful techniques in reframing your mindset toward self-acceptance.

Setting realistic goals and celebrating even small achievements fosters a sense of self-worth and accomplishment. By recognizing and honoring your progress, you reinforce the idea that you are capable and worthy of success. Challenge yourself to step outside of your comfort zone and face your fears, embracing the opportunities for personal growth along the way.

Self-acceptance plays a crucial role in building confidence and overcoming fear. By practicing mindfulness to detach from negative self-perceptions, engaging in self-care activities to reinforce self-worth, challenging negative self-talk, and setting achievable goals, you can promote a positive self-image and increase assertiveness. Embrace the journey of self-acceptance, knowing that accepting and loving yourself unconditionally is the foundation of personal growth and a fulfilling life.

CHAPTER THREE SUMMARY: BUILDING CONFIDENCE - OVERCOMING FEAR OF ASSERTIVENESS

Chapter Three explores building confidence and overcoming the fear of assertiveness. It delves into the roots of fear, including past experiences and societal expectations, and provides strategies to challenge and overcome these fears.

The chapter emphasizes the importance of assertiveness and its benefits, such as improved self-esteem, stronger relationships, increased personal satisfaction, and enhanced emotional well-being. It also highlights the significance of self-awareness in understanding and overcoming fears related to assertiveness, providing exercises and techniques for developing self-awareness.

Strategies for building confidence are discussed, including setting achievable goals, practicing assertive communication, cultivating self-compassion, challenging negative self-talk, visualizing success, embracing failure, building a support network, and practicing self-care.

The chapter addresses common obstacles, such as fear of conflict or rejection, and provides strategies to navigate them effectively. It emphasizes the importance of building a support network for encouragement, guidance, reassurance, accountability, and emotional support.

Finally, the chapter focuses on cultivating self-acceptance as a crucial step in building confidence and overcoming fear, discussing mindfulness, self-care, challenging negative self-talk, and setting realistic goals as techniques for cultivating self-acceptance.

CHAPTER 4

EFFECTIVE COMMUNICATION: EXPRESSING YOURSELF CLEARLY AND ASSERTIVELY

UNDERSTANDING THE POWER OF EFFECTIVE COMMUNICATION:

E	ffective communication is a fundamental skill that plays a pivotal role in various parts of our lives. Whether it is in personal relationships, professional settings, or even casual interactions, the ability to express oneself clearly and assertively is essential for creating understanding and achieving positive outcomes.

The power of effective communication lies in its ability to build strong relationships. When we communicate effectively, we establish a sense of trust and rapport with others. By expressing our thoughts, feelings, and ideas in a way easily understood, we create an environment where others feel comfortable opening up and sharing their own perspectives. This fosters a deeper level of connection and mutual respect, strengthening the bonds between individuals.

In addition to fostering relationships, effective communication also plays a significant role in achieving positive outcomes. When we can clearly and assertively articulate our needs, wants, and expectations, we increase the likelihood of our messages being received and understood accurately. This reduces the chances of misinterpretation, misunderstandings, and conflicts, ultimately leading to improved collaboration, problem-solving, and decision-making.

Effective communication lets us navigate and resolve conflicts more constructively. By expressing ourselves assertively, we can address issues or concerns in a direct and respectful manner. This approach promotes open dialogue, encourages active listening, and enables all parties involved to collaborate on finding mutually beneficial solutions. It enables us to manage disagreements and differences of opinion effectively, making sure conflicts are resolved in a productive and respectful manner, rather than escalating into harmful situations.

Effective communication also enables us to influence and inspire others. When we have a clear and confident communication style, we are more likely to convey our ideas and persuade others to adopt our viewpoint. Whether it is in a professional presentation, a negotiation, or a personal discussion, the ability to express our thoughts convincingly can lead to positive outcomes, such as gaining support for a project, securing a business deal, or even inspiring others to act toward a common goal.

Finally, effective communication empowers individuals to express their identities and values authentically. By using clear and assertive language, we can confidently share our beliefs, experiences, and perspectives. This authenticity fosters trust and respect, enabling us to establish meaningful connections with others who share similar values or who appreciate different perspectives. It lets us express ourselves and be understood for who we are, fostering a sense of belonging and acceptance in our personal and professional lives.

The power of effective communication cannot be underestimated. It forms the foundation for building strong relationships, achieving positive outcomes, resolving conflicts constructively, influencing others, and expressing our authentic selves. By recognizing and understanding the significance of clear and assertive expression, we can enhance our communication skills and ultimately lead more fulfilling and successful lives.

BREAKING DOWN BARRIERS TO EFFECTIVE EXPRESSION: OVERCOMING COMMUNICATION OBSTACLES

Clear and assertive communication is crucial for fostering meaningful relationships and achieving successful outcomes. However, many barriers often impede our ability to express ourselves effectively. This chapter will explore common obstacles, such as fear of conflict, lack of confidence, and passive-aggressive behavior, and provide practical tips and techniques for overcoming these barriers.

Fear of Conflict:

Many individuals find it challenging to engage in conflicts or difficult conversations due to fear of rejection, confrontation, or negative consequences. This fear often results in avoiding or sidestepping important issues, leading to misunderstandings and unresolved conflicts.

- **Acknowledge the fear:** Recognizing the existence of our fears is the first step toward overcoming them. Understand that conflicts and disagreements are natural and addressing them can lead to growth and resolution.
- **Manage emotions:** Before engaging in a difficult conversation, take a moment to regulate your emotions. Practice deep breathing, self-reflection, or other relaxation techniques to maintain a calm and composed state of mind.
- **Focus on mutual understanding:** Emphasize that you intend to find a resolution, not to attack or blame the other party. Use "I" statements, listen actively, and seek to understand their perspective to foster constructive dialogue.

Lack of Confidence:

Low self-esteem and a lack of confidence can hinder effective expression, as individuals may doubt the value of their thoughts and ideas. This often leads to hesitancy in asserting oneself, resulting in ineffective communication.

- **Recognize your worth:** Understand that your opinions and ideas carry weight and deserve to be heard. Acknowledge your accomplishments, strengths, and unique perspectives to boost your self-confidence.
- **Practice assertiveness:** Start by asserting yourself in low-stakes situations and gradually work your way up to more challenging conversations. Use confident body language, maintain eye contact, and speak with clarity and conviction.
- **Seek support:** Enlist the help of trusted friends, mentors, or therapists to provide guidance and encouragement. They can help you build your self-esteem and offer constructive feedback on your communication skills.

Passive-Aggressive Behavior:

Passive-aggressive behavior is a communication style characterized by indirect expressions of hostility or frustration. This approach avoids direct confrontation but often undermines relationships and inhibits honest two-way communication.

- **Develop awareness:** Recognize passive-aggressive tendencies in your own communication style. Pay attention to subtle signs such as sarcasm, backhanded compliments, or withholding information.
- **Communicate openly and directly:** Practice expressing your thoughts and feelings honestly, without resorting to passive-aggressive tactics. Use "I" statements to convey assertiveness and provide specific examples to avoid ambiguity.
- **Encourage open dialogue:** Foster an environment of trust and openness where others feel comfortable expressing their concerns directly. Lead by example and encourage constructive feedback to promote effective communication.

Effective expression and communication are essential for building healthy relationships and achieving personal and professional growth. Breaking down barriers such as fear of conflict, lack of confidence, and passive-aggressive behavior requires self-awareness, practice, and a commitment to open dialogue. By implementing the practical tips and techniques outlined in this chapter, you can overcome communication obstacles and foster more effective and assertive expression in all parts of your life.

THE ART OF ACTIVE LISTENING:

The art of active listening is a cornerstone of effective communication. It goes beyond simply hearing the words being spoken; it encompasses understanding and connecting with the speaker. By actively listening, we show our genuine interest in the other person's thoughts and experiences, fostering a deeper level of engagement and empathy.

To become a better active listener, certain strategies can be employed. One such technique is maintaining eye contact. By looking directly at the speaker, we show we are fully present and focused on their words. This nonverbal communication can help put them at ease and encourage them to open up further.

Asking clarifying questions is another powerful tool for active listening. It shows we are engaged and seeking to understand the speaker's perspective. By asking open-ended questions, we invite them to elaborate and provide more details, letting us grasp the complete picture.

Providing feedback is crucial for active listening as well. It involves summarizing or paraphrasing what the speaker has said to make sure we have correctly understood their message. Not only does this affirm that we are actively listening, but it also offers a chance for the speaker to clarify any misunderstandings or misconceptions.

Active listening also requires being fully present and reducing distractions. This means putting aside our own thoughts, agendas, and judgments, and fully immersing ourselves in the conversation. It involves being patient, giving the speaker ample time to express themselves, and avoiding interrupting or finishing their sentences.

To master the art of active listening, one must also pay attention to nonverbal cues. These cues include facial expressions, body language, and tone of voice. While words convey meaning, these nonverbal signals offer more insights into the speaker's emotions and intentions.

Last, being mindful of our own biases and prejudices is essential for active listening. By recognizing and setting aside our own preconceived notions, we can approach conversations with an open mind and a genuine desire to understand the speaker's perspective.

Active listening is a fundamental skill for effective communication. By using techniques such as maintaining eye contact, asking clarifying questions, providing feedback, reducing distractions, and being mindful of nonverbal cues and personal biases, we can become proficient active listeners. This skill not only enhances our relationships but also lets us foster deeper connections and understanding with others.

ASSERTIVENESS: FINDING YOUR VOICE:

Communication is a vital part of our everyday lives, and expressing our thoughts and feelings effectively is crucial. However, many of us struggle to find our voice and assert ourselves confidently. This chapter aims to delve into the idea of assertiveness and its significance in effective communication. By understanding assertiveness and using various tools and techniques, we can develop essential skills to express ourselves clearly and confidently.

Understanding Assertiveness:

Assertiveness lies between passive and aggressive communication styles. It involves expressing our thoughts, feelings, and needs without belittling or disrespecting others. Assertive individuals are self-assured, able to establish boundaries, and effectively communicate their desires and expectations.

Benefits of Assertiveness:

Developing assertiveness skills can significantly improve our relationships, both personal and professional. It lets us communicate our needs and desires effectively, build trust, and establish healthy boundaries. Additionally, assertiveness helps develop self-confidence, reduces stress, and leads to better problem-solving and conflict resolution.

Tools and Techniques:

Using "I" Statements: When expressing our thoughts and emotions, using "I" statements instead of blaming or accusatory language can prevent defensiveness and conflict. For example, instead of saying, "You never listen to me," rephrase it as, "I feel unheard when I'm not given the opportunity to share my thoughts."

Setting Boundaries: Establishing boundaries is crucial in maintaining healthy relationships. Clearly communicate your limits, expectations, and needs to others. This includes saying "no" when necessary and not feeling guilty about it. Respect of your boundaries by others is essential for healthy communication.

Expressing Thoughts and Emotions Confidently: Speak clearly, using a confident and calm tone. Practice active listening by showing genuine interest and empathy toward others' perspectives. When expressing emotional states, use specific and descriptive language to convey your feelings effectively.

Self-Awareness and Self-Reflection: Acknowledge your emotions, needs, and values. Take the time to reflect on your communication patterns, identifying areas where you may be passive, aggressive, or lack assertiveness. Understanding yourself better will enhance your ability to express yourself authentically.

Assertiveness in Non-Verbal Communication: Pay attention to your body language, eye contact, and tone of voice. Maintain an open and confident posture. Avoid aggressive gestures such as pointing or invading personal space, while ensuring you are not overly passive by slouching or avoiding eye contact.

Assertiveness is a crucial skill for effective communication. Developing assertiveness lets us express our thoughts, feelings, and needs confidently without disrespecting others. Using tools such as "I" statements, setting boundaries, expressing thoughts and emotions confidently, and cultivating self-awareness, we can find our voice and communicate more authentically. Practice these techniques consistently, and you will see positive changes in your relationships and overall self-confidence.

NON-VERBAL COMMUNICATION: THE UNSUNG HERO

Non-verbal communication is a powerful tool that often goes unnoticed and overlooked in our daily interactions. While verbal communication may take center stage, it is non-verbal cues that can convey a clearer and more assertive message. This section aims to shed light on the significance of non-verbal communication and how it can enhance the effectiveness of expressing oneself.

Body Language:

Body language is a primary and universal form of non-verbal communication that unconsciously reveals our thoughts, emotions, and attitudes. Posture, gestures, and overall body movements play a vital role in conveying our message more effectively. For example, standing tall with open arms creates an impression of confidence and openness, while crossed arms and slouching may suggest defensiveness or disinterest. By being aware of our body language, we can align it with our verbal communication to reinforce our message and establish authenticity.

Facial Expressions:

Our faces serve as a canvas for countless emotions, and our facial expressions can provide valuable insights into our thoughts and feelings. Expressions such as smiles, frowns, raised eyebrows, or narrowed eyes can significantly affect how our messages are received. A warm smile can create a friendly and inviting atmosphere, while a frown or grimace can communicate displeasure or disagreement. Being mindful of our facial expressions lets us express ourselves genuinely and helps make sure our words are not misunderstood.

Tone of Voice:

While verbal communication relies on the words we speak, our tone of voice carries another layer of meaning. How we say something can drastically change its interpretation. Tone of voice encompasses factors such as volume, pitch, rhythm, and emphasis. A calm and soothing tone may signify empathy and reassurance, but a harsh and loud tone might convey anger or frustration. By aligning our tone with our words, we make sure our message is delivered clearly and assertively, leaving no room for misinterpretation.

Aligning Non-verbal and Verbal Communication:

To express oneself clearly and assertively, it is essential to align non-verbal and verbal communication seamlessly. Inconsistencies between the two can create confusion or lead to a lack of credibility. By consciously paying attention to body language, facial expressions, and tone of voice, we can enhance the impact of our verbal message and create a more powerful overall communication experience. This alignment helps establish trust, build rapport, and show authenticity, ultimately leading to more effective communication.

Non-verbal communication is the unsung hero in expressing oneself clearly and assertively. By acknowledging and understanding the power of body language, facial expressions, and tone of voice, we can unlock its potential for enhanced clarity and impact. Integrating non-verbal cues with verbal communication lets us communicate more authentically, build stronger connections, and make sure our message is received as intended. So, let us recognize the value of non-verbal communication and harness its power to become more effective communicators in all parts of life.

CONFLICT RESOLUTION: NAVIGATING CHALLENGING CONVERSATIONS

Understanding the Importance of Clear Communication:

Clear communication plays a crucial role in conflict resolution. It enables individuals to express their thoughts, needs, and perspectives in a concise and understandable manner. By stating ideas, misunderstandings and assumptions can be avoided, leading to more effective dialogue.

Managing Emotions:

Emotions can often escalate during conflicts, hindering productive conversations. It is important to recognize and manage emotions to prevent them from influencing our ability to communicate effectively. Strategies such as deep breathing, taking breaks, and self-reflection can help in regulating emotions and maintaining composure.

Staying Calm and Focused:

Maintaining a calm and focused mindset during challenging conversations is key to resolving conflicts. This involves actively listening to the other person's viewpoint without interrupting or becoming defensive. It also requires avoiding personal attacks or disrespectful language. Staying calm lets individuals think clearly, respond appropriately, and work toward a resolution.

Finding Common Ground:

Building common ground is an essential part of conflict resolution. It involves seeking areas of agreement or shared interests with the other person, even in the midst of disagreement. By focusing on common goals or values, individuals can bridge gaps and foster a cooperative atmosphere. This approach fosters mutual understanding and increases the likelihood of finding solutions that satisfy both parties.

Assertive Expression:

Assertiveness is a crucial skill when navigating challenging conversations. It involves expressing one's thoughts, needs, and boundaries confidently and respectfully. By practicing assertiveness, individuals can avoid passive or aggressive communication styles that often escalate conflicts. Clear communication can help establish a positive tone, encourage open dialogue, and contribute to successful conflict resolution.

The ability to express oneself clearly and assertively during conflicts and challenging conversations is an indispensable skill. By using strategies to manage emotions, stay calm, and find common ground, individuals can engage in constructive dialogue while expressing their thoughts and needs effectively. Remember, conflict resolution is not about winning an argument but finding a resolution that satisfies all parties involved.

THE POWER OF EMPATHY AND UNDERSTANDING:

Empathy and understanding play a significant role in fostering effective communication. By actively listening and putting ourselves in the shoes of others, we can create meaningful connections and achieve more successful communication outcomes.

One powerful technique for practicing empathy is active listening. It involves fully engaging with the person speaking, maintaining eye contact, and giving our full attention. By doing so, we not only understand their words but also try to comprehend the emotions, thoughts, and experiences behind their message. Active listening shows we value and respect the other person's perspective, which encourages them to open up and share more authentically. This helps build trust and strengthens the connection between individuals.

Additionally, putting ourselves in other's shoes lets us understand their experiences and emotions better. This technique requires us to imagine what it feels like to be in their situation, considering their background, beliefs, and values. By doing so, we can gain a more comprehensive understanding of their perspective and respond in a way that acknowledges their feelings and needs. This fosters mutual respect and shows we genuinely care about the other person's well-being.

Empathy and understanding enhance communication outcomes by bridging differences and resolving conflicts. When we strive to understand others, we create a safe space for open dialogue and collaboration. We are more likely to find common ground and reach mutually beneficial solutions. Instead of becoming defensive or dismissive, we can approach disagreements with curiosity and empathy. This promotes a constructive exchange of ideas and can lead to creative problem-solving.

Ultimately, empathy and understanding should be woven into the fabric of our communication. By focusing on these qualities, we can create a more compassionate and inclusive society where everyone feels heard and valued. Whether in personal relationships, professional settings, or broader communities, practicing empathy enables us to connect on a deeper level and build stronger, more meaningful relationships.

The power of empathy and understanding in effective communication cannot be overstated. By actively listening and putting ourselves in other's shoes, we can foster meaningful connections, build trust, and achieve more successful communication outcomes. Let us embrace empathy as a guiding principle, for it has the potential to transform our relationships and the world around us.

CHAPTER FOUR SUMMARY: EFFECTIVE COMMUNICATION: EXPRESSING YOURSELF CLEARLY AND ASSERTIVELY

Chapter Four delves into the power of effective communication and its impact on various parts of our lives. It highlights the role of effective communication in building strong relationships, achieving positive outcomes, resolving conflicts constructively, influencing others, and expressing our authentic selves. The chapter emphasizes the significance of clear and assertive expression in creating understanding and fostering meaningful connections.

The chapter also addresses common obstacles to effective expression and provides practical tips and techniques for overcoming them. It explores the fear of conflict, lack of confidence, and passive-aggressive behavior as barriers to effective communication and offers strategies to manage and overcome these challenges.

Active listening is identified as a fundamental skill for effective communication. The chapter provides techniques for active listening, including maintaining eye contact, asking clarifying questions, providing feedback, reducing distractions, and being mindful of nonverbal cues and personal biases. By becoming proficient active listeners, individuals can foster deeper connections and understanding with others.

The idea of assertiveness is introduced as a vital skill for expressing oneself clearly and confidently. The chapter explores the benefits of assertiveness in personal and professional relationships and offers tools and techniques for developing assertiveness, such as using "I" statements, setting boundaries, expressing thoughts and emotions confidently, and cultivating self-awareness.

Nonverbal communication is highlighted as an essential part of expressing oneself clearly and assertively. The chapter emphasizes the significance of body language, facial expressions, and tone of voice in conveying messages effectively. It encourages aligning nonverbal and verbal communication to enhance the impact and authenticity of one's message.

The chapter also addresses conflict resolution and provides strategies for expressing oneself clearly and assertively during challenging conversations. It emphasizes the importance of clear communication, managing emotions, staying calm and focused, finding common ground, and using assertive expression to navigate conflicts effectively.

Last, the power of empathy and understanding in effective communication is explored. The chapter emphasizes the role of active listening and putting oneself in others' shoes to foster meaningful connections and achieve successful communication outcomes. It highlights the impact of empathy on building trust, resolving conflicts, and creating a compassionate and inclusive society.

Overall, Chapter Four emphasizes the significance of effective communication, provides practical strategies for expressing oneself clearly and assertively, and highlights the importance of active listening, assertiveness, nonverbal communication, conflict resolution, and empathy in enhancing communication skills and fostering meaningful connections.

SETTING BOUNDARIES: LEARNING TO SAY 'NO' RESPECTFULLY

THE POWER OF BOUNDARIES: NURTURING PERSONAL WELL-BEING AND HEALTHY RELATIONSHIPS

Setting boundaries is essential for maintaining personal well-being and fostering healthy relationships. Boundaries serve as guidelines that define and protect our physical, emotional, and psychological space. They help us establish a sense of self-respect, promoting positive interactions and reducing conflicts with others. Understanding the reasons behind setting boundaries can support personal growth and contribute to overall happiness.

First, setting boundaries is crucial for personal well-being. It lets us prioritize our own needs and take care of ourselves. By defining limits on how others treat us, we establish a level of self-respect and make sure our emotional and physical well-being are safeguarded. This is important in relationships where others may have different expectations or interests. Setting boundaries enables us to give time and energy for self-care, which reduces stress and prevents burnout, ultimately leading to improved mental health.

Second, boundaries are vital for maintaining healthy relationships. Clear and well-communicated boundaries establish mutual respect, trust, and understanding between individuals. By articulating our needs and limits, we provide others with a framework for interacting with us. This can prevent misunderstandings, resentment, and conflicts that may arise due to unspoken expectations. Healthy relationships require mutual respect for each other's boundaries, fostering an environment of trust and emotional safety.

Additionally, boundaries contribute significantly to personal growth and self-awareness. When we set boundaries, we practice self-reflection and learn of our values, desires, and limits. This process lets us gain a deeper understanding of ourselves and identify what is essential to our well-being. By recognizing and respecting our own boundaries, we are better equipped to communicate them to others effectively. This self-awareness also enables us to establish healthier relationships, as we are more aware of what we require from others and can avoid codependent or toxic dynamics.

Setting boundaries is crucial for personal well-being and maintaining healthy relationships. By defining our limits, we focus on our own self-care, leading to improved mental health. Additionally, clear boundaries foster mutual respect and understanding in relationships, preventing conflicts and misunderstandings. Last, boundaries contribute to personal growth and self-awareness, letting us understand our needs and desires better. So, understanding the importance of setting boundaries supports our overall happiness and helps with healthy interactions with others.

BALANCING BOUNDARIES: IDENTIFYING OVERCOMMITMENT AND SAFEGUARDING MENTAL AND PHYSICAL WELL-BEING

In our modern society, overcommitment has become a common issue affecting individuals from various walks of life. Whether due to work-related demands, social obligations, or personal goals, many people continuously push their limits and struggle to balance their commitments. While having a busy schedule may seem like a testament to productivity, it is crucial to recognize the signs of overcommitment and understand the negative consequences it can have on mental and physical health.

Physical Exhaustion: Overcommitment often leads to physical exhaustion, as individuals constantly juggle multiple tasks and lack adequate time for rest. This exhaustion can manifest as chronic fatigue, a weakened immune system, and even various physical illnesses such as headaches or gastrointestinal issues.

Emotional Turmoil: When overburdened with commitments, individuals may experience emotional turmoil. Feelings of stress, anxiety, and overwhelm become common, affecting their overall emotional well-being. This can lead to irritability, frequent mood swings, and even depression or anxiety disorders.

Reduced Productivity: Contrary to the belief that overcommitment enhances productivity, it often has the opposite effect. When one is overwhelmed with many responsibilities, it becomes challenging to give the necessary time and attention to each task. This results in reduced productivity and quality of work. Procrastination and increased errors become more likely as mental clarity and focus decline.

Decreased Satisfaction: Overcommitment can rob individuals of the joy and satisfaction they once derived from their commitments. When overwhelmed, people often merely go through the motions without experiencing true fulfillment or a sense of accomplishment. This, in turn, can lead to decreased motivation and loss of interest in previously enjoyable activities.

Strained Relationships: Maintaining healthy relationships requires time and energy, both of which can become compromised when over-committed. As individuals struggle to find a balance, their social connections may suffer. They may become less available for family, friends, or romantic partners, resulting in strained relationships that may lead to feelings of isolation and loneliness.

Sleep Disturbances: Overcommitment can significantly disrupt one's sleep patterns. Constantly trying to meet multiple obligations can cause restlessness and intrusive thoughts, making it difficult to wind down and fall asleep. Lack of quality sleep not only exacerbates physical exhaustion but also impairs cognitive function and increases the risk of various health issues.

Neglected Self-Care: Overcommitment often leads to neglecting self-care practices crucial for maintaining mental and physical well-being. With limited time available, exercise routines, healthy eating habits, relaxation techniques, and hobbies may be pushed aside. This neglect further underscores the negative impact of overcommitment on overall health.

Recognizing the signs of overcommitment and its consequences is vital for preventing long-term negative effects on mental and physical health. It is essential to focus on self-care, set realistic boundaries, and learn to say no when necessary. By understanding the limitations of our time and energy, we can strive for a healthier balance, leading to improved well-being and a more fulfilling life.

ASSERTIVE COMMUNICATION: NAVIGATING BOUNDARIES WITH CLARITY, RESPECT, AND SENSITIVITY

Effective communication techniques for asserting boundaries without causing offense or guilt are essential for maintaining healthy relationships and ensuring mutual respect. Here are some strategies to explore:

Be clear and specific in expressing your boundaries: Clearly articulate what you need or don't want in a calm and confident manner. Use "I" statements to communicate how a particular behavior affects you personally. For example, say, "I feel overwhelmed when you constantly ask me for favors after work," instead of saying, "You are so demanding, and I can't handle it anymore."

Use non-blaming language: Avoid blaming or accusing the other person, as it can lead to defensiveness. Focus on your feelings and needs instead. Frame your statements in a way that emphasizes your perspective, such as "I need some alone time to recharge" instead of "You're always suffocating me."

Maintain a respectful tone and body language: Keep your communication respectful, both in verbal and non-verbal cues. Be mindful of your tone of voice, maintaining a calm and assertive demeanor. Non-verbal cues like maintaining eye contact, open body language, and a relaxed posture can also contribute to effective communication.

Offer alternatives or compromises: If saying "no" to someone's request, offer alternatives or compromises you are comfortable with. This shows that you acknowledge their needs while still asserting your boundaries. For example, say, "I can't help you both Saturday and Sunday, but I can do it on Monday."

Practice active listening: Give the other person a chance to express their feelings or concerns about your boundaries. Actively listen to their perspective without interrupting or getting defensive. Showing empathy and understanding can help them recognize the validity of your boundaries.

Repeat your commitment to the relationship: Emphasize that maintaining healthy boundaries does not mean you value the relationship any less. Express your desire to continue having a positive connection while ensuring your personal well-being. This reassurance can help alleviate any guilt the other person may feel.

Be consistent and firm: Once you establish your boundaries, stick to them consistently. Reinforcing your boundaries over time will show you are serious and committed to your own well-being. This helps others understand and respect your limits.

Reflect and offer space for discussion: After expressing your boundaries, allow space for both parties to reflect and discuss them. Encourage open dialogue and address any concerns or misunderstandings that arise. This approach fosters mutual understanding and paves the way for stronger boundaries.

Effective communication is a skill that requires practice and patience. By adopting these techniques, you can assert your boundaries confidently and respectfully without causing offense or guilt to others.

SAYING 'NO' WITH PURPOSE: PRIORITIZING PERSONAL NEEDS AND EMPOWERING DECISION-MAKING

Learning how to focus on one's own needs and desires is crucial for making informed decisions about what to say 'no' to. It involves recognizing and understanding our own limitations, setting boundaries, and valuing our own well-being. Here are some steps to help develop this important skill:

Self-reflection: Begin by taking the time to understand your own needs, desires, and values. Reflect on what truly matters to you and what brings you happiness and fulfillment. This self-awareness will serve as a guide when deciding what to focus on and say 'no' to.

Identify your priorities: Once you clearly understand your needs and desires, focus on them. List them in order of importance and relevance to your life. By doing so, you can consider these priorities when faced with various demands or requests.

Establish boundaries: Setting boundaries is crucial to protect your time, energy, and well-being. Identify what you are comfortable with and what you are not willing to compromise. This could be related to work demands, personal commitments, or social obligations. Remember, it's okay to say 'no' when something goes against your boundaries.

Assess the consequences: Before deciding on saying 'no,' consider the potential outcomes, both positive and negative. Evaluate how it aligns with your priorities and how it may affect your overall well-being. This step will help you make informed decisions and assess the importance of each request.

Practice assertiveness: Learning to say 'no' assertively is a skill that can be developed over time. Be clear, honest, and respectful when declining requests. Express your priorities, limitations, and reasons calmly, without feeling the need to justify or apologize excessively. Remember, you have the right to protect your time and energy.

Reinforce self-care: Prioritizing your own needs and desires means recognizing the importance of self-care. Taking care of your physical, mental, and emotional well-being is essential for making informed decisions. Allow yourself time for rest, relaxation, and activities that bring you joy. By doing so, you'll have a clearer vision of what to say 'no' to in order to protect your well-being.

Learning how to focus on your own needs and desires is a continual process. It requires practice and self-reflection. By doing so, you'll develop the ability to make informed decisions about what to say 'no' to, leading to a more balanced and fulfilling life.

THE ART OF RESPECTFUL REFUSALS: STRATEGIES FOR SAYING 'NO' WITH GRACE AND GRATITUDE

Developing strategies for saying 'no' respectfully can be a valuable skill in both personal and professional settings. By offering alternative solutions or expressing gratitude for the opportunity, you can decline requests while still maintaining positive relationships. Here are some strategies to consider:

Express gratitude: Start your response by appreciating the person's offer or request. Showing gratitude sets a positive tone and ensures the other person feels valued. For example, you can say, "Thank you so much for thinking of me. I really appreciate the opportunity."

Offer an alternative solution: Instead of simply declining, propose another option that could be more feasible or convenient for both parties. This shows that you are still willing to help. For example, you might say, "I'm unable to take on this project right now, but I can recommend someone who would be perfect for it."

Be honest and concise: It's important to be straightforward and honest about your limitations without going into too much detail. Being straightforward helps avoid confusion or misunderstandings. A simple, clear statement like, "I'm sorry, but I won't be able to commit to that at the moment" can signal your inability to fulfill the request without causing offense.

Suggest an alternative time frame: Sometimes, it's not possible to say 'yes' immediately, but you're open to considering the request later. In that case, indicate your willingness to revisit the matter at a different time. For example, you could say, "I'm unavailable right now, but if this opportunity arises in the future, please feel free to reach out again."

Offer help within your bounds: If you cannot fulfill the entire request, offer a partial solution, or assist in a way that aligns with your capabilities. This approach lets you contribute while still respecting your own boundaries. For example, you may say, "I'm unable to take on the whole project, but I can provide guidance and support during the initial stages."

Be empathetic and understanding: Acknowledge the importance of the request to the person making it. Let them know you understand their needs and concerns, even if you cannot accommodate them. Showing empathy helps have positive relationships and shows your consideration. You can say, "I understand this is important to you, but unfortunately, I won't be able to assist this time."

Reflect on your priorities: It's crucial to consider your own priorities and workload before committing to more tasks. If you are already overloaded with responsibilities, be honest about your current commitments and explain that you cannot take on more at the moment. This highlights your dedication to your existing responsibilities and avoids overstretching yourself.

It is important to be kind, respectful, and considerate when saying 'no' to others. By offering alternative solutions or expressing gratitude for the opportunity, you can decline requests while still maintaining positive relationships.

NAVIGATING CHALLENGES: OVERCOMING PUSHBACK WITH ASSERTIVE BOUNDARY MANAGEMENT

Asserting boundaries can be a powerful and necessary practice for maintaining healthy relationships and personal well-being. However, it is common to face challenges and pushbacks when establishing and maintaining these boundaries. Here are some common challenges and tips on how to handle them with confidence:

Guilt and fear of disappointing others: One of the biggest challenges in asserting boundaries is the guilt or fear of letting down or disappointing others. Remember that it is important to focus on your own needs and well-being. Recognize that setting boundaries is not selfish, but essential for maintaining healthy relationships and personal growth.

Lack of understanding or respect from others: Some individuals may not understand or respect your boundaries. Clearly communicate your needs and boundaries in a direct yet respectful manner. Use assertive communication, expressing your preferences and feelings without being aggressive or overly accommodating. Stay firm and consistent and explain why these boundaries are important to you.

Emotional manipulation: Some people may try to manipulate you into feeling guilty or changing your boundaries. They might use emotional blackmail or try to make you feel responsible for their emotions or actions. Recognize these manipulative tactics and stay firm in your boundaries. Remember that you are not responsible for other people's emotions or actions, and it's important to focus on your own well-being.

Fear of confrontation and conflict: Many individuals avoid asserting boundaries because they fear confrontation or conflict. However, avoiding these conversations can lead to resentment and dissatisfaction. Practice assertiveness by using "I" statements, expressing your feelings and needs in a calm and confident manner. Be prepared for potential disagreements and remember that healthy relationships can withstand respectful disagreements.

Feeling like you're being unreasonable: It is common to doubt whether your boundaries are reasonable or fair. Remember that boundaries are subjective and unique to everyone. Trust your instincts and judgments about what feels right for you. Seek support from trusted friends, family, or professionals who can confirm your boundaries and provide guidance if needed.

Setting and maintaining consistent boundaries: Consistency is crucial in maintaining boundaries. Some individuals may test your boundaries to see if they are firm or negotiable. Stay consistent in enforcing your boundaries and avoid making exceptions, as this can lead to confusion and undermine your confidence. Practice self-care and focus on yourself to reinforce the importance of your boundaries.

Struggling with assertiveness: Assertiveness is a skill that can be developed with practice. Engage in assertiveness training or seek support from a therapist or counselor to enhance your communication and assertiveness skills. Remember that being assertive is not synonymous with being harsh or rude, but rather expressing your needs and boundaries in a respectful and confident manner.

Asserting boundaries is a journey that requires self-reflection, self-awareness, and consistent practice. Embrace the process, trust yourself, and remember that setting boundaries is an act of self-love and self-respect.

BOUNDARIES UNLEASHED: UNLOCKING PERSONAL GROWTH AND TRANSFORMING RELATIONSHIPS

Setting and maintaining boundaries is crucial for personal growth and the development of healthy relationships. Boundaries define our limits and create a safe space for us to protect our mental, emotional, and physical well-being. While some may associate boundaries with a negative connotation, it is important to understand the positive impact they have on our lives and those around us.

One significant effect of setting boundaries is the empowerment it brings. By clearly communicating our needs and limits, we gain a sense of control over our lives. Instead of allowing others to dictate our choices, boundaries let us make decisions based on what aligns with our values and priorities. This empowers us to live authentically and with a greater sense of self-worth.

Additionally, boundaries promote personal growth by fostering self-awareness and self-care. When we establish boundaries, whether it's giving time for self-reflection or engaging in activities that bring us joy, we focus on our own well-being. This self-care practice enables personal growth by providing us with the necessary time and energy to invest in our own personal development. As we continuously work on ourselves, setting and maintaining boundaries becomes an integral part of our growth and personal transformation.

Setting boundaries can have a positive impact on our relationships. It sets a framework of respect, trust, and communication between individuals. Boundaries make sure each person's needs and limits are acknowledged and respected, leading to healthier and more fulfilling connections. By clearly defining our boundaries, we create open and honest relationships where both parties feel valued and understood.

In relationships where boundaries are upheld, conflicts are reduced, and misunderstandings are reduced. Each person knows where they stand and what is expected from them, which cultivates a sense of security and stability. This enables individuals to more effectively support and care for one another, leading to enhanced intimacy and stronger connections.

Last, maintaining boundaries lets us better manage stress and avoid burnout. By respecting our own limits and saying 'no' when necessary, we prevent ourselves from spreading too thin and becoming overwhelmed. When we focus on our well-being, we are better equipped to handle life's challenges and have the energy to invest in our relationships and personal growth.

Setting and maintaining boundaries has many positive impacts on our personal growth and relationships. Empowerment, self-awareness, and self-care are all fostered through boundary-setting, allowing an individual to flourish and grow. Boundaries also promote healthier and more fulfilling relationships, as they establish a foundation of respect, trust, and open communication. By focusing on our well-being and managing stress effectively, we create an environment for personal growth and enhanced connections. Ultimately, boundaries are not restrictive barriers, but rather liberating tools that pave the way for a more enriching and fulfilling life.

CHAPTER FIVE SUMMARY: SETTING BOUNDARIES: LEARNING TO SAY 'NO' RESPECTFULLY

In Chapter Five, the importance of setting boundaries for personal well-being and healthy relationships is explored. The chapter begins by highlighting how boundaries serve as guidelines that define and protect our physical, emotional, and psychological space, contributing to self-respect, positive interactions, and reduced conflicts. Setting boundaries is crucial for personal well-being as it lets individuals prioritize their needs and take care of themselves. By defining limits on how others treat them, individuals establish self-respect and safeguard their emotional and physical well-being. This prioritization of self-care reduces stress, prevents burnout, and leads to improved mental health.

The chapter also emphasizes that boundaries are vital for maintaining healthy relationships. Clear and well-communicated boundaries establish mutual respect, trust, and understanding between individuals. By articulating needs and limits, boundaries provide others with a framework for interacting, preventing misunderstandings, resentment, and conflicts arising from unspoken expectations. Healthy relationships require mutual respect for each other's boundaries, fostering an environment of trust and emotional safety.

In addition to personal well-being and healthy relationships, boundaries contribute significantly to personal growth and self-awareness. Setting boundaries involves self-reflection, letting individuals understand their values, desires, and limits. This process deepens self-understanding and helps individuals identify what is essential to their well-being. By recognizing and respecting their own boundaries, individuals can effectively communicate them to others and establish healthier relationships. Self-awareness also enables individuals to avoid codependent or toxic dynamics and develop stronger connections based on mutual respect and understanding.

The chapter concludes by reaffirming that setting boundaries is crucial for personal well-being and maintaining healthy relationships. By defining limits, individuals focus on self-care, leading to improved mental health. Clear boundaries foster mutual respect and understanding, preventing conflicts and misunderstandings. Additionally, boundaries contribute to personal growth and self-awareness, letting individuals understand their needs and desires better. Understanding the importance of setting boundaries supports overall happiness and promotes healthy interactions with others.

CHAPTER 6

CONFLICT RESOLUTION: NAVIGATING DIFFICULT CONVERSATIONS WITH ASSERTIVENESS

UNDERSTANDING THE IMPORTANCE OF CONFLICT RESOLUTION:

Conflict is an inherent part of human interactions, and conflict resolution plays a vital role in maintaining healthy relationships and creating a positive work or personal environment. Understanding the importance of conflict resolution helps individuals embrace its positive aspects, rather than avoiding or dismissing conflicts altogether. This chapter aims to explore why resolving conflicts is crucial for the well-being of relationships and environments.

Foremost, conflict resolution leads to improved communication and understanding. Conflicts often arise due to misunderstandings, differences in perspectives, or unmet expectations. By addressing conflicts and engaging in open and honest dialogue, individuals can gain a deeper understanding of each other's viewpoints, needs, and concerns. This increased understanding fosters empathy and enables parties to find common ground or compromise, leading to a more harmonious and respectful relationship.

Conflict resolution promotes personal growth and self-awareness. Engaging in conflict requires individuals to reflect on their own behavior, attitudes, and emotions. By examining their contributions to the conflict, individuals can identify areas for self-improvement and enhance their emotional intelligence. Conflict resolution lets individuals recognize their biases, defensiveness, or triggers, and develop better coping mechanisms. Consequently, individuals become more self-aware and are better equipped to handle future conflicts effectively, promoting personal growth and development.

Resolving conflicts also strengthens trust and strengthens relationships. Trust is the foundation on which relationships are built, be it personal or professional. When conflicts remain unresolved, resentment, frustration, and mistrust can fester, damaging the bond between individuals. Conversely, actively addressing and resolving conflicts shows a genuine commitment to the relationship. By showing respect, empathy, and a willingness to find mutually beneficial solutions, individuals can rebuild trust and strengthen their connection. Resolving conflicts in a healthy way also sets a positive example for others, encouraging open communication and trust in group dynamics.

In the workplace, conflict resolution contributes to a positive and productive environment. Conflicts among coworkers can create tension and reduce productivity. However, addressing conflicts promptly and effectively makes sure issues do not escalate and spread negativity throughout the team. By fostering a workplace culture that encourages open dialogue and conflict resolution, organizations can create an environment where diverse opinions and ideas are valued, leading to higher levels of innovation, cooperation, and job satisfaction.

Lastly, conflict resolution reduces stress and promotes well-being. Lingering conflicts can take a toll on individuals' mental and emotional health. The unresolved tension and anxiety associated with conflicts can negatively affect personal happiness, job satisfaction, and overall well-being. By actively addressing and resolving conflicts, individuals can experience a sense of relief and release the emotional burden they were carrying. This promotes better mental health, increased happiness, and a positive overall environment.

Understanding the importance of conflict resolution is crucial for maintaining healthy relationships and creating a positive work or personal environment. Conflict resolution enhances communication, promotes personal growth and self-awareness, strengthens trust, fosters productive relationships, reduces stress, and contributes to overall well-being. By embracing conflict resolution as a fundamental skill, individuals can transform conflicts into opportunities for growth and true connection, leading to happier and more fulfilling relationships and environments.

IDENTIFYING COMMON BARRIERS TO EFFECTIVE CONFLICT RESOLUTION:

Effective conflict resolution is crucial in maintaining healthy relationships and promoting productive outcomes. However, several common barriers can hinder the successful resolution of conflicts. These barriers often include fear of confrontation, lack of communication skills, and emotional reactivity. Understanding these obstacles is essential for improving conflict resolution abilities.

Fear of Confrontation: Many individuals avoid conflict due to a fear of confrontation. This fear may arise from concerns about damaging relationships, creating hostility, or not handling the emotions that may arise during the conflict. Conflicts may remain unresolved, helping to accumulate unresolved tension and potential long-term damage to the relationship.

Lack of Communication Skills: Poor communication skills are a significant barrier to effective conflict resolution. It is common for people to struggle with expressing their viewpoints, actively listening to others, or using appropriate non-verbal cues. Ineffective communication can lead to misunderstandings, escalating tensions, and an inability to reach a resolution.

Emotional Reactivity: Emotions play a critical role in conflict situations. When individuals become emotionally reactive, their ability to engage in rational discussions diminishes. Emotional outbursts, defensiveness, aggression, or withdrawal can prevent a healthy dialogue and make conflict resolution challenging. Addressing conflicts with emotional intelligence is essential for finding common ground and resolving issues effectively.

Lack of Empathy: Empathy is crucial for understanding different perspectives and fostering effective conflict resolution. When individuals are unable or unwilling to empathize with others, conflicts often escalate rather than being resolved. Empathy helps individuals acknowledge and confirm the feelings and experiences of others, creating a foundation for constructive problem-solving.

Power Imbalances: Power imbalances can create significant barriers to conflict resolution. When one party has more authority, influence, or control, it can prevent the other party from feeling comfortable expressing their concerns or opinions. This imbalance may result in one party dominating the conversation while the other feels powerless, leading to an unfair resolution or unresolved conflict.

Cultural Differences: Cultural diversity can present challenges in conflict resolution. Different cultural backgrounds may shape individuals' communication styles, conflict management strategies, and expectations for resolving conflicts. Misunderstandings related to cultural differences can lead to confusion, frustration, and difficulty in finding common ground.

Lack of Problem-Solving Skills: Conflicts arise due to differing needs, interests, and perspectives. Without effective problem-solving skills, parties may struggle to identify and evaluate potential solutions. This barrier prevents the development of mutually beneficial outcomes, hindering conflict resolution.

To overcome these barriers, individuals can engage in conflict resolution training, practice active listening, develop emotional intelligence, cultivate empathy, and strive for equitable power dynamics. By recognizing and addressing these common obstacles, individuals can enhance their conflict resolution skills and strengthen their relationships.

DEVELOPING ASSERTIVENESS SKILLS: EFFECTIVE STRATEGIES FOR EXPRESSING NEEDS RESPECTFULLY

In various parts of life, being assertive is crucial for effective communication and maintaining healthy relationships. Developing assertiveness skills empowers individuals to express their needs, opinions, and concerns confidently, while still respecting others. By understanding and implementing effective strategies, individuals can foster respectful and constructive interactions. This chapter will discuss key strategies for developing assertiveness skills while promoting respectful communication.

Self-Awareness:

Before you can express yourself assertively, it is essential to reflect on your emotions, beliefs, and values. Understanding your needs and boundaries enables you to communicate them confidently. This self-awareness helps avoid aggressive or passive behavior and ensures respectful communication.

Clear Communication:

Assertiveness relies on expressing thoughts and feelings clearly, using direct and concise language. Focus on using "I" statements to share your emotions and experiences, rather than pointing fingers or making assumptions. Clearly state your needs, opinions, or concerns, while avoiding ambiguity or aggressive language.

Active Listening:

Active listening is key to developing assertiveness skills. Pay attention to the speaker, maintain eye contact, and provide verbal or non-verbal cues to show attentiveness and interest. Reflecting and paraphrasing the speaker's thoughts and emotions not only shows respect but fosters a deeper understanding of their perspective.

Respectful Tone and Body Language:

While expressing your needs and opinions, maintain a calm and respectful tone of voice. Avoid raising your voice or using aggression to make your point. Additionally, practice open body language by maintaining eye contact, standing or sitting in an upright position, and using appropriate facial expressions. These non-verbal cues communicate attentiveness and respect.

Practice Assertiveness Techniques:

Developing assertiveness skills often requires practice. Start techniques such as "broken record" by calmly repeating your point when faced with resistance or diversion. Use the "fogging" technique to acknowledge valid concerns without negating your own needs. Role-playing various scenarios can also be helpful in building confidence in expressing assertiveness effectively.

Set Boundaries:

Assertiveness involves setting personal boundaries and respecting the boundaries of others. Communicate your limits and expectations while being receptive to those of others. By respecting boundaries, you can foster an environment of mutual respect and open communication.

Conflict Resolution:

Assertiveness skills are crucial for resolving conflicts assertively and respectfully. Learn constructive conflict resolution strategies, such as using "I" statements, active listening, and finding common ground. Seek a win-win solution that honors both parties' needs, opinions, and concerns.

Developing assertiveness skills is essential for effective communication and maintaining healthy relationships. By practicing self-awareness, clear communication, active listening, and respectful body language, individuals can express their needs, opinions, and concerns assertively while respecting others. Setting boundaries and learning conflict resolution techniques further enhance assertiveness skills. Embracing assertiveness lets individuals navigate challenging situations confidently and build strong, respectful connections with others.

ACTIVE LISTENING: DISCOVER THE POWER OF ACTIVE LISTENING FOR SUCCESSFUL CONFLICT RESOLUTION

Conflict is an inevitable part of human interactions, occurring in various parts of our lives, be it at work, within relationships, or even within families. However, conflict does not necessarily have to result in heated arguments or broken relationships. Active listening, a key part of successful conflict resolution, holds the power to transform conflicts into opportunities for growth and understanding. This chapter will explore the techniques of empathetic listening and paraphrasing as essential tools for ensuring understanding and fostering empathy in conflict resolution.

Empathetic Listening:

Empathetic listening involves genuinely connecting with the speaker by understanding and sharing their feelings and emotions. It requires creating a safe and non-judgmental space for the speaker to express themselves. Here are techniques to enhance empathetic listening:

Give your full attention: Put away distractions such as phones and other devices. Maintain eye contact, face the speaker, and show you are fully present and engaged. Non-verbal cues like nodding and maintaining an open posture can also convey your attentiveness.

Use encouraging prompts: Encouraging prompts, such as "tell me more," "I understand," or "how did that make you feel?" show you are actively interested in understanding the speaker's perspective. These prompts invite further elaboration and help the speaker feel heard.

Show empathy through validation: Validate the speaker's emotions by acknowledging their feelings without judgment. Reflect on their emotions, saying things like, "It seems like you're really frustrated by this situation," or "I can imagine this has been challenging for you."

Paraphrasing for Understanding:

Paraphrasing is a crucial skill that shows your understanding of the speaker's message. It involves restating or summarizing the speaker's ideas using your own words. Here's how to paraphrase effectively:

Reflect the content: Recap the main points of what the speaker said, using your own words. This shows that you have actively listened to and understood their message. For example, you can say, "If I understand correctly, you're concerned about the lack of communication from the team members."

Capture emotions: Besides reflecting the content, paraphrasing should also include the emotional nuances expressed by the speaker. Reflect on the underlying emotions, saying something like, "It sounds like you're feeling overwhelmed and undervalued by the recent workload increase."

Seek confirmation: After paraphrasing, seek confirmation from the speaker to make sure you accurately understood their message. Ask open-ended questions like, "Did I capture your concerns accurately?" or "Is there anything else you'd like to add?"

Benefits of Active Listening in Conflict Resolution:

By using active listening techniques, conflicts can transform into constructive conversations, fostering understanding and empathy. Active listening benefits conflict resolution by:

Improving comprehension: Active listening makes sure all parties understand each other's perspectives, reducing the chances of miscommunication or misunderstanding.

Promoting empathy: By actively listening and confirming the speaker's emotions, empathy is fostered, creating an atmosphere of openness and trust.

Resolving conflicts: Through active listening, conflicts can be de-escalated, as it provides an opportunity for each party to feel heard and valued, increasing the chances for mutually beneficial resolutions.

Active listening is a powerful tool that can transform conflicts into opportunities for growth and understanding. By using techniques such as empathetic listening and paraphrasing, we can make sure all parties involved feel heard, understood, and respected. Integrating active listening into conflict resolution processes can pave the way for more harmonious relationships, both personally and professionally. So, let's embrace the power of active listening and unlock its potential for successful conflict resolution.

MANAGING EMOTIONS DURING DIFFICULT CONVERSATIONS:

Managing emotions during difficult conversations can be a challenging task. However, with some techniques and strategies, it is possible to navigate these discussions while keeping emotions in check. It is equally important to know how to support others in expressing their emotions constructively. Here are some techniques for managing emotions during difficult conversations and supporting others:

Self-Awareness: Begin by cultivating self-awareness. Recognize your own emotions and be aware of how they can influence your responses during a difficult conversation. Take a moment to check in with yourself and understand what you are feeling before engaging in the discussion.

Pause and Breathe: When emotions start to escalate or become overwhelming, take a pause. Deep breathing exercises can help calm your body and mind. By giving yourself a moment to breathe, you allow yourself to regain composure and respond more effectively.

Active Listening: Practice active listening skills during difficult discussions. Give your full attention to the person speaking, focus on their words, and try to empathize with their perspective. Listening attentively can help diffuse tension and create a more open dialogue.

Reflect and Reframe: Instead of reacting impulsively to emotional triggers, take a moment to reflect on the situation. Consider alternative viewpoints or interpretations of what is being discussed. This can prevent emotional escalation and help you approach the conversation with a more balanced perspective.

Use "I" Statements: When expressing your own emotions, use "I" statements to avoid sounding accusatory. For example, say "I feel hurt when..." instead of "You always make me feel..." This way, you are expressing your emotions without attacking the other person, which can keep the conversation more constructive.

Practice Empathy: Empathy is crucial when supporting others in expressing their emotions constructively. Actively try to understand their feelings and genuinely confirm them. Let them know that their emotions are heard and acknowledged, even if you may not agree with their perspective.

Create a Safe Space: During difficult conversations, create an environment where everyone feels safe to express themselves. Encourage open, respectful communication, and establish ground rules that foster a non-judgmental atmosphere. This can help individuals feel more comfortable sharing their emotions.

Confirm Emotions: Validate the emotions of others by acknowledging and accepting their feelings as valid. Avoid dismissing or trivializing their experiences. Confirming emotions shows empathy and promotes a more productive conversation.

Seek Solutions: When emotions are high, it's easy to get caught up in the heat of the moment. Shift the focus toward finding solutions rather than dwelling on the issue. Encourage brainstorming and problem-solving to move the conversation forward.

Take Breaks if Needed: If emotions become overwhelming, or the discussion reaches a stalemate, it may help to take a break. Allow for disconnected time to calm down and collect thoughts. Returning to the conversation with a fresh perspective can lead to more constructive outcomes.

Managing emotions during difficult conversations requires practice and self-awareness. By implementing these techniques, individuals can navigate challenging discussions more effectively while supporting others in expressing their emotions constructively.

CONSTRUCTIVE CONFLICT RESOLUTION TECHNIQUES:

Constructive conflict resolution techniques are essential in effectively navigating difficult conversations and finding mutually satisfactory solutions. Here are four techniques you can employ:

Win-Win Negotiation:

In a win-win negotiation approach, both parties focus on cooperative problem-solving rather than competing against each other. The goal is to reach a solution that benefits everyone involved. This technique encourages active listening, empathy, and understanding the underlying interests and needs of each party. By brainstorming creative ideas and exploring different options, win-win negotiation helps generate a solution that satisfies both parties.

Compromise:

When there is no single solution that fully satisfies both parties, compromise is often a proper approach. In this technique, each side gives up something to gain something else in return. Compromise requires open communication and a willingness to listen, understand, and value the perspectives of others. By finding common ground and reaching a middle ground on specific issues, compromise enables a resolution that may not be ideal for either party, but still acceptable.

Problem-Solving:

Problem-solving is a collaborative approach where all parties work together to find a solution that addresses the root causes of the conflict. This technique involves identifying and defining the problem, gathering information, generating and evaluating different options, and ultimately selecting and implementing the best solution. By focusing on shared goals and the common interest of all parties involved, problem-solving allows for a more comprehensive and lasting resolution.

Mediation:

Mediation involves the use of a neutral third party to help with communication and guide the conflict resolution process. The mediator does not impose a solution but encourages dialogue, active listening, and understanding between the parties. They help in exploring underlying concerns, clarifying issues, and finding common ground. Mediation is useful when emotions are high, and direct communication may prove challenging. It provides a safe and structured environment for open and respectful discussion, helping the parties come to an agreement independently.

In all conflict resolution techniques, effective communication is key. Active listening, expressing oneself assertively yet respectfully, and seeking to understand the perspectives of others are fundamental skills for constructive conflict resolution. It is important to approach conflicts with an open mind, genuine curiosity, and a willingness to work toward a solution that benefits everyone involved.

BUILDING A CULTURE OF CONFLICT RESOLUTION:

Building a culture of conflict resolution is essential for promoting an environment that values open communication, collaboration, and ultimately leads to a more harmonious and productive workplace. Here are strategies to create such a culture:

Education and Training: Begin by educating employees about the importance of conflict resolution and its positive impact on the workplace. Offer training programs to build conflict management skills, emphasizing effective communication, active listening, negotiation, and problem-solving techniques. This will enable employees to resolve conflicts independently and constructively.

Establish Clear Policies and Procedures: Develop and communicate clear policies and procedures for conflict resolution within the organization. These policies should emphasize respect, professionalism, and fairness while outlining a step-by-step process for resolving conflicts. Make sure employees have access to these policies and understand how to use them.

Encourage Open Communication: Foster an environment that encourages open and honest communication. Promote transparency, active listening, and empathy among team members. Create opportunities for open dialogue, such as regular team meetings, suggestion boxes, or anonymous feedback platforms. When communication channels are open, conflicts are more likely to be addressed and resolved proactively.

Lead by Example: Leaders and managers play a crucial role in shaping the organizational culture. To build a culture of conflict resolution, leaders must model positive behaviors themselves. Show effective conflict resolution skills, encourage collaboration, and provide constructive feedback. Leaders should also focus on resolving conflicts promptly to avoid escalation and set the tone for others to follow.

Encourage Collaboration and Teamwork: Promote a collaborative work environment where teamwork is valued. Encourage employees to work together toward common goals, emphasizing shared success rather than individual achievements. Foster an atmosphere that celebrates collaboration and encourages employees to resolve conflicts through constructive dialogue.

Provide Mediation Support: Offer mediation services, either internally or through trained professionals, for conflicts that cannot be resolved independently. Mediation provides a safe and neutral space for employees to express their concerns and work toward mutually beneficial solutions. Having a mediation process in place shows employees that the organization is committed to addressing conflicts effectively.

Recognize and Reward Positive Conflict Resolution: Encourage and acknowledge employees who show exceptional conflict resolution skills. Recognize individuals who effectively manage conflicts and contribute to a positive workplace environment. This recognition can be as verbal praise, rewards, or bonuses, showing others that resolving conflicts constructively is valued and encouraged.

Regularly Evaluate and Improve Processes: Continuously assess the effectiveness of conflict resolution strategies within the organization. Seek feedback from employees through surveys or focus groups to identify areas that require improvement. Regularly review and update conflict resolution policies, procedures, and training materials to ensure they remain relevant and effective.

By implementing these strategies, organizations can foster a culture that values open communication, collaboration, and conflict resolution. Ultimately, this will create a more harmonious and productive environment where employees feel valued and empowered to address conflicts in a constructive way.

CHAPTER SIX SUMMARY: CONFLICT RESOLUTION: NAVIGATING DIFFICULT CONVERSATIONS WITH ASSERTIVENESS

Chapter Six explores the importance of conflict resolution and provides strategies for navigating difficult conversations with assertiveness. It emphasizes the positive aspects of conflict resolution and its impact on maintaining healthy relationships and creating a positive work or personal environment. The chapter highlights the benefits of conflict resolution, including improved communication, personal growth and self-awareness, strengthened trust and relationships, a positive and productive workplace environment, reduced stress, and overall well-being.

The chapter also identifies common barriers to effective conflict resolution, such as fear of confrontation, lack of communication skills, emotional reactivity, lack of empathy, power imbalances, cultural differences, and a lack of problem-solving skills. Understanding these barriers is essential for improving conflict resolution abilities.

The chapter focuses on developing assertiveness skills and provides effective strategies for expressing needs respectfully. It emphasizes the importance of self-awareness, clear communication, active listening, respectful tone and body language, practicing assertiveness techniques, setting boundaries, and using conflict resolution skills.

Another section discusses the power of active listening in successful conflict resolution. It explores empathetic listening techniques and the skill of paraphrasing, highlighting their role in understanding others' perspectives, fostering empathy, and transforming conflicts into opportunities for growth and understanding.

Additionally, the chapter addresses managing emotions during difficult conversations and offers techniques for keeping emotions in check. It emphasizes self-awareness, pausing and breathing, active listening, reflection, and reframing, using "I" statements, practicing empathy, creating a safe space, confirming emotions, seeking solutions, and taking breaks if needed.

Last, the chapter covers constructive conflict resolution techniques, including win-win negotiation, compromise, problem-solving, and mediation. It underscores the importance of effective communication and highlights active listening, expressing oneself assertively yet respectfully, and understanding others' perspectives as fundamental skills for resolving conflicts constructively.

The chapter concludes by discussing strategies for building a culture of conflict resolution, including education and training, establishing clear policies and procedures, encouraging open communication, leading by example, fostering collaboration and teamwork, providing mediation support, recognizing and rewarding positive conflict resolution, and regularly evaluating and improving processes.

Overall, Chapter Six provides a comprehensive overview of conflict resolution, assertiveness skills, active listening, managing emotions, constructive conflict resolution techniques, and building a culture of conflict resolution. It equips individuals with the knowledge and strategies to navigate difficult conversations with confidence and promote healthy relationships and environments.

CHAPTER 7

NEGOTIATION SKILLS: HOW BEING ASSERTIVE CAN LEAD TO WIN-WIN OUTCOMES

ASSERTIVE NEGOTIATION: THE PATH TO WIN-WIN SOLUTIONS

Assertiveness in negotiation refers to the ability to confidently and respectfully express one's needs, wants, and opinions, while also remaining open to the needs and interests of the other party involved. It is a crucial skill in negotiation as it lets individuals advocate for their own goals while working toward mutually beneficial solutions.

The connection between assertiveness and win-win outcomes can be understood through the principles of collaborative negotiation. In a negotiation, both parties usually have different goals and interests. By being assertive, individuals can clearly articulate their own priorities, making sure their needs are met. This open communication helps establish trust and transparency between parties, enabling them to better understand each other's requirements.

At the same time, assertiveness also involves actively listening and acknowledging the concerns of the other party. By fully understanding their goals and interests, individuals can identify areas of common ground, helping with the development of creative and mutually beneficial solutions. This collaborative approach fosters a sense of cooperation and promotes win-win outcomes where both parties feel satisfied with the final agreement.

Assertiveness in negotiation makes sure individuals do not compromise their own interests or values excessively. By respectfully advocating for what they believe is fair and reasonable, negotiators can prevent being taken advantage of or settling for unfavorable agreements. This sense of self-assurance helps maintain a balanced power dynamic between parties and promotes fairness in the negotiation process.

Assertiveness in negotiation is vital for achieving win-win outcomes. It enables individuals to clearly communicate their needs and actively listen to the concerns of the other parties involved. By successfully balancing their own interests while working toward mutually beneficial solutions, negotiators can create agreements that satisfy all parties involved and build long-term relationships based on trust and cooperation.

DIFFERENTIATING ASSERTIVENESS FROM AGGRESSION AND PASSIVE BEHAVIOR IN NEGOTIATIONS.

Assertiveness in negotiations is a communication style that involves confidently expressing one's needs, interests, and desires, while also respecting and considering the needs of the other party. It is about standing up for oneself and advocating for one's own interests, but without disregarding the concerns and interests of the other party.

Aggression is a forceful and confrontational communication style that aims to dominate and win at any cost. Aggressive negotiators often focus on their own interests above all else and may resort to intimidation, personal attacks, or other aggressive tactics to achieve their objectives. They tend to disregard the needs and concerns of the other party, leading to a breakdown in communication and collaboration.

Passive behavior in negotiations, however, involves avoiding confrontation and conflict by not expressing one's true needs, interests, or desires. Passive negotiators often put the needs and concerns of the other party above their own, often leading to dissatisfaction and resentment. They may accommodate the demands of the other party without advocating for their own interests or assertively expressing their viewpoints.

Assertiveness in negotiations involves confidently expressing one's interests while considering the needs of the other party. Aggression seeks to dominate and win at any cost, disregarding the other party's concerns. Passive behavior involves avoiding confrontation and sacrificing one's own needs. A successful negotiator should aim for assertive behavior, as it allows for effective communication, cooperation, and a mutually beneficial outcome.

ASSERTIVE EXPRESSION: TECHNIQUES FOR CONFIDENTLY COMMUNICATING NEEDS AND WANTS

Assertive communication techniques are powerful tools that can help individuals express their needs and wants confidently and clearly. By using assertiveness, people can effectively communicate their desires while respecting the rights and boundaries of others. Let's explore some assertive communication techniques that can aid in expressing needs and wants:

Use "I" statements: When voicing your needs or wants, start your sentences with "I" instead of "you." For example, instead of saying, "You never listen to me," say, "I feel unheard when...". This approach focuses on your feelings and experiences rather than blaming or attacking the other person.

Be direct and specific: Clearly state what you want or need. Avoid beating around the bush or relying on hints. For example, instead of saying, "It would be nice if you could help me sometimes," say, "I would appreciate it if you could help me with this task." Being direct helps avoid confusion and clearly communicates your desires.

Use confident body language: Your non-verbal cues also play a crucial role in assertive communication. Stand tall, make eye contact, and maintain good posture. Use gestures to emphasize your points but avoid aggressive or defensive body language.

Be mindful of your tone: The tone of your voice can influence how your message is received. Speak in a clear, calm, and confident tone. Avoid aggressive or passive-aggressive tones, as they can undermine your assertiveness.

Practice active listening: When the other person responds or shares their perspective, actively listen, and confirm their experiences. Show empathy and understanding. Active listening fosters open communication and helps build rapport.

Set boundaries: Clearly define your boundaries and communicate them assertively. For example, say, "I cannot continue working on this project past 7 pm as I have personal commitments." Setting boundaries makes sure your needs are respected and prevents others from taking advantage of you.

Use "the broken record" technique: If someone tries to dismiss your needs or wants, calmly and respectfully repeat your request. By repeating your message, you reinforce your assertiveness and show your commitment to your wants and needs.

Practice self-compassion: Assertive communication requires courage and self-assurance. Remind yourself that it's okay to express your needs and wants. Give yourself permission to focus on your feelings and desires, without feeling guilty or selfish.

Assertive communication helps build healthier relationships based on open and honest communication. By practicing these techniques, you can confidently express your needs and wants while maintaining respect for others.

THE POWER OF ACTIVE LISTENING: BUILDING RAPPORT THROUGH UNDERSTANDING PERSPECTIVES

Active listening is a valuable skill that can greatly improve communication and help in building strong relationships. When applied effectively, it can help us understand the perspective of others, create rapport, and foster a deeper connection. Here are some ways to leverage active listening skills to achieve these outcomes:

Give undivided attention: When engaging in a conversation, eliminate distractions and concentrate only on the speaker. Maintain eye contact, nod occasionally, and use positive body language to show you are fully present and genuinely interested in what they have to say.

Avoid interrupting: Allow the speaker to express themselves fully before interjecting or asking clarifying questions. Interrupting may hinder the flow of conversation and prevent them from expressing their thoughts.

Practice empathy: Put yourself in the other person's shoes and try to understand their emotions, perspectives, and experiences. Avoid judging or making assumptions. By acknowledging their feelings and confirming their experiences, you can create a safe space for open and honest communication.

Reflect and paraphrase: After the speaker has shared, summarize, or reflect on their main points to ensure you have understood them correctly. Paraphrase their perspective or feelings to show you were actively listening and trying to comprehend their thoughts.

Ask open-ended questions: Encourage the other party to elaborate on their ideas by asking open-ended questions. This shows your willingness to learn more and engage in a deeper conversation. Questions like "Can you tell me more about that?" or "How do you feel about this situation?" can open channels for further discussion.

Avoid jumping to conclusions: Be careful not to assume you know what the other person will say before they finish speaking. This can lead to miscommunication or misunderstandings. Stay engaged and be patient until they have fully expressed their thoughts and feelings.

Be non-judgmental: Maintain an open mind and not pass judgment or make evaluative statements. Everyone has their own unique perspective, and by listening without criticism, you create a space where the other party feels comfortable sharing their thoughts openly.

Summarize and confirm: Once the conversation is ending, summarize the main points and feelings expressed. This shows you have actively listened to and understood their perspective. Let them know that you appreciate their viewpoint, even if you may not necessarily agree with it.

By actively practicing these techniques, you can leverage your active listening skills to better understand the other party's perspective and build rapport. This not only strengthens relationships but also promotes effective communication and mutual understanding.

GOAL-ORIENTED NEGOTIATION: HARNESSING ASSERTIVENESS FOR SUCCESSFUL OUTCOMES

Setting clear goals before entering a negotiation is crucial for success. It provides a clear direction and purpose, making sure all parties involved are on the same page. Without clear goals, negotiations can become chaotic and unproductive.

Here are steps to setting clear goals:

Define your desired outcomes: Determine what you hope to achieve from the negotiation. Be specific and consider both short-term and long-term goals. For example, you might aim to reach a certain agreement or secure a favorable deal that benefits your company in the long run.

Focus on your goals: Rank your goals in order of importance. Understand which goals are critical and which are negotiable. This helps you stay focused during the negotiation process and know when to be flexible.

Research and gather information: Collect as much information as possible about the other party involved in the negotiation. Understand their needs, desires, limitations, and expectations. This knowledge lets you tailor your goals to accommodate their perspective and increase your chances of a successful negotiation.

Write down your goals: Put your goals in writing. This helps you organize your thoughts and serves as a reference during the negotiation. Writing down your goals also makes them more concrete and memorable, making sure you do not lose sight of them during the negotiation.

Now, once you have set clear goals, the next step is to use assertiveness to ensure they are met. Assertiveness is a critical skill that lets you express your needs and wants while respecting the needs and wants of others. Here's how you can be assertive during negotiations:

Communicate your goals: Articulate your goals to the other party in a clear and concise manner. Be specific about what you want to achieve and why it is important to you. This clear communication helps set the tone for the negotiation and ensures both parties are on the same page.

Be confident and stand your ground: Confidence is vital during negotiations. Believe in the value and importance of your goals and confidently express them. Do not be afraid to defend your points and be persistent in your pursuit.

Listen actively and empathetically: While assertiveness is important, it is equally crucial to listen to the other party. Actively listen to their needs, concerns, and expectations. Show empathy and try to understand their perspective. This creates a collaborative and respectful negotiation environment.

Explore win-win solutions: Assertiveness should not come at the expense of a win-lose outcome. Instead, look for win-win solutions where both parties feel their goals are met. Maintain an open mindset and be willing to compromise when necessary.

Setting clear goals before entering a negotiation provides clarity and purpose. Using assertiveness ensures these goals are met by clear communication, confidence, active listening, and striving for win-win solutions. Combining these two strategies increases the chances of a successful negotiation outcome.

UNLEASHING ASSERTIVENESS: OVERCOMING BARRIERS FOR SUCCESSFUL NEGOTIATIONS

Overcoming common barriers to assertiveness, such as fear of conflict or rejection, is crucial in the negotiation process. Assertiveness plays a significant role in making sure your needs are met and that you achieve successful outcomes. Below are strategies to help you overcome these barriers and maintain assertiveness throughout negotiations:

Change Your Perspective: Instead of viewing conflict as something negative, reframe it as an opportunity for growth and understanding. Conflict can lead to better solutions by uncovering different perspectives and needs. Embrace the idea that assertiveness is not about winning or losing but finding mutually beneficial outcomes.

Self-Confidence and Self-Belief: Building self-confidence is essential for assertiveness. Remind yourself of your skills, knowledge, and the value you bring to the negotiation table. Increase your self-belief by practicing positive self-talk and visualizing successful outcomes.

Preparation and Research: Thoroughly prepare for negotiations by researching the other party's needs, desires, and potential objections. This knowledge will increase your confidence and help you formulate persuasive arguments. By being well-prepared, you can assert your position effectively without fear of rejection or conflict.

Active Listening and Empathy: Actively listen to the other party's perspective and try to understand their needs and concerns. By displaying empathy, you create a more collaborative environment, reducing the fear of conflict. Acknowledge their concerns, confirm their feelings, and find common ground that enables win-win solutions.

Use "I" Statements and Assertive Language: When expressing your needs or concerns, use "I" statements instead of aggressive or passive language. For example, instead of saying, "You always fail to meet the deadlines," say "I feel frustrated when deadlines are not met." Assertive language focuses on expressing your thoughts, feelings, and desires without attacking or blaming others.

Practice Effective Nonverbal Communication: Your body language and tone of voice play a significant role in assertiveness. Stand or sit up straight, maintain eye contact, and speak clearly and confidently. A strong nonverbal presence will boost your assertiveness and command respect.

Set Boundaries and Prioritize: Be clear about your boundaries and priorities before entering negotiations. This clarity empowers you to assertively communicate what is acceptable and what is not. By focusing on your priorities, you can maintain assertiveness while accommodating the other party's needs where possible.

Practice Assertiveness in Small Steps: Overcoming fear of conflict or rejection is a gradual process. Start by practicing assertiveness in low-stakes situations before moving to more significant negotiations. This incremental approach lets you build confidence and skills.

Seek Support: If you continue to struggle with assertiveness barriers, seek support from a mentor, coach, or therapist. They can provide guidance, offer new perspectives, and help you develop personalized strategies to overcome specific barriers.

Assertiveness is a skill that can be learned and strengthened over time. By applying these strategies and remaining committed to your growth, you can overcome common barriers to assertiveness and achieve successful negotiation outcomes.

ASSERTIVE SUCCESS: CASE STUDIES OF WIN-WIN OUTCOMES IN NEGOTIATIONS

Case Study 1: Win-Win Outcome in Salary Negotiation

In this case study, two parties engaged in a salary negotiation, where being assertive led to a win-win outcome. Sarah, a skilled professional with several years of experience, was offered a job at a reputable company. However, the initial salary offered was lower than her expectations.

Sarah decided to be assertive and scheduled a meeting with the human resources manager to discuss her concerns. During the meeting, she confidently presented her case, highlighting her qualifications, achievements, and the value she could bring to the organization. She also researched industry standards to support her request for a higher salary.

Instead of being confrontational, Sarah approached the negotiation with professionalism and respect. She listened attentively to the HR (Human Resources) manager's perspective and tried to understand their limitations. By remaining assertive yet open to compromise, she proposed a salary range that aligned with her expectations but also considered the company's constraints.

The outcome was a win-win situation. Sarah negotiated a higher salary, which fairly reflected her skills and knowledge. Simultaneously, the company recognized the value she could provide and would invest in her, increasing employee motivation and retention.

Real-Life Example: Business Partnership Negotiation

Two business owners, John and Lisa, were considering a partnership to expand their respective businesses. To ensure a successful negotiation, both individuals adopted an assertive approach.

John believed that merging their companies could create synergy, increasing profitability for both parties. However, he acknowledged Lisa's hesitation due to concerns like control over the business and brand identity.

During the negotiation process, John and Lisa engaged in open discussions, letting each party express their fears, concerns, and expectations. They actively listened to each other and brainstormed collaborative solutions to address these issues.

Instead of getting defensive or manipulative, John and Lisa remained assertive but also empathetic toward each other's concerns. They explored alternative scenarios and carefully crafted a partnership agreement that ensured both companies' interests were protected.

Their assertiveness and willingness to find mutually beneficial solutions resulted in a win-win outcome. The businesses merged successfully, leveraging their respective strengths, expanding their customer base, and thriving as a unified entity.

By showing assertive negotiation skills, both parties in these case studies communicated their needs effectively, considered the other party's perspective, and found a mutually beneficial solution. These examples illustrate how assertiveness can lead to successful negotiations and win-win outcomes in various contexts.

CHAPTER SEVEN SUMMARY: NEGOTIATION SKILLS: HOW BEING ASSERTIVE CAN LEAD TO WIN-WIN OUTCOMES

Chapter Seven explores the importance of assertiveness in negotiation and how it can lead to win-win outcomes. The chapter emphasizes that assertiveness involves confidently and respectfully expressing one's needs and opinions while remaining open to the needs and interests of the other party. By being assertive, individuals can advocate for their own goals while working toward mutually beneficial solutions.

The chapter highlights the principles of collaborative negotiation and how assertiveness helps establish trust and transparency between parties. It explains that assertiveness involves listening to the concerns of the other party and finding areas of common ground, which leads to the development of creative and mutually beneficial solutions.

The chapter also differentiates assertiveness from aggression and passive behavior in negotiations. It explains that assertiveness seeks to find a balance between advocating for one's interests and respecting the needs of the other party, while aggression aims to dominate and win at any cost, and passive behavior involves avoiding confrontation and not expressing one's true needs.

The chapter provides techniques for confidently communicating needs and wants through assertive expression. It suggests using "I" statements, being direct and specific, using confident body language, being mindful of tone, practicing active listening, setting boundaries, using the "broken record" technique, and practicing self-compassion.

The chapter then explores the power of active listening in negotiation and building rapport. It emphasizes the importance of giving undivided attention, avoiding interruption, practicing empathy, reflecting and paraphrasing, asking open-ended questions, avoiding jumping to conclusions, being non-judgmental, summarizing and confirming.

Additionally, the chapter discusses goal-oriented negotiation and how assertiveness can be harnessed for successful outcomes. It emphasizes the importance of setting clear goals, focusing on priorities, researching and gathering information, and using assertiveness to communicate goals, be confident, listen actively, and explore win-win solutions.

The chapter concludes by addressing common barriers to assertiveness and providing strategies to overcome them. It suggests changing perspectives on conflict, building self-confidence and self-belief, preparing and researching, practicing active listening and empathy, using assertive language, practicing effective nonverbal communication, setting boundaries, practicing assertiveness in small steps, and seeking support when needed.

Finally, the chapter presents case studies that show win-win outcomes achieved through assertiveness in salary negotiation and business partnership negotiation. These examples illustrate how assertiveness can lead to successful negotiations and mutually beneficial solutions in various contexts.

Overall, the chapter emphasizes that assertiveness is a vital skill in negotiation that lets individuals effectively communicate their needs, listen to the concerns of the other party, and work toward win-win outcomes.

DEVELOPING EFFECTIVE LEADERSHIP SKILLS THROUGH ASSERTIVENESS

THE ASSERTIVE LEADER: EMPOWERING EFFECTIVE LEADERSHIP THROUGH CLEAR COMMUNICATION AND RESPECTFUL ENGAGEMENT

Assertiveness is the ability to express oneself confidently, directly, and respectfully, while still considering the rights and opinions of others. It is an important communication skill that plays a significant role in effective leadership. Here, we will delve into the idea of assertiveness and explore its relationship with effective leadership.

Assertive leaders are those who can confidently express their thoughts, ideas, and expectations, while also actively listening to and acknowledging the viewpoints of others. They balance being responsive and standing up for themselves and their team. This ability to communicate openly and honestly fosters an environment of trust, collaboration, and productivity.

One key trait of assertive leaders is their clear and concise communication style. They can articulate their expectations, goals, and directions, avoiding ambiguity and confusion. This clarity lets employees understand their roles and responsibilities, which leads to increased efficiency and reduced conflict within the team.

Assertive leaders are not afraid to provide constructive feedback and address performance issues. They approach these conversations with empathy and respect, focusing on the behavior or the task rather than attacking the person. By doing so, they help with growth and development, and create a culture of continuous improvement.

Assertiveness also empowers leaders to set and maintain boundaries. They know when to say "no" and how to delegate tasks effectively, ensuring a balanced workload within the team. This skill prevents burnout and overwhelm, ultimately enhancing employee satisfaction and overall team performance.

In addition, assertive leaders actively help with open and honest discussions, inviting diverse perspectives and opinions. They encourage their team members to express themselves authentically without fear of judgment or reprisal. By valuing the input of others and actively seeking their thoughts, assertive leaders promote inclusion, engagement, and innovation within the team.

Despite these benefits, it's important to note that assertiveness should not be confused with aggression or dominance. Assertiveness is about standing up for oneself while still respecting others, fostering collaboration and mutual understanding. It involves actively listening, considering different viewpoints, and finding common ground.

Assertiveness is an essential quality for effective leadership. It lets leaders communicate clearly, address issues constructively, set boundaries, and cultivate an inclusive and collaborative team culture. By balancing their own needs and the needs of their team members, assertive leaders inspire trust, enhance productivity, and ultimately achieve success.

THE POWER OF COMMUNICATION: EXPLORING COMMUNICATION STYLES AND THEIR IMPACT ON EFFECTIVE LEADERSHIP

Effective communication is a crucial part of successful leadership. It helps leaders establish and maintain strong relationships with their team members, inspire and motivate them, and drive organizational success. However, different communication styles can have varying impacts on leadership effectiveness. This chapter aims to explore various communication styles and their impact on leadership effectiveness.

Authoritarian Style:

The authoritarian communication style is characterized by top-down communication, where the leader dictates instructions and expects immediate obedience. This style can be effective in situations that require quick decision-making and maintaining order. However, it often stifles creativity and discourages team members from contributing their ideas or perspectives. This can lead to decreased job satisfaction and reduced engagement among team members, ultimately affecting leadership effectiveness.

Democratic Style:

The democratic communication style encourages participation, collaboration, and open dialogue within the team. Leaders adopting this style seek input and opinions from their team members, using consensus-based decision-making. This style fosters a sense of ownership and empowerment among team members, as they feel valued and have their voices heard. By encouraging participation and involving team members in decision-making, leaders foster trust, motivation, and job satisfaction, enhancing leadership effectiveness.

Laissez-faire Style:

The laissez-faire communication style is characterized by minimal interference or direction from the leader. While this style allows individuals the freedom to work independently, it can hinder effective communication and coordination. This lack of guidance may lead to confusion, decreased accountability, and inefficient work processes. Although some employees may thrive in an autonomous work environment, the lack of structure and guidance often negatively affects the team's overall productivity and leadership effectiveness.

Transformational Style:

The transformational communication style focuses on inspiring and motivating team members to reach their full potential. Leaders adopting this style communicate their vision, goals, and values clearly, inspiring a shared sense of purpose among their team members. This style emphasizes active listening, empathy, and effective feedback, fostering trust and building strong relationships. By empowering and developing their team members, transformational leaders enhance their leadership effectiveness.

Transactional Style:

The transactional communication style emphasizes clear expectations and rewards/punishments based on performance. Leaders using this style establish a set of predetermined goals, rules, and communicate them to their team members. They provide feedback, rewards, or disciplinary actions based on individual or team performance. While this style can be effective in achieving short-term goals and maintaining control, it may limit innovation, creativity, and employee autonomy. This can hinder leadership effectiveness, especially in dynamic and rapidly changing work environments.

Communication styles significantly affect leadership effectiveness. While authoritarian and laissez-faire styles can limit engagement and motivation, democratic, transformational, and transactional styles can enhance teamwork, collaboration, and overall performance. Effective leaders understand the significance of adapting their communication style to specific situations, individuals, and organizational contexts, ultimately maximizing their leadership effectiveness.

THE ASSERTIVE LEADER: INSPIRING AND MOTIVATING THROUGH CONFIDENCE, COLLABORATION, AND GROWTH

Assertive leaders are characterized by their confident and self-assured demeanor. They display strong communication skills and have a clear vision for the future. These leaders inspire and motivate others by setting high standards, fostering collaboration, providing support and guidance, and promoting personal growth.

One key characteristic of assertive leaders is their ability to set high standards. They establish clear goals and expectations for their teams and hold everyone accountable for their actions. This determination to achieve excellence creates a sense of purpose and drives individuals to perform at their best.

Assertive leaders also excel in fostering collaboration. They value the input of others and create an inclusive environment where diverse perspectives are encouraged. By involving team members in decision-making processes, they make everyone feel valued and motivated to contribute their ideas and knowledge. This approach not only enhances the quality of decisions but also promotes a sense of ownership and commitment among team members.

In addition, assertive leaders provide support and guidance. They actively listen to the concerns and challenges of their team members and offer help whenever necessary. By being approachable and empathetic, they create an environment that encourages open communication and enables individuals to seek help when needed. This support helps to build trust and confidence within the team, and ultimately motivates them to overcome obstacles and meet their goals.

Assertive leaders also focus on personal growth. They recognize the potential in their team members and provide them with opportunities for development. Whether through training programs, challenging assignments, or mentoring relationships, they actively invest in the growth and success of their employees. This investment in personal growth not only inspires individuals to reach their full potential but also creates a culture of continuous learning and improvement.

Overall, assertive leaders inspire and motivate others by embodying confidence and setting high standards, fostering collaboration, providing support and guidance, and promoting personal growth. Through their leadership style, they create a positive and empowering environment where individuals feel motivated to excel, collaborate, and develop their skills.

MASTERING ASSERTIVENESS: TECHNIQUES FOR SETTING BOUNDARIES AND EXPRESSING OPINIONS WITH CONFIDENCE

Developing assertiveness skills is crucial for effective communication and self-confidence. Here are some learning techniques to help improve assertiveness:

Know your boundaries: Identify your personal limits and what makes you uncomfortable. Reflect on instances when you felt your boundaries were crossed. This awareness helps you establish clear boundaries and determine when to assert yourself.

Practice self-awareness: Understand your thoughts, emotions, and behavioral patterns. Recognize any passive or aggressive tendencies you may have and strive to adopt an assertive mindset instead. Regular self-reflection can aid in understanding your own needs and desires.

Set realistic goals: Start with small, achievable goals to assert yourself gradually. Practice speaking up in low-stakes situations such as ordering food or expressing preferences. Gradually move to more challenging scenarios, like voicing opinions in group discussions or saying no to requests that you are uncomfortable with.

Effective communication skills: Enhance your communication abilities by learning active listening, paraphrasing, and using "I" statements. Mastering these skills lets you express your thoughts and opinions clearly and confidently. Practice assertive body language, such as maintaining eye contact and having a confident posture.

Role play and rehearse: Enlist the help of a trusted friend or mentor to role play different scenarios where assertiveness is required. Practice asserting yourself in various situations to build your skills. Rehearsing helps reduce anxiety and build confidence.

Seek feedback: Ask for honest feedback from people you trust regarding your assertiveness skills. Understand how your behavior affects others and learn from their perspectives. Use constructive criticism to improve your approach.

Manage confrontation: Learn techniques to handle conflict and assertively address disagreements. Use strategies like active listening, empathy, and finding common ground to prevent conflicts from escalating. Practice keeping calm and composed during difficult conversations.

Positive self-talk and self-esteem: Cultivate self-confidence through positive self-talk. Remind yourself of your worth and abilities. Developing self-esteem empowers you to assert yourself and express your opinions confidently.

Learn negotiation skills: Improve your ability to compromise and find win-win solutions. Understanding a give-and-take approach lets you assert your needs while appreciating the perspective of others.

Seek professional help if needed: If you struggle excessively with assertiveness, consider seeking support from a therapist or counselor. They can provide guidance, techniques, and personalized strategies to help you develop assertiveness skills effectively.

Developing assertiveness takes time and practice. Embrace patience and persistence, honoring your progress along the way.

THE POWER OF LISTENING AND FEEDBACK:
ENHANCING LEADERSHIP SKILLS FOR SUCCESS

Active listening and constructive feedback are crucial parts in developing effective leadership skills. Leaders who have these skills are more successful in fostering positive relationships with their team members, understanding their needs and concerns, and guiding them toward achieving their full potential. Let's delve into why active listening and constructive feedback are so important in leadership development.

Active listening is the ability to fully focus on the speaker, understand their message, and provide appropriate responses. It involves empathetically listening without interruption, maintaining eye contact, and using non-verbal cues to show interest. By actively listening, leaders can gain a deep understanding of their team members' perspectives, emotions, and motivations. This understanding enables leaders to make informed decisions, provide relevant guidance, and show genuine care for their employees' well-being.

Active listening encourages open communication and trust within the team. When leaders give their undivided attention and show they value the opinions and ideas of their team members, it creates an inclusive environment where everyone feels comfortable sharing their thoughts. This not only fosters creativity and innovation but also enhances collaboration and problem-solving.

Constructive feedback is another crucial part of effective leadership. Instead of simply criticizing or praising, constructive feedback focuses on specific behaviors and actions that need improvement or recognition. It is delivered in a respectful and constructive manner, highlighting areas for growth while also pointing out strengths. Constructive feedback helps individuals understand their strengths and weaknesses, identify areas for development, and ultimately grow both personally and professionally.

Leaders who provide constructive feedback not only help their team members in improving their performance but also build strong relationships based on trust and respect. When employees feel valued and supported, they are more likely to be engaged, committed, and loyal to their leader and the organization.

Constructive feedback lets leaders address potential issues or conflicts in a proactive way. By openly discussing areas for improvement, leaders can prevent misunderstandings, identify barriers to success, and work collaboratively toward finding solutions. This not only strengthens the team but also helps in maximizing individual and collective performance.

Active listening and constructive feedback are indispensable tools in developing effective leadership skills. By actively listening, leaders can understand their team members' perspectives, build trust, and create an inclusive and collaborative environment. Constructive feedback enables leaders to guide their team members toward growth, build strong relationships, and address potential issues proactively. Leaders who focus on active listening and constructive feedback are more likely to inspire and empower their team, leading to enhanced performance, productivity, and overall success.

NAVIGATING CONFLICT WITH ASSERTIVENESS: STRATEGIES FOR CONSTRUCTIVE RESOLUTION

Conflict is a natural part of human relationships, whether it is in personal or professional settings. It is important to have strategies in place to handle conflict assertively and resolve disputes constructively. Here are some strategies to explore:

Maintain open communication: Effective communication is vital to handling conflict assertively. Make sure all parties involved have the opportunity to express their thoughts and feelings. Listen actively, without interrupting, and try to understand the other person's perspective.

Focus on interests, not positions: During conflict, individuals tend to take rigid positions. Instead of arguing over positions, try to identify the underlying interests and concerns. This can help find common ground and help with constructive solutions.

Collaborate to find win-win solutions: When conflicts arise, approach the situation with a mindset of collaboration and cooperation. Encourage brainstorming and problem-solving techniques that let all parties contribute to finding mutually beneficial solutions.

Use "I" statements: When expressing your concerns or frustrations, use "I" statements instead of "you" statements. This helps to avoid placing blame and promotes a more non-confrontational approach. For example, say "I feel upset when..." instead of "You always do this..."

Practice active listening: Active listening involves fully immersing yourself in the conversation and showing you understand the other person's perspective. Use verbal and non-verbal cues, such as nodding, eye contact, and summarizing their points, to show you are actively engaged in the conversation.

Remain calm and composed: Conflict can easily escalate when emotions run high. It is crucial to remain calm and composed, even in difficult situations. Take deep breaths, pause before responding, and avoid getting defensive or aggressive. Responding assertively instead of reactively will help create a more constructive atmosphere.

Seek mediation if necessary: Sometimes, conflict may become too complex to handle on your own. In such situations, it's helpful to involve a neutral third party to mediate and help with the resolution process. This mediator can guide the discussion, making sure each party has an equal opportunity to be heard and help find a resolution.

Focus on the bigger picture: During conflicts, it is easy to get caught up in the details and lose sight of the bigger picture. Remind yourself of the shared goals or common interests you have with the other person. This can help put the conflict into perspective and encourage a more collaborative approach to resolving the dispute.

Reflect and learn from conflicts: After a conflict is resolved, take time to reflect on the situation. Assess your own behavior and identify areas where you could have handled the conflict more assertively or constructively. Use this self-reflection as an opportunity for personal growth and development.

By exploring these strategies for handling conflict assertively and resolving disputes constructively, individuals can promote healthy relationships, effective communication, and positive outcomes in both personal and professional settings.

ASSERTIVE LEADERSHIP: CULTIVATING A POSITIVE AND PRODUCTIVE WORK ENVIRONMENT

Assertive leadership is a critical part in creating a positive and productive work environment. It involves leaders who confidently communicate their expectations, listen to, and address the concerns of their team members, and promote open and honest dialogue.

One of the key aspects of assertive leadership is the ability to recognize and handle conflict in an assertive way. Instead of avoiding or escalating conflicts, assertive leaders resolve disputes constructively. Here are some strategies for handling conflict assertively and promoting a positive work environment:

Proactive Communication: Encouraging open and honest communication among team members is essential for resolving conflicts. Assertive leaders create an environment where individuals feel comfortable expressing their concerns, opinions, and ideas.

Active Listening: Listening attentively to all parties involved in a conflict is crucial for understanding the root cause of the disagreement. An assertive leader actively listens to both verbal and nonverbal cues, allowing everyone to feel heard and confirmed.

Collaboration and Mediation: Assertive leaders encourage collaboration and seek common ground between conflicting parties. They act as mediators, helping with discussions and helping individuals find mutually beneficial solutions.

Constructive Feedback: Providing timely and constructive feedback is important for conflict resolution. Assertive leaders offer feedback in a respectful and non-threatening manner, focusing on the behavior or issue rather than attacking the person.

Setting Boundaries: Establishing clear boundaries and expectations helps prevent conflicts from arising. Assertive leaders communicate the team's values and standards, making sure everyone understands the acceptable behaviors and consequences for crossing boundaries.

Conflict Resolution Training: Providing conflict resolution training for team members can help them develop assertive communication and problem-solving skills. These skills enable employees to handle conflicts effectively and contribute to a positive and harmonious work environment.

Emotional Intelligence: Leaders with high emotional intelligence are more capable of recognizing emotions in themselves and others. This enables them to approach conflicts with empathy, understanding, and a focus on finding resolutions that benefit all parties involved.

Encouraging Accountability: Assertive leaders hold themselves and their team members accountable for their actions. This helps create a culture where individuals take responsibility for their behaviors, learn from mistakes, and work toward preventing conflicts.

Role Modeling: Leaders who show assertive behavior serve as role models for their team members. By exemplifying assertive communication and conflict resolution techniques, they inspire others to adopt similar approaches, fostering a positive work environment.

Overall, assertive leadership plays a vital role in creating a positive and productive work environment. By recognizing and handling conflicts assertively, leaders contribute to healthy communication, trust, collaboration, and overall team effectiveness.

CHAPTER SUMMARY: DEVELOPING EFFECTIVE LEADERSHIP SKILLS THROUGH ASSERTIVENESS

Chapter Eight explores the importance of assertiveness in developing effective leadership skills. Assertive leaders are those who can confidently express their thoughts, ideas, and expectations while actively listening to and acknowledging the viewpoints of others. They communicate openly and honestly, fostering trust, collaboration, and productivity within their teams.

The chapter emphasizes that assertive leaders have clear and concise communication styles. They articulate expectations, goals, and directions, which reduces ambiguity and conflict within the team. They also provide constructive feedback and address performance issues with empathy and respect, focusing on behavior rather than attacking the person. This approach promotes growth and development and creates a culture of continuous improvement.

Additionally, assertive leaders know how to set and maintain boundaries, preventing burnout and overwhelm within their teams. They delegate tasks effectively, ensuring a balanced workload. By valuing open and honest discussions, they encourage diverse perspectives and opinions, promoting inclusion, engagement, and innovation.

The chapter distinguishes assertiveness from aggression or dominance, emphasizing that assertiveness is about standing up for oneself while still respecting others. It involves active listening, considering different viewpoints, and finding common ground.

Overall, assertiveness is an essential quality for effective leadership. It enables leaders to communicate clearly, address issues constructively, set boundaries, and cultivate an inclusive and collaborative team culture. By balancing their own needs and the needs of their team members, assertive leaders inspire trust, enhance productivity, and ultimately achieve success.

CHAPTER 9

OVERCOMING GENDER BIAS: EMPOWERING WOMEN TO EMBRACE ASSERTIVENESS

UNDERSTANDING THE HISTORY AND IMPACT OF GENDER BIAS: EXPLORING ORIGINS AND PERVASIVENESS IN SOCIETY, ITS EFFECTS ON WOMEN'S SELF-PERCEPTION, AND ASSERTIVENESS

Gender bias has been a predominant issue throughout human history, influencing societal beliefs, norms, and expectations. Often rooted in a patriarchal structure, gender bias has a profound impact on women's self-perception and assertiveness. Examining the origins of gender bias and understanding its pervasiveness in society is crucial to address and overcome its adverse effects on women.

Historical Origins of Gender Bias:

a. Early societal structures and patriarchy: Gender bias can be traced back to ancient societies, where men dominated decision-making processes and held positions of power. This led to cultural narratives that emphasized male superiority and female subservience.

b. Traditional gender roles: The industrial revolution solidified the separation between public (male) and private (female) spheres, further entrenching gender stereotypes and bias. Women were assigned domestic duties, limiting their opportunities for self-expression and individual growth.

Manifestations of Gender Bias in Society:

a. Employment and career opportunities: Historically, women faced limited access to education and were excluded from certain professions. Even though we have made progress, gender bias persists in occupational segregation and wage gaps, hindering women's professional growth and financial independence.

b. Media and popular culture: The media often portrays women in stereotypical roles, objectifying and sexualizing them. This reinforces societal biases and affects women's self-perception, perpetuating harmful beauty standards and undermining their self-confidence.

c. Political and leadership positions: Despite advancements, women are underrepresented in politics and top leadership positions globally. Gender bias in electoral processes, social expectations, and lack of support prevents women from taking on decision-making roles, limiting their influence and representation.

Impact on Women's Self-Perception:

a. Body image and beauty standards: Media imagery and societal pressures lead women to internalize unrealistic standards of beauty, contributing to body dissatisfaction and low self-esteem. This can impair women's assertiveness and overall self-perception.

Imposter syndrome: Due to consistent societal messages of male superiority, women often experience imposter syndrome – feeling inadequate or undeserving of their success. This self-doubt can hinder their ability to assert themselves and contribute fully in various domains.

c. Self-limiting beliefs and ambitions: Gender bias can influence women's perception of their capabilities and limit their aspirations. A lack of confidence and fear of judgment can prevent them from pursuing leadership positions or taking risks in their personal and professional lives.

Fostering Gender Equality and Empowerment:

a. Education and awareness: Promoting education about gender bias, its history, and its impact is essential to challenge societal norms and break the cycle. By empowering women with knowledge, they can recognize and resist gender bias in their lives.

b. Equal opportunities and policies: Implementing policies that promote gender equality in education, employment, and leadership positions is crucial. By addressing structural biases, women can have greater access to opportunities and resources.

c. Breaking societal stereotypes: Encouraging a shift in cultural narratives that challenge traditional gender roles is essential. This involves fostering diversity and representation in media, supporting women's voices, and promoting different notions of success and beauty.

Gender bias, deeply rooted in history, continues to pervade society and affect women's self-perception and assertiveness. Understanding its origins and prevalence is imperative in combating gender bias. By advocating for equal opportunities, empowering women, and challenging societal norms, we can strive toward an equal and inclusive future.

UNVEILING THE INNER STRENGTH: OVERCOMING GENDER BIASES AND CULTIVATING SELF-AWARENESS AND CONFIDENCE FOR WOMEN

Building self-awareness and confidence is crucial for women to navigate the challenges and opportunities they encounter. In society, gender biases can often hinder women's progress and limit their belief in themselves. So, it is important for women to recognize and challenge these internalized gender biases to cultivate a strong sense of self and confidence in their abilities. Here are some strategies that can help in this endeavor:

Educate yourself: Start by educating yourself about the pervasive gender biases that exist in society. Read books, chapters, and research on the subject to better understand the historical context and the impact these biases can have on a woman's self-perception and confidence.

Identify and challenge internalized biases: Reflect on your own beliefs and thoughts about gender roles, abilities, and expectations. Recognize where you might have internalized gender biases and challenge them. Ask yourself if your self-perceptions are influenced by societal norms or if they are authentic to who you truly are. Be open to questioning and reevaluating your beliefs and assumptions.

Surround yourself with positive influences: Build a support network of individuals who uplift and encourage you. Connect with mentors, role models, or peers who can provide a positive influence and boost your self-confidence. Seek communities and organizations that empower women and provide a safe space to share experiences and challenges.

Celebrate achievements and strengths: Take the time to acknowledge and celebrate your accomplishments, no matter how big or small they may be. Keep a record of your achievements and the skills you have developed. This self-reflection will help you recognize your abilities and build a stronger sense of self.

Set realistic goals and take risks: Set goals that align with your passions and values. Break down these goals into smaller, achievable tasks. By carrying out these smaller tasks, you will build a sense of accomplishment and confidence to tackle bigger challenges. Don't fear taking risks and stepping out of your comfort zone. Embrace opportunities to challenge yourself and learn new skills.

Practice self-care: Nurturing both your physical and mental well-being is essential for self-awareness and confidence. Take time for self-care activities that help you relax, rejuvenate, and reflect. Engage in activities that make you feel good about yourself and boost your self-esteem.

Embrace failure as a learning opportunity: Everyone faces setbacks and failures. Learn to view these as opportunities for growth and learning, rather than personal shortcomings. Use failure as a chance to evaluate your approach, make changes, and improve for the future.

Support other women: Lift other women up and celebrate their achievements. By supporting and empowering other women, you contribute to a more inclusive and supportive environment. This can reinforce your own self-worth and confidence.

Building self-awareness and confidence is an ongoing process. Recognizing and challenging internalized gender biases is a crucial step toward cultivating a strong sense of self. By applying these strategies, women can empower themselves and create a positive impact within themselves and in the world around them.

EMBRACING ASSERTIVENESS AS A POWERFUL TOOL:

Assertiveness is a valuable trait that can empower women to communicate effectively, negotiate for their needs, and break through gender stereotypes. Despite societal expectations that often discourage women from expressing their opinions and desires assertively, embracing assertiveness can bring about many benefits and lead to personal and professional growth.

One of the primary benefits of assertiveness is effective communication. Women who embrace assertiveness confidently express their thoughts, opinions, and needs, making sure their voice is heard and respected. Assertive communication lets women clearly state their boundaries, preferences, and expectations, enabling them to build healthier relationships and avoid being taken advantage of. By embracing assertiveness, women can stand up for themselves and confidently navigate various social, professional, or personal situations.

Assertiveness empowers women to negotiate for their needs successfully. Often, women face unequal power dynamics, such as pay disparities or limited opportunities for advancement. By being assertive, women can negotiate more effectively, advocating for fair treatment and better outcomes. Assertive negotiation skills help women command respect and assert their value in the workplace, resulting in improved earning potential and increased career opportunities.

Embracing assertiveness also lets women break through gender stereotypes and societal expectations. Society often associates assertiveness with aggressiveness, and women are often discouraged from being too assertive due to cultural biases. However, when women embrace assertiveness, they challenge these stereotypes and pave the way for gender equality. By showing their competence, confidence, and leadership skills through assertive behavior, women can dismantle preconceived notions and inspire other women to do the same.

Additionally, assertiveness can enhance women's self-esteem and self-confidence. By speaking assertively and standing up for themselves, women build a stronger sense of self-worth and belief in their capabilities. This newfound confidence enables them to take on challenges, pursue their goals, and strive for success without compromising their values or authenticity.

Embracing assertiveness as a powerful tool empowers women to communicate effectively, negotiate for their needs, and break through gender stereotypes. By becoming assertive, women can cultivate their voice, build stronger relationships, and advocate for their rights. Embracing assertiveness is not only beneficial for individual growth but also contributes to a more inclusive and equal society. So, women must recognize the power of assertiveness and embrace it as a tool for personal and professional success.

OVERCOMING THE FEAR OF BACKLASH: EMPOWERING WOMEN TO ASSERT THEMSELVES

Asserting oneself can be challenging, particularly for women who often face a fear of negative reactions or pushback. The fear of backlash can hinder their personal growth, professional success, and overall well-being. However, by understanding and addressing this fear head-on, women can overcome it and learn practical strategies to manage situations effectively. This chapter aims to shed light on the common fear of backlash, provide insightful advice, and equip women with useful tools to assert themselves confidently.

Recognize the Societal Context:

- Understand that women historically faced limited opportunities to assert themselves, leading to the fear of backlash becoming deeply ingrained.
- Acknowledge that society is evolving, and women have every right to assert themselves without fear of negative reactions.
- Recognize that progress is being made, and the fear of backlash should not overshadow personal growth.

Build Self-Confidence:

- Develop a strong sense of self-worth and confidence in your abilities.
- Focus on past achievements and positive feedback to reinforce your self-esteem.
- Surround yourself with individuals who uplift and support you, providing valuable reassurance during challenging situations.

Cultivate Assertiveness Skills:

- Practice assertive communication techniques to effectively express thoughts, needs, and expectations.
- Use confident body language, maintain eye contact, and speak with a clear and steady voice when asserting yourself.
- Learn to respect your feelings and opinions and understand that they hold value like anyone else's.

Prepare in Advance:

- Prioritize research and gather facts before engaging in discussions or presenting ideas.
- Anticipate potential disagreements or pushbacks and prepare well-reasoned counterarguments.

- Approach conversations with empathy and respect, promoting a constructive dialogue rather than confrontation.

Seek Support Networks:

- Connect and engage with like-minded individuals or support groups who have experienced similar fears and challenges.
- Share stories and discuss strategies with others who have successfully managed backlash.
- Collaborate on joint initiatives to amplify your collective voice and build a more supportive environment.

Embrace Feedback:

- View feedback, even if it is critical, as an opportunity for growth and improvement.
- Strive to separate emotionally charged comments from constructive criticism.
- Respond gracefully, using feedback as a steppingstone toward growth and self-improvement.

Set Boundaries:

- Establish clear boundaries regarding what is acceptable behavior toward you.
- Communicate these boundaries assertively and consistently.
- Be prepared to assertively enforce these boundaries if they are crossed, ensuring respect and fair treatment.

Overcoming the fear of backlash is an essential step toward personal growth, professional success, and self-empowerment. By recognizing the societal context, building self-confidence, acquiring assertiveness skills, preparing in advance, seeking support networks, embracing feedback, and setting boundaries, women can alleviate their fears and assert themselves without hesitation. With practice and determination, the fear of backlash will gradually fade, paving the way for a more fulfilling and empowered life.

NURTURING SUPPORTIVE NETWORKS:

To empower women and promote assertiveness, it is crucial to nurture and encourage the development of supportive networks. These networks can provide women with invaluable guidance, encouragement, and a sense of belonging as they strive to assert themselves and navigate various professional and personal challenges. Here are some strategies to help with the creation and maintenance of these supportive networks:

Raise awareness: Start by raising awareness about the importance of supportive networks and the role they can play in cultivating assertiveness. Highlight the benefits of peer, mentor, and ally relationships in promoting growth, confidence, and resilience.

Organize networking events: Arrange networking events specifically targeted at women, where they can connect with like-minded individuals and potential mentors or allies. These events can include workshops, panel discussions, or casual meetups to foster meaningful connections.

Establish mentorship programs: Develop formal mentorship programs that pair experienced individuals with women looking to enhance their assertiveness skills. Encourage these partnerships to focus on building self-confidence, professional development, and assertive communication techniques.

Encourage participation in affinity groups: Encourage women to participate in affinity groups or professional associations aligned with their interests or career goals. These groups provide opportunities to connect with individuals who face similar challenges, fostering a sense of solidarity and support.

Promote mental health support: Recognize the importance of mental health in building assertiveness. Promote access to mental health resources and encourage women to seek counseling or therapy if necessary. These support systems can help navigate anxiety or self-doubt that may hinder assertiveness practices.

Foster collaboration and peer learning: Create spaces for women to collaborate and learn from one another. This can be facilitated through workshops, group projects, or online forums where individuals can share experiences, discuss challenges, and guide one another.

Advocate for change at the organizational level: Encourage organizations to invest in employee resource groups or affinity networks focused on women's empowerment. These initiatives can be instrumental in providing a sense of community, fostering mentorship opportunities, and influencing organizational policies and practices.

Emphasize the value of reciprocity: Encourage women to not only seek support but also offer guidance to others. Emphasize the value of a mutually beneficial dynamic within supportive networks where each participant contributes to the growth and empowerment of others.

Provide role models and success stories: Highlight successful women who have embraced assertiveness and the positive impact it has had on their personal and professional lives. Sharing stories of inspiration can motivate and instill confidence in women as they navigate assertiveness.

Emphasize long-term connections: Encourage women to maintain and nurture their support networks even after meeting their goals. These networks can continue to provide ongoing support, professional opportunities, and personal growth.

By actively promoting the establishment and growth of supportive networks for women, we can enhance their sense of empowerment and enable the practice of assertiveness in all parts of life.

BREAKING SOCIETAL BARRIERS: CHALLENGING AND DISMANTLING GENDER BIASES FOR WOMEN'S EQUITY

Gender biases continue to persist in various spheres of life, limiting women's potential and perpetuating inequality. To create a more just and equitable society, it is crucial to challenge and dismantle these biases. This chapter explores ways to break societal barriers by addressing gender biases in the workplace, relationships, and societal expectations, empowering women to thrive in all parts of life.

Workplace:

a. Promote equal opportunities: Encourage organizations to provide equal opportunities for women in leadership roles, promotions, and career growth. Implement programs that support diversity and inclusion, ensuring gender balance at all levels.

b. Address pay gaps: Advocate for pay transparency and policies that ensure equal pay for equal work. Evaluate salary structures and review compensation policies to close existing gender pay gaps.

c. Combat stereotypes: Challenge stereotypes that pigeonhole women into specific roles or industries. Encourage girls to pursue careers in STEM fields and provide mentors who can guide and inspire them.

Relationships:

a. Foster mutual respect: Promote healthy relationships based on mutual respect, encouraging open communication, and shared decision-making. Encourage both partners to support each other's goals and aspirations.

b. Share household responsibilities: Challenge traditional gender roles by fostering an equal distribution of household chores and child-rearing. Encourage men to actively participate in domestic work to create a more balanced environment.

c. Support education: Advocate for comprehensive sexual education that includes discussions on consent, healthy relationships, and gender equality. Enable girls and boys to challenge harmful gender norms and stereotypes from an early age.

Societal Expectations:

a. Challenge gender norms: Encourage individuals to challenge societal expectations and stereotypes surrounding gender roles. Promote the idea that everyone should have the freedom to choose their own path, despite societal expectations.

b. Amplify women's voices: Support platforms that amplify women's voices and experiences, providing opportunities for them to share their stories, knowledge, and expertise. Encourage balanced representation in media, literature, and public discourse.

c. Engage men as allies: Engage men in conversations about gender equality, encouraging them to question existing biases and take proactive steps to dismantle them. Promote male allies who advocate for women's rights and challenge toxic masculinity.

Breaking societal barriers and challenging gender biases is essential to creating a more equitable environment for women. By addressing biases in the workplace, relationships, and societal expectations, we can empower women to rise to their full potential. It is crucial to foster an inclusive society where women are given equal opportunities, where relationships are based on respect and equality, and where societal expectations are not limiting but supportive. By challenging existing norms, we can dismantle gender biases and build a more just and equitable world for future generations.

INSPIRING FUTURE GENERATIONS: EMPOWERING YOUNG WOMEN AND GIRLS TO EMBRACE ASSERTIVENESS

Empowering young women and girls to embrace assertiveness is crucial in breaking down gender biases and encouraging them to navigate their personal and professional lives with confidence. By providing them with tools and examples, we can equip them to overcome societal constraints and achieve their full potential. This chapter will discuss the importance of empowering young females to be assertive, highlighting the benefits it brings to their lives and to society.

Overcoming Gender Biases:

a) Encouraging Confidence: Empowering young girls to be assertive helps them challenge stereotypes and societal expectations. By cultivating confidence from an early age, they gain the courage to challenge limiting gender biases and pursue their own interests and aspirations.

b) Breaking Stereotypes: Through assertiveness, young females can actively defy limited gender roles. By engaging in activities traditionally dominated by males or pursuing careers in fields such as science, technology, engineering, and mathematics (STEM), they break down societal limitations and pave the way for future generations.

Navigating Personal Lives:

a) Building Healthy Relationships: Assertiveness enables young females to establish healthy boundaries, communicate effectively, and develop meaningful relationships. Encouraging them to express their thoughts and emotions assertively empowers them to demand respect, thus reducing the risk of exploitation and fostering mutual understanding.

b) Developing Self-Worth: Embracing assertiveness helps young girls foster a strong sense of self-worth. Encouraging them to voice their opinions and make decisions instills confidence, ensuring they are active participants in their own lives.

Excelling in Professional Lives:

a) Encouraging Ambition: Empowering young women to embrace assertiveness from an early age motivates them to pursue ambitious goals and aspirations. It cultivates a belief in their abilities and helps overcome the barriers they may face in male-dominated industries.

b) Negotiation Skills: Assertiveness equips young women with vital negotiation skills, enabling them to advocate for themselves in the workplace. By instilling these skills, we help bridge the gender pay gap and create a more equitable society.

Empowering young women and girls to embrace assertiveness is a crucial step toward creating an inclusive and equal society. By providing them with examples and tools to overcome gender biases, we enable them to navigate their personal and professional lives with confidence. By embracing assertiveness, the barriers that restrict their potential can be dismantled, inspiring future generations to believe in themselves and manifest their dreams. Let us all play our part in empowering young women to embrace assertiveness and create a brighter and more equitable future for all.

CHAPTER NINE SUMMARY: OVERCOMING GENDER BIAS: EMPOWERING WOMEN TO EMBRACE ASSERTIVENESS

Chapter Nine focuses on addressing gender bias and empowering women to embrace assertiveness. It explores the historical origins and manifestations of gender bias in society, as well as its impact on women's self-perception and assertiveness.

The chapter emphasizes the importance of fostering gender equality and empowerment through education, equal opportunities, and breaking societal stereotypes. It highlights the benefits of embracing assertiveness as a powerful tool for effective communication, negotiation, and breaking through gender stereotypes.

The chapter also provides strategies for overcoming the fear of backlash, nurturing supportive networks, challenging, and dismantling gender biases, and inspiring future generations to embrace assertiveness.

By recognizing and addressing gender bias, empowering women, and challenging societal norms, an equal and inclusive future can be achieved.

CHAPTER 10

UNDERSTANDING CULTURAL DIFFERENCES: ASSERTIVENESS IN A GLOBAL CONTEXT

CULTURAL PERSPECTIVES ON ASSERTIVENESS: UNVEILING COMMUNICATION NORMS AND SIGNIFICANCE ACROSS CULTURES

Assertiveness is a social behavior that involves the expression of one's thoughts, desires, and needs in a confident and direct manner while respecting the rights and boundaries of others. It is a communication style that varies across cultures, shaped by societal norms, values, and beliefs. Exploring the idea of assertiveness and its significance in various cultures around the world unveils the fascinating diversity in interpersonal interactions.

In Western cultures, such as the United States or European countries, assertiveness is generally valued and encouraged. Openly expressing one's opinions and standing up for oneself is seen as a positive trait. Assertiveness is often associated with confidence, autonomy, and self-esteem. Individuals are taught from a young age to be assertive, as it is believed to enhance personal growth, personal agency, and the ability to achieve one's goals.

But in many Eastern and collectivist cultures, such as Japan or China, assertiveness is often downplayed or even discouraged. These cultures prioritize harmony, group cohesion, and avoiding direct confrontation. Modesty, respect for authority, and maintaining interpersonal relationships take precedence over individual assertiveness. Expressing oneself forcefully or assertively may be perceived as disruptive or disrespectful.

In Confucian-influenced cultures, such as those found in East Asia, assertiveness is often replaced by indirect communication styles. People use non-verbal cues, subtle hints, and contextual understanding to convey their thoughts and desires. The focus is on preserving relationships and maintaining social harmony rather than individual self-expression.

Similarly, in many African and Latin American cultures, assertiveness may be overshadowed by communal values. Relationships and collectivism are paramount, and individuals often focus on group needs over their own. Communicating assertively can be seen as confrontational or aggressive, and people rely on implicit communication strategies, such as body language and context, to express their needs indirectly.

Generalizations about assertiveness across cultures can oversimplify the complexities and variations within each culture. Different regions within a single country, and even different generations, may have diverse perspectives on assertiveness. Cultural values and norms are evolving over time due to globalization and cross-cultural influences.

Still, understanding the significance of assertiveness within different cultural contexts is crucial for effective cross-cultural communication. It helps individuals navigate intercultural interactions with sensitivity and adapt their communication style to be more inclusive and respectful. Recognizing and appreciating cultural diversity in assertiveness promotes empathy, reduces misunderstandings, and fosters mutual understanding among individuals from various backgrounds.

Assertiveness is an idea that varies significantly across cultures. While Western cultures value and encourage assertiveness, many Eastern and collectivist cultures focus on harmony and indirect communication. Understanding these cultural differences is essential for effective cross-cultural communication and building respectful relationships in today's interconnected world.

CULTURAL INFLUENCES ON ASSERTIVENESS: ANALYZING THE IMPACT OF VALUES AND NORMS ON EXPRESSION ACROSS CULTURES

Cultural values and norms play a significant role in shaping the expression of assertiveness in different cultures. Assertiveness refers to the ability to communicate and express oneself confidently, directly, and effectively while respecting the rights and opinions of others. However, cultural variations exist in the way assertiveness is perceived and practiced. This analysis aims to explore how cultural values and norms influence the expression of assertiveness in different cultures.

Cultural values, which are deeply ingrained beliefs about what is considered desirable, shape the behavior and interpersonal communication patterns of individuals within a culture. In some cultures, such as those with collectivist values, the emphasis is on harmony, cooperation, and maintaining relationships. Collectivist cultures, commonly found in East Asian countries like China and Japan, focus on the needs and goals of the group over the individual's desires. Assertiveness tends to be less valued in these cultures as it may be seen as disruptive to the harmony of the group.

In contrast, individualistic cultures, common in Western countries like the United States and many European nations, emphasize personal goals, autonomy, and self-expression. In these cultures, assertiveness is considered important, as individuals are encouraged to advocate for their rights and opinions. Here, assertiveness is viewed as a positive trait that leads to personal growth and assertive communication is often encouraged and rewarded.

Norms, which are established rules of behavior within a society, further influence the expression of assertiveness in different cultures. In high-context cultures, such as those found in many Asian and Middle Eastern countries, indirect communication is often favored. These cultures heavily rely on non-verbal cues, contextual information, and respecting social hierarchies. Consequently, assertiveness might be expressed more subtly, with individuals using non-verbal communication or relying on hierarchical relationships to convey their opinions or desires.

But low-context cultures, commonly found in countries like the United States, Canada, and many European countries, value direct and explicit communication. Assertiveness is expected in these cultures, and individuals are encouraged to express themselves clearly and directly to avoid misunderstandings. In low-context cultures, assertiveness is often associated with being confident, independent, and in control of one's own destiny.

While these generalizations provide insights into how cultural values and norms influence assertiveness, individual differences still exist within cultures. Not every person adheres strictly to the norms or values of their culture, and there can be variations in assertiveness even within the same cultural group. Additionally, globalization and increased intercultural interactions have led to the mixture and adaptation of cultural values and norms, influencing the expression of assertiveness in various ways.

Cultural values and norms significantly influence the expression of assertiveness in different cultures. Collectivist cultures prioritize harmony and cooperation, leading to less emphasis on assertiveness, but individualistic cultures value personal goals and self-expression, promoting assertiveness. Norms related to communication styles, such as direct or indirect communication, also shape assertiveness expression. However, individual variations and the influence of globalization should be considered when analyzing assertiveness in different cultures.

UNRAVELING MISCONCEPTIONS AND STEREOTYPES: EXPLORING THE MULTICULTURAL DIMENSIONS OF ASSERTIVENESS

Common misconceptions and stereotypes related to assertiveness can vary across different cultures and societies around the world. Here are some common ones:

Misconception: Assertiveness is synonymous with aggression.

Explanation: Many people confuse assertiveness with aggression, assuming that being assertive means being rude, pushy, or confrontational. However, assertiveness is actually a communication style that involves expressing one's thoughts, needs, and boundaries in a respectful and direct manner, without violating the rights of others.

Misconception: Assertiveness is only for extroverted individuals.

Explanation: Assertiveness is often associated with extroverted behaviors such as being outspoken, confident, and outgoing. However, introverted individuals can also be assertive by effectively expressing their opinions, setting boundaries, and standing up for themselves in a respectful and calm manner. Assertiveness is not limited to any specific personality type.

Stereotype: Assertiveness is not culturally appropriate in collectivist societies.

Explanation: Assertiveness can be misunderstood or not align with cultural norms in some collectivist societies where harmony and group cohesion are highly valued. This stereotype suggests that assertive individuals are seen as disrupting group harmony. However, note that assertiveness can be practiced in various cultural contexts, and its expression may differ based on cultural values.

Stereotype: Assertive women are viewed as aggressive or bossy.

Explanation: Society often imposes gender stereotypes that portray assertive women as too aggressive or bossy. This stereotype suggests that women should adhere to traditional gender roles and should not be assertive, as it goes against societal expectations. However, this stereotype is unfair and disempowering to women, as assertiveness is a crucial skill for everyone, regardless of gender.

Misconception: Assertiveness is only about expressing oneself.

Explanation: Assertiveness is not just about expressing oneself but also includes active listening, understanding, and respecting the perspectives and needs of others. Assertive individuals can communicate effectively and find mutually beneficial solutions through open and respectful dialogue, rather than dominating or imposing their ideas.

It is essential to recognize these common misconceptions and stereotypes to foster cultural understanding and promote effective communication in a global context. Appreciating the diverse ways assertiveness can be expressed in different cultures allows for more inclusive and respectful interactions.

NAVIGATING AND ADAPTING TO CULTURALLY DIVERSE ASSERTIVENESS STYLES: PRACTICAL STRATEGIES FOR PROFESSIONAL AND PERSONAL SETTINGS

In an increasingly globalized world, cultural diversity has become an integral part of our personal and professional lives. However, these cultural differences often manifest in varying assertiveness styles, posing challenges when communicating and collaborating with individuals from different cultural backgrounds. To ensure successful interactions and build strong relationships, it is essential to navigate and adapt to these culturally diverse assertiveness styles. This chapter provides practical strategies to help individuals effectively communicate and work with diverse groups, both in professional and personal settings.

Develop cultural self-awareness:

The first step toward navigating cultural differences in assertiveness is to develop self-awareness of your own cultural biases and communication style. Recognize that your assertiveness may be perceived differently by others from distinct cultural backgrounds. By reflecting on your own cultural upbringing, values, and communication norms, you can better appreciate and adapt to different assertiveness styles.

Practice active listening:

Active listening is crucial when interacting with individuals from culturally diverse backgrounds. Pay attention not only to the spoken words but also to non-verbal cues and cultural nuances. Avoid assumptions and be open to exploring and understanding perspectives that may differ from your own. This practice not only builds trust but also creates a foundation for effective communication.

Respect cultural norms:

Different cultures have varying expectations around assertiveness. While some cultures focus on directness and assertiveness, others place more significance on indirect communication and harmonious dialogue. Understanding and respecting these cultural norms is key to adapting your communication style appropriately. Observe the assertiveness styles of individuals from different cultures and adjust your approach without compromising your authenticity.

Cultivate empathy and sensitivity:

Cultivating empathy and sensitivity toward cultural differences is essential for successful interactions. Strive to understand the underlying reasons behind assertiveness styles in different cultures. This understanding helps create an environment of inclusivity and encourages open dialogue, enabling collaboration and effective decision-making within culturally diverse teams.

Seek feedback and clarify expectations:

In both professional and personal settings, it is important to seek feedback from individuals of different cultural backgrounds. Regularly check in to ensure effective communication and understand if any miscommunication or misunderstandings have occurred due to conflicting assertiveness styles. Clarify expectations regarding communication channels, decision-making processes, and preferred methods of feedback within diverse groups to foster an open and collaborative environment.

Develop cross-cultural communication skills:

Invest time in developing your cross-cultural communication skills. Educate yourself about cultural dimensions, communication styles, and business practices specific to the cultures you often interact with. Go to training sessions or workshops designed to enhance cross-cultural competence. By continuously improving your knowledge and skills, you will become more comfortable in adapting to and navigating culturally diverse assertiveness styles.

Navigating culturally diverse assertiveness styles requires awareness, sensitivity, and adaptability. By developing cultural self-awareness, practicing active listening, respecting cultural norms, cultivating empathy, seeking feedback, and enhancing cross-cultural communication skills, individuals can overcome hurdles and build thriving professional and personal relationships across cultural boundaries. Embracing these strategies not only promotes effective collaboration but also fosters a deeper understanding and appreciation of diverse assertiveness styles, leading to a more inclusive and harmonious global community.

BRIDGING THE GAP: CHALLENGES AND OPPORTUNITIES IN INTERACTIONS BETWEEN ASSERTIVE AND NON-ASSERTIVE CULTURES

When individuals from assertive and non-assertive cultures come together, they often face unique challenges and opportunities in their interactions. Understanding and navigating these differences requires sensitivity, respect, and open-mindedness. Let's delve into some challenges and opportunities that arise when these cultures interact.

One of the primary challenges in such interactions is the stark contrast in communication styles. Assertive cultures, such as those found in Western societies, value directness, speaking up, and expressing opinions freely. Non-assertive cultures, which are often common in Asian and some Latin American countries, emphasize harmony, politeness, and the avoidance of conflict. This disparity can lead to misunderstanding and miscommunication, further exacerbating the differences in perspectives.

For individuals from assertive cultures, the lack of directness and frankness in non-assertive cultures might be perceived as evasiveness or lack of honesty. Conversely, people from non-assertive cultures might perceive assertive communication as aggressive, rude, or disrespectful. These challenges can hinder effective collaboration, decision-making, and problem-solving.

However, despite the challenges, interactions between assertive and non-assertive cultures can also offer valuable opportunities. The fusion of different communication styles can lead to enhanced creativity and a wider range of perspectives in problem-solving. By combining the directness of assertive cultures with the diplomacy and empathy of non-assertive cultures, individuals can find innovative solutions that cater to both sides' needs.

Another opportunity that arises from these interactions is the potential for personal growth and cultural understanding. When individuals from assertive and non-assertive cultures engage in open dialogue, they have the chance to challenge their own assumptions, learn from different perspectives, and expand their worldview. This can help build empathy, acceptance, and respect for cultural diversity, leading to greater inclusiveness and collaboration in various contexts.

To effectively navigate these interactions, individuals must adopt a culturally sensitive approach. This involves recognizing and respecting the different cultural norms and adapting one's communication style. It is crucial to actively listen, seek clarification when needed, and be mindful of non-verbal cues that may carry hidden messages. Cultural intelligence, empathy, and a willingness to learn and adapt are key to overcoming the challenges and leveraging the opportunities presented by these cross-cultural interactions.

When individuals from assertive and non-assertive cultures come together, they encounter both challenges and opportunities. The differences in communication style can lead to misunderstandings, but they can also foster creativity and broader perspectives. By embracing these interactions with cultural sensitivity, individuals can learn from each other and build stronger relationships, leading to enhanced collaboration and understanding across cultures.

THE POWER OF EMPATHY AND CULTURAL SENSITIVITY: FOSTERING EFFECTIVE COMMUNICATION AND COLLABORATION ACROSS CULTURAL DIFFERENCES

In a world becoming increasingly interconnected and diverse, it is essential to recognize the significance of empathy, understanding, and cultural sensitivity in fostering effective communication and collaboration across cultural differences. These qualities are not only crucial for maintaining harmonious relationships but also for helping with progress in a globalized society.

Empathy, the ability to understand and share someone else's feelings, is the foundation of effective communication. By putting ourselves in another person's shoes and considering their perspective, we can communicate in a way that resonates with others. Empathy helps us overcome barriers that language alone cannot, as it lets us decode the underlying emotions and motivations behind a person's words or actions. When we approach interactions with individuals from different cultures with empathy, we show respect and confirm their experiences, which builds trust and lays the groundwork for meaningful connections.

Understanding is another key element of successful communication across cultures. It involves gaining knowledge of different cultural norms, values, and practices. By actively seeking to understand cultural differences, we can avoid making assumptions based on our own experiences and beliefs. Recognizing there are various ways of thinking and that each culture has its distinct features enables us to appreciate diversity, expand our horizons, and enhance our adaptability when collaborating with individuals from different backgrounds.

Cultural sensitivity goes hand in hand with empathy and understanding. It refers to being aware of and respectful toward cultural differences. It means recognizing that certain gestures, words, or symbols may hold significance in one culture but carry a different meaning or even offend in another. Culturally sensitive individuals are mindful of these nuances and endeavor to communicate in a way that is inclusive and considerate of diverse cultural backgrounds. By showing cultural sensitivity, we can create an atmosphere of inclusivity and foster an environment where people are comfortable expressing themselves.

The importance of empathy, understanding, and cultural sensitivity in communication and collaboration across cultural differences cannot be overstated. When these qualities are not present, misunderstandings and conflicts can easily arise, hampering progress and hindering the effectiveness of teamwork. But when individuals actively practice empathy, seek understanding, and exhibit cultural sensitivity, communication becomes more open and inclusive. This leads to enhanced collaboration, creativity, and problem-solving as diverse perspectives are embraced and valued.

Fostering effective communication and collaboration in multicultural settings has ripple effects beyond individual relationships and organizations. It contributes to building bridges between different nations and cultures, promoting peace, and helping with dialogue on a global scale. By recognizing the significance of empathy, understanding, and cultural sensitivity, we enable everyone to be heard, respected, and included in the conversation, ultimately leading to a more harmonious and interconnected world.

Empathy, understanding, and cultural sensitivity are crucial ingredients in fostering effective communication and collaboration across cultural differences. By valuing and practicing these qualities, we can break down barriers, build bridges, and create a more inclusive and interconnected global society. From interpersonal relationships to international cooperation, empathy, understanding, and cultural sensitivity serve as the keys to unlocking the full potential of multiculturalism and helping with progress in our increasingly diverse world.

CHAPTER TEN SUMMARY: UNDERSTANDING CULTURAL DIFFERENCES - ASSERTIVENESS IN A GLOBAL CONTEXT

Chapter Ten explores the idea of assertiveness in a global context, highlighting the cultural differences in its expression and significance. The chapter begins by discussing how assertiveness varies across cultures, with Western cultures valuing and encouraging assertiveness while many Eastern, collectivist, African, and Latin American cultures focus on harmony and indirect communication over individual assertiveness. The chapter emphasizes that cultural values and norms shape assertiveness and that generalizations can oversimplify the complexities within each culture.

The next section focuses on the impact of cultural values and norms on assertiveness expression. It explains how collectivist cultures focus on group harmony, while individualistic cultures emphasize personal goals and self-expression. It discusses communication norms and how high-context and low-context cultures influence assertiveness expression through indirect and direct communication styles, respectively.

The chapter then addresses misconceptions and stereotypes associated with assertiveness. It challenges the belief that assertiveness is synonymous with aggression and clarifies that it is not limited to extroverted individuals. It also dispels the stereotype that assertiveness is not appropriate in collectivist societies and that assertive women are viewed as aggressive or bossy. Additionally, it highlights that assertiveness involves active listening and respect for others' perspectives.

Practical strategies for navigating culturally diverse assertiveness styles are provided in the following section. The strategies include developing cultural self-awareness, practicing active listening, respecting cultural norms, cultivating empathy and sensitivity, seeking feedback, and improving cross-cultural communication skills.

The chapter then discusses the challenges and opportunities that arise when individuals from assertive and non-assertive cultures interact. It addresses the contrasting communication styles and the potential for misunderstanding. However, it also recognizes the opportunities for creativity and personal growth that arise from combining different assertiveness styles.

Finally, the chapter emphasizes the power of empathy and cultural sensitivity in fostering effective communication and collaboration across cultural differences. It explains how empathy helps decode underlying emotions, understanding promotes knowledge of cultural norms, and cultural sensitivity ensures respectful and inclusive communication.

Overall, the chapter underscores the importance of understanding cultural differences in assertiveness for effective cross-cultural communication. It encourages individuals to develop cultural sensitivity, embrace diverse perspectives, and foster empathy to promote harmonious interactions and collaboration in our increasingly interconnected world.

LEVERAGING ASSERTIVENESS TO TAKE CHARGE OF YOUR CAREER GROWTH

RECOGNIZING THE IMPORTANCE OF ASSERTIVENESS IN CAREER GROWTH

I n today's competitive job market, it is crucial to recognize the significance of assertiveness in career growth. Assertiveness refers to the ability to express oneself confidently and respectfully, standing up for one's rights and opinions without being aggressive. By understanding the role of assertiveness in taking control of one's career growth, individuals can empower themselves to pursue opportunities, overcome challenges, and achieve long-term success.

Taking Ownership of Career Growth:

Assertiveness plays a vital role in taking ownership of one's career growth. When individuals are assertive, they actively seek opportunities for professional development, such as training programs, networking events, and mentorship. By enhancing their skills and knowledge, assertive individuals position themselves for career advancement.

Being Proactive in Pursuing Opportunities:

Assertiveness encourages individuals to pursue career opportunities. Rather than waiting for opportunities to come their way, assertive individuals take active steps to seek new challenges, projects, and responsibilities. They understand that by taking the initiative, they can showcase their capabilities and show their value to their employers or clients, thus opening doors to new and exciting prospects.

Building Confidence and Self-Worth:

Assertiveness fosters confidence and self-worth, key factors in career growth. When individuals are assertive, they believe in their abilities and feel empowered to take risks. By advocating for themselves and their ideas, they gain the recognition they deserve and develop a strong sense of self-worth. This self-assuredness not only opens up new opportunities but also improves overall job satisfaction and fulfillment.

Overcoming Challenges and Negotiating:

Assertiveness is essential in addressing and overcoming challenges that may hinder career growth. Whether it's dealing with difficult colleagues, facing professional setbacks, or negotiating for a higher salary or better working conditions, assertive individuals are more likely to effectively navigate these hurdles. Their ability to express their needs and concerns assertively enables them to find constructive solutions, ultimately propelling their career growth.

Developing Strong Relationships:

Building and maintaining strong professional relationships is fundamental for career growth. Assertiveness lets individuals communicate effectively and express their viewpoints while respecting others' perspectives. By being assertive in a respectful way, individuals can prove themselves to be reliable and trustworthy colleagues or leaders. This fosters collaboration and opens doors to beneficial connections, mentoring opportunities, and professional support networks.

In today's competitive career landscape, recognizing the importance of assertiveness is crucial for individuals aiming to take control of their career growth. Being proactive, confident, and assertive empowers individuals to pursue opportunities, overcome challenges, build strong relationships, and negotiate for what they deserve. By mastering assertiveness, individuals can shape their professional destiny and create a fulfilling and successful career path.

UNDERSTANDING YOUR CAREER GOALS AND ASPIRATIONS

In today's competitive job market, it is crucial to clearly understand your career goals and aspirations. Many professionals spend years working without a clear direction, leading to dissatisfaction and a lack of fulfillment. This chapter aims to guide readers through articulating their career goals and aspirations, emphasizing the need to be clear about what they want to achieve in their professional journey.

Reflecting on Your Passions and Interests:

The first step in understanding your career goals is to reflect on your passions and interests. Ask yourself what excites you and brings you joy. Consider the activities or subjects you could spend hours immersed in without feeling drained. Reflecting on your passions will provide insights into the work that aligns with your natural inclinations.

Identifying Your Strengths and Skills:

To set realistic career goals, it is important to identify your strengths and skills. Assess your abilities, both technical and interpersonal. Determine the areas where you excel and the skills that come naturally to you. Recognizing your strengths will help you align them with your career aspirations, guiding you toward roles that will let you use your abilities effectively.

Evaluating Your Values and Priorities:

Understanding your values and priorities is crucial when defining your career goals and aspirations. Consider what matters most to you in life and make sure your professional journey aligns with these values. Determine whether work-life balance, making a positive impact, or achieving financial success is a priority for you. Aligning your values and priorities with your career goals will lead to greater fulfillment and satisfaction.

Setting SMART Goals:

Once you have reflected on your passions, strengths, skills, values, and priorities, it is time to set SMART goals. SMART goals are Specific, Measurable, Achievable, Relevant, and Time bound. Define clear objectives specific to your desired career path, ensure they are measurable so that progress can be tracked, set achievable goals that are within your reach, ensure their relevance to your long-term aspirations, and set a timeframe for their achievement.

Seeking and Utilizing Resources:

You need not navigate the process alone. Seek resources that can help you gain a better understanding of your career goals and aspirations. Contact mentors, career counselors, or professionals in your desired field who can provide guidance and advice. Use online platforms, industry publications, and networking events to gain knowledge and insights that will help you in shaping your professional journey.

Being clear about your career goals and aspirations is a fundamental step toward building a fulfilling career. By reflecting on your passions, strengths, skills, values, and priorities, you can set SMART goals that align with your long-term aspirations. Utilize available resources to gain a deeper understanding of your chosen path and seek guidance from mentors and professionals. Remember, a well-defined career goal is a roadmap to success and fulfillment in your professional journey.

COMMUNICATING EFFECTIVELY TO ASSERT YOUR NEEDS AND DESIRES:

One of the first steps in effectively communicating your needs and desires is to have a clear understanding of what they are. Take the time to reflect on your goals, aspirations, and what you need to accomplish them. This self-awareness will not only help you articulate your needs better but also give you the confidence to assert them.

When communicating your needs and desires, it is important to be direct and straightforward. Use clear and concise language to convey your message without being overly aggressive or passive. Be confident in expressing yourself and avoid apologizing for your needs. Remember, you have the right to advocate for yourself.

Active listening is also crucial in effective communication. When engaging in a conversation, pay attention to the other person's responses and validate their opinions. Listen carefully, ask clarifying questions, and show empathy toward their perspective. This will create a more open and respectful dialogue, increasing the chances of your needs being understood and met.

Another effective strategy is to use "I" statements rather than "you" statements. For example, instead of saying, "You never give me the resources I need," say, "I need more resources to complete my tasks effectively." This way, you express your needs without blaming or accusing others, which can help prevent defensiveness and conflict.

Non-verbal communication also plays a significant role in asserting your needs and desires effectively. Pay attention to your body language, tone of voice, and facial expressions. Maintain a confident posture, speak clearly and assertively, and maintain eye contact. These non-verbal cues can add weight to your words and convey your assertiveness more effectively.

In team meetings or job interviews, be ready to articulate your needs and desires by providing concrete examples or evidence. Prepare in advance, brainstorming relevant achievements and experiences that support your requests. Use facts, data, and specific examples to back up your statements and support what you need.

Last, practice assertiveness in everyday conversations. Look for opportunities to express your needs and desires in a respectful and confident manner. It could be as simple as asking for help when you need it or expressing your preferences when making decisions. The more you practice assertive communication, the more comfortable and effective you will become in asserting your needs and desires in all areas of your life.

Effective communication is vital in asserting your needs and desires. By being clear, direct, and confident in expressing yourself, actively listening, using "I" statements, paying attention to non-verbal cues, and providing evidence, you can effectively communicate your needs, desires, and career aspirations in various situations. Practice assertiveness in everyday conversations and continue to refine your communication skills to ensure your voice is heard and your needs are met.

OVERCOMING FEAR AND SELF-DOUBT: TAKING CHARGE OF CAREER GROWTH

In the journey of career growth, fear and self-doubt can be significant barriers that hinder assertiveness and hold us back from reaching our full potential. Overcoming these obstacles is crucial to take charge of our professional lives and achieve the success and fulfillment we desire. This chapter will explore common barriers that impede assertiveness, offering practical tips and techniques to build self-confidence and eliminate self-limiting beliefs.

Understanding the Barriers:

a. Self-Doubt: Many individuals experience self-doubt, questioning their abilities, skills, and worth. This lack of confidence can prevent us from taking risks, seeking new opportunities, or advocating for ourselves.

b. Fear of Failure: The fear of failing often paralyzes us, causing us to avoid stepping outside our comfort zones or pursuing ambitious goals. This fear can undermine our self-belief and hinder our career growth.

c. Imposter Syndrome: Imposter syndrome is the persistent feeling of being inadequate or fraudulent despite evidence of competence and accomplishments. Many successful individuals experience this syndrome, which can lead to self-sabotage and inhibiting career progression.

Building Self-Confidence:

a. Recognize Your Achievements: Reflect on your past successes and acknowledge your accomplishments. Celebrating even small wins can help boost your self-confidence.

b. Embrace Continuous Learning: Invest in your personal and professional development. Acquiring new skills and knowledge will make you feel more competent and confident in your abilities.

c. Surround Yourself with Positive Influences: Seek supportive relationships and surround yourself with individuals who uplift and encourage you. Their positivity can counteract self-doubt and provide a solid support system.

Challenging Self-Limiting Beliefs:

a. Identify and Challenge Negative Thoughts: Pay attention to your thought patterns and challenge negative self-talk. Replace them with positive affirmations and realistic beliefs that support your growth and potential.

b. Visualize Success: Envision yourself overcoming challenges, meeting your goals, and excelling in your career. Visualization techniques can help rewire your mind for success, enhancing belief in your capabilities.

c. Experiment with Small Risks: Gradually expose yourself to manageable risks, step outside your comfort zone, and prove to yourself that you can handle challenges. These small victories can collect and strengthen your self-belief.

Seeking Support and Professional Development:

a. Seek Mentorship: Find a mentor who can provide guidance, support, and encouragement. Their experience can help you navigate challenges, boost your confidence, and broaden your perspective.

b. Invest in Personal Development Programs: Participate in workshops, seminars, or coaching programs that focus on building assertiveness, self-confidence, and overcoming fear and self-doubt. These structured learning environments can provide valuable tools and strategies for personal growth.

Overcoming fear and self-doubt is essential to take charge of your career growth. By understanding common barriers, building self-confidence, challenging self-limiting beliefs, and seeking support, you can break free from the grip of fear and self-doubt. Embrace the journey of self-improvement and unlock your potential to create a fulfilling and successful professional life.

BUILDING RAPPORT AND INFLUENCING OTHERS:

Building rapport and influencing others are essential skills for success in any field. While assertiveness is crucial for advocating for yourself, it is equally important to build connections and persuade others to support your career growth. This section will provide techniques for building strong relationships, effective networking, and influencing others.

Active Listening: One of the most effective ways to build rapport is through active listening. Show genuine interest in others by giving them your full attention, maintaining eye contact, and nodding or using verbal cues to show engagement. Reflecting on what others say and asking clarifying questions shows you value their opinions and perspectives.

Empathy and Understanding: Being empathetic enables you to understand others better and build stronger relationships. Put yourself in their shoes and try to see things from their perspective. This will help you create connections based on mutual understanding and trust.

Authenticity: Building rapport requires authenticity. Be yourself and let your true personality shine through. People are more likely to connect with and trust someone who is genuine. Authenticity also creates an environment where others feel comfortable being themselves, fostering better relationships.

Networking: Effective networking is essential for career growth. Go to industry events, conferences, and workshops to connect with professionals from diverse backgrounds. Actively participate in networking activities by introducing yourself, engaging in conversations, and exchanging contact information. Follow up with personalized messages after the event to maintain the connection.

Building a Supportive Network: Cultivate a network of individuals who support and mentor your career growth. Seek mentors who can guide you and provide valuable insights. By surrounding yourself with supportive and knowledgeable individuals, you can enhance your skills and increase your influence **within your field.**

Influencing Others: Persuading others to support your career growth requires effective communication and a compelling argument. Articulate your goals and the potential benefits of supporting you. Use evidence, data, and personal examples to support your claims. Tailor your approach to the person you are trying to influence, considering their values, needs, and interests.

Collaboration and Relationship Building: Foster collaboration and build relationships by offering your support and knowledge to others. By being generous with your knowledge and helping others meet their goals, you become a valuable resource within your network. This reciprocity can lead to increased influence and support for your own career growth.

Adaptability: Being adaptable lets you navigate different personalities and situations effectively. Recognize that different people require different approaches and be willing to adjust your style to connect with others. Adapting to new circumstances and being open to others' perspectives enhances your ability to influence and build rapport.

Building rapport and influencing others is an ongoing process. Continuous effort and practice will help you develop and refine these skills, ultimately leading to long-lasting connections and increased support for your career growth.

SEIZING OPPORTUNITIES AND TAKING CALCULATED RISKS

In today's fast-paced and competitive world, assertiveness plays a crucial role in career growth. It enables individuals to express their thoughts, take charge of situations, and make bold decisions. However, to leverage assertiveness for career advancement, individuals must also be willing to seize opportunities and take calculated risks. This chapter aims to provide guidance on how to identify and evaluate opportunities while overcoming the fear of stepping out of one's comfort zone.

Identifying Opportunities:

To effectively leverage assertiveness, individuals must first learn to identify opportunities that align with their career goals. This requires staying informed and seeking out possibilities. Here are strategies to identify opportunities:

a. Networking: Building a robust network of contacts can provide valuable insights into potential opportunities. Go to industry events, connect with professionals through social media, and participate in relevant forums or groups.

b. Research and stay updated: Keep yourself updated with industry trends, market shifts, and emerging technologies. This knowledge will equip you to identify potential gaps or areas for growth.

c. Embrace challenges: Be open to challenges and embrace them as opportunities for growth. Often, when faced with a problem, individuals with an assertive mindset can envision solutions and turn challenges into opportunities.

Evaluating Opportunities:

Once opportunities are identified, it is vital to evaluate their potential and determine their suitability. Applying a systematic approach can help in making informed decisions:

a. Assess alignment with career goals: Evaluate how the opportunity aligns with your long-term career aspirations. Will it provide the desired skill development, growth, or exposure?

b. Evaluate potential risks and rewards: Consider the potential risks involved and weigh them against the potential rewards. Calculate the potential impact on your career trajectory to make a well-informed choice.

c. Seek advice and insights: Engage with mentors, colleagues, or industry experts to gain different perspectives on the opportunity. Their insights can help you make a more objective evaluation.

Overcoming the Fear:

Fear of taking risks and stepping out of one's comfort zone can often hinder assertiveness and career growth. To overcome this fear:

a. Cognitive reframing: Challenge negative thoughts and self-doubt that may hold you back. Instead, focus on the potential gains and what you can learn from the experience.

b. Gradual exposure: Start small by taking calculated risks in low-stakes situations. As you gain confidence and experience positive outcomes, gradually take on more significant challenges.

c. Embrace failure as a learning opportunity: Recognize that failure is a part of growth and a steppingstone toward success. Learn from your failures, adapt, and persevere.

Seizing opportunities and taking calculated risks are essential parts of leveraging assertiveness for career growth. By identifying and evaluating opportunities, individuals can make informed decisions that align with their career goals. Overcoming the fear of stepping out of one's comfort zone and embracing risks will propel individuals toward continuous growth and advancement in their careers. With the guidance provided in this chapter, individuals can equip themselves to seize opportunities and thrive in their professional journeys.

NAVIGATING SETBACKS:

Navigating setbacks is an essential part of any journey toward career growth. Inevitably, along the way, we will encounter challenges, setbacks, and even failures. However, it is our response to these obstacles that can make a significant difference in our ability to overcome them and continue progressing toward our goals.

The first step in navigating setbacks is to accept that they are a natural part of the growth process. Instead of being discouraged or disheartened when faced with a setback, view it as an opportunity for learning and growth. Recognize that setbacks are temporary and can provide invaluable lessons that can propel you forward in your career.

Resilience plays a crucial role in bouncing back from setbacks. Cultivating resilience lets you bounce back from failures, adapt to changing circumstances, and stay strong in the face of adversity. Building resilience involves developing a positive mindset, focusing on your strengths, and seeking support from mentors or a support network. Remember that setbacks do not define your capabilities or potential; it is how you respond and bounce back from them that matters.

Learning from setbacks is another critical part of taking charge of your career growth. Reflect on the reasons behind the setback and identify areas where you can improve. It is crucial to approach setbacks with a growth mindset, seeing them as opportunities for development rather than as permanent roadblocks. Take the time to analyze what went wrong, gather feedback from mentors or colleagues, and necessarily adjust your approach or strategy.

Setbacks provide an opportunity to reassess your goals and priorities. Use this time to reflect on your career aspirations, evaluate whether they still align with your values and interests, and make any necessary changes. Sometimes setbacks can lead us to discover new paths or opportunities we may not have considered before.

Seeking support during setbacks is also crucial. Contact mentors, colleagues, or a support network to discuss your challenges and gain insight from their experiences. They can offer guidance, feedback, and encouragement to help you navigate through setbacks more effectively. Remember that you need not face setbacks alone; seeking support can provide you with fresh perspectives and renewed motivation.

Finally, it is essential to stay persistent and committed to your career growth, even in the face of setbacks. Have faith in your abilities and stay focused on your long-term goals. Remember that setbacks are just temporary hurdles - they do not dictate your ultimate success. Maintain a positive attitude, celebrate small victories along the way, and continue taking proactive steps toward your career growth.

Setbacks are an inevitable part of the career journey. However, by embracing setbacks as learning opportunities, cultivating resilience, learning from challenges, seeking support, and staying persistent, you can navigate and overcome setbacks to continue progressing toward your goals. The path to career growth may not always be smooth sailing, but with the right strategies and mindset, you can steer through any storm and come out stronger on the other side.

CHAPTER ELEVEN SUMMARY: LEVERAGING ASSERTIVENESS TO TAKE CHARGE OF YOUR CAREER GROWTH

Chapter Eleven emphasizes the importance of assertiveness in career growth. It highlights how assertiveness enables individuals to take ownership of their career growth, pursue opportunities, build confidence and self-worth, overcome challenges, and develop strong professional relationships.

The chapter also provides practical advice on understanding career goals and aspirations, communicating effectively to assert needs and desires, overcoming fear and self-doubt, building rapport and influencing others, seizing opportunities and taking calculated risks, and navigating setbacks.

By mastering assertiveness and applying the strategies outlined in the chapter, individuals can shape their professional destiny and achieve a fulfilling and successful career path.

CHAPTER 12
SETTING AND ACHIEVING ASSERTIVE CAREER GOALS

UNDERSTANDING THE IMPORTANCE OF SETTING ASSERTIVE CAREER GOALS:

Setting assertive career goals is crucial for personal and professional development because they provide direction, motivation, and a clear roadmap for success. Without goals, individuals may quickly find themselves aimless and lacking the drive to advance in their careers. Assertiveness plays a key role in meeting these goals by making sure individuals confidently advocate for themselves, seize opportunities, and overcome obstacles.

One of the main reasons setting career goals is so important is that they provide a sense of purpose and direction. When individuals have a clear vision of what they want to achieve, they can focus their energy and resources toward reaching those goals. This sense of purpose also helps to create a positive mindset, increasing motivation and dedication to reach career milestones. Without specific goals, individuals may find themselves stuck in a repetitive cycle, lacking growth and progress.

Assertiveness is essential when pursuing and achieving career goals. It involves the ability to confidently express ideas, ask for what one wants, and negotiate effectively. By actively advocating for oneself, individuals are more likely to seize opportunities that come their way. They can voice their aspirations, show their capabilities, and show their commitment to meeting their goals. Assertive individuals also are more willing to take calculated risks, pushing themselves outside of their comfort zones to make significant strides in their careers.

Assertiveness helps individuals overcome obstacles and setbacks that may impede their progress toward their career goals. It lets them address conflicts, navigate challenging situations, and resolve issues effectively. By standing up for themselves and their aspirations, individuals can make sure they are not held back by external factors or discouraged by others' opinions. Assertiveness builds resilience and enables individuals to stay focused and determined in the face of adversity.

In addition to personal development, setting assertive career goals is also crucial for professional development. Employers often seek individuals who are self-driven and have a clear plan for their careers. Setting and achieving goals shows ambition, dedication, and goal-oriented thinking. It shows employers that individuals are proactive in their personal and professional growth, which can result in increased opportunities for advancement, promotions, and salary increases.

Understanding the importance of setting assertive career goals is essential for personal and professional development. Career goals provide direction, motivation, and a clear roadmap for success, while assertiveness empowers individuals to confidently pursue and meet those goals. By setting clear goals and being assertive, individuals can take control of their careers, overcome challenges, and create opportunities for growth and advancement.

UNVEILING INNER FOUNDATIONS: IDENTIFYING PERSONAL VALUES AND STRENGTHS

Understanding one's personal values and strengths is crucial when shaping a fulfilling professional journey. By aligning our career goals with our inherent motivations and abilities, we can create a path that not only resonates with us on a deeper level but also leads to long-lasting success and satisfaction. In this chapter, we will embark on a journey of self-discovery, letting readers uncover their core values and strengths, ultimately aiding them in finding the perfect alignment between their aspirations and their true selves.

Section 1: Unraveling Core Values

1.1 The Importance of Identifying Personal Values:

- Recognizing the impact of personal values on career satisfaction

Personal values play a significant role in determining career satisfaction. When individuals align their personal values with the values of their chosen career or work environment, it creates a sense of fulfillment and happiness. Recognizing the impact of personal values on career satisfaction is crucial for making informed decisions and finding a meaningful career path.

Self-reflection: The first step in recognizing the impact of personal values on career satisfaction is to engage in self-reflection. Identify and understand your own values—what matters to you in life, work, and relationships. This may include values like independence, creativity, helping others, or dedication to a cause.

Identify career-related values: Once you clearly understand your personal values, consider how they align with different career options. Research various careers and industries to identify which ones resonate with your values. For example, if creativity is important to you, you may find satisfaction in artistic or design-related fields.

Aligning values with work environment: Besides considering specific careers, it is also important to evaluate how your values align with different work environments. Do you prefer a collaborative or individual work setting? Are you motivated by financial rewards or making a positive impact on society? Understanding how your values fit into different work environments will help you find a career that aligns with your values on a deeper level.

Focus on your values: It is unlikely to find a career that aligns with all your values. However, it is essential to focus on your values and determine which ones are non-negotiable for your career satisfaction. This will help you make difficult decisions and avoid compromising on values vital to your overall happiness and fulfillment.

Seek alignment in your current job: If you realize that your current job or career does not align with your values, consider ways to seek alignment within your current circumstances. Can you find opportunities within your current job to align your values? Are there specific tasks you can take on that align more closely with your values?

Explore different career paths: If you feel that your personal values are significantly compromised in your current job or career, it may be time to explore different career paths. Look for opportunities that offer closer alignment with your values and consider taking professional development courses or seeking guidance from career counselors to help you in understanding the prospects that best match your values.

Recognizing the impact of personal values on career satisfaction is an ongoing process. It requires periodic introspection, reassessment, and changes to make sure your career remains fulfilling and aligned with your values throughout your professional journey. By consciously considering your values and seeking alignment, you can increase your chances of finding a career path that brings you satisfaction and fulfillment.

- Realizing how values act as guiding principles in decision-making

Values are the deeply rooted beliefs and principles that shape our thoughts, actions, and decisions. They serve as a moral compass and guide us on the path we take in life. Through our values, we make choices that align with our beliefs and have a significant impact on our overall well-being and happiness.

Realizing the role of values in decision-making is a critical step towards understanding why we make certain choices and how they reflect our character and goals. When we are aware of our values, we can make decisions in harmony with our authentic selves, leading to a sense of integrity and fulfillment.

Values provide a framework for decision-making by offering a set of criteria against which we can weigh our options. They act as a filter through which we analyze the potential outcomes, consequences, and ethical implications of our choices. By evaluating decisions based on our values, we make sure our actions are in line with what we believe to be right and just.

For example, suppose honesty and integrity are among our core values. Where we face the choice of whether to lie or tell the truth, our values would guide us to choose honesty, even if it means facing consequences or difficulties. These values help us build strong relationships, maintain trust, and stay true to ourselves.

Values also give us a sense of purpose and direction in decision-making. By understanding what is most important, we can set goals and focus on our actions. For example, if our values revolve around family and work-life balance, we may focus on spending quality time with our loved ones, even if it means sacrificing certain professional opportunities.

Values enable us to make consistent decisions across different parts of our lives. They provide a sense of continuity, making sure our choices align with our core principles despite the situation. This consistency strengthens our character and builds a reputation as someone who is reliable, trustworthy, and true to their convictions.

But it's important to note that values can sometimes clash, making decision-making more challenging. In such cases, we must weigh the relative importance of different values and find a balance that aligns with our overall principles. It is through reflection, introspection, and self-awareness that we can navigate these conflicts and make choices authentic to ourselves.

Realizing how values act as guiding principles in decision-making is essential for a purposeful and meaningful life. By understanding and aligning our choices with our values, we can live a life in harmony with our beliefs, fostering personal growth, happiness, and integrity.

1.2 Reflecting on Core Values:

- Engaging in self-reflection exercises to explore intrinsic values

Self-reflection exercises are valuable tools for exploring our intrinsic values. By engaging in these exercises, we can gain a deeper understanding of what matters to us, allowing us to live a more authentic and fulfilled life. Here are a few engaging self-reflection exercises to help you explore your intrinsic values:

Values Map: Start by creating a values map, which is essentially a visual representation of your core values. Grab a large piece of paper or use a digital platform and write down different values that come to mind. Next, categorize those values into broader themes such as relationships, personal growth, career, community, etc. Make sure to prioritize them in terms of importance to you. Reflect on each value and why it holds significance in your life. This exercise lets you see the bigger picture of what truly matters to you.

Life Narrative: Take time to reflect on the events and experiences that have shaped you into who you are today. Write down your life narrative, starting from your earliest memories and going until the present moment. Identify key moments, relationships, successes, and challenges that have had a significant impact on you. Then, analyze how these experiences align with your intrinsic values. What behaviors, choices, or parts of your life align with your values? What areas may need further exploration or improvement?

Ideal Day Visualization: Close your eyes and imagine your ideal day from start to finish. Dive into vivid details – where are you, who are you with, what are you doing, how do you feel? Pay attention to the activities and emotions that arise during this visualization. As you reflect on this ideal day, think about how it aligns with your intrinsic values. Which values are being fulfilled in this visualization? Are there any values you would like to focus on more in your daily life?

Strengths and Passions: Reflect on your strengths and passions – the activities or skills that come naturally to you, and that you truly enjoy doing. List these strengths and passions, and then consider how they tie in with your underlying values. What value does each strength or passion honor? How can you make more room for these activities in your life or align them with your overall values?

Gratitude Practice: Engaging in a gratitude practice can also help you explore your intrinsic values. Take a few moments each day to reflect on what you are grateful for. Notice patterns in your gratitude – what values are being expressed through these moments of appreciation? Look for common threads and consider how you can incorporate more of these values into your life.

Self-reflection is an ongoing process, and these exercises may take time to fully explore your intrinsic values. By engaging in these activities, you will develop a clearer understanding of what matters to you, allowing you to live a more purposeful and fulfilling life.

- Determining values' hierarchy and impact on different areas of life

Determining values' hierarchy and their impact on different areas of life involves assessing the importance of different values in relation to various parts of our lives. Values can be defined as guiding principles or fundamental beliefs that inform our behaviors and decision-making processes. They play a significant role in shaping our attitudes, motivations, and overall well-being. Understanding the hierarchy of values lets us prioritize and align our actions with what matters to us, leading to a more fulfilling and balanced life.

To begin determining values' hierarchy, it is essential to reflect on various parts of our lives, such as personal relationships, career, health, spirituality, personal growth, and community involvement. Ask yourself these questions:

What values are most important in each area of my life?

Consider the principles or beliefs that hold the most significance in different areas. For example, in personal relationships, values like trust, love, and loyalty might be crucial, while in career, values such as professionalism, ambition, or work-life balance might matter more.

How do these values influence my decision-making?

Evaluate whether these values guide your choices, actions, and behaviors in the different areas of life. When faced with a dilemma or decision, pay attention to the values that come into play and determine the importance they hold in shaping your response.

Once you have identified the values in each area, consider their impact on your life:

How do these values align or conflict with each other?

Sometimes, different values may clash or seem contradictory. Assess how these conflicting values impact your decision-making and whether there are potential areas where compromises or changes need to be made.

How do these values contribute to personal fulfillment?

Reflect on how these values contribute to your overall happiness and satisfaction in life. Investing time and effort into understanding and living according to your highest values often leads to a sense of purpose and fulfillment.

Once you clearly understand your values and their impact, it's time to establish a hierarchy:

Rank your values according to their importance in each area of your life.

Take each area and assign a level of importance to each value within that specific context. This ranking process will help you identify the primary values that hold the most significance in each area.

Determine the overall hierarchy of values.

Review the rankings across different areas of life and identify any patterns or consistencies. These patterns can guide you in determining the overall hierarchy of values, which reflects the core principles that matter most to you.

The hierarchy of values is a personal and ever-evolving process. As life circumstances change and personal growth occurs, the importance of certain values may also shift. Continually reassessing and adjusting your values' hierarchy can help you stay aligned with your evolving priorities and lead a more authentic and fulfilling life.

1.3 Aligning Values with Career Goals:

- Recognizing the significance of values-based goal setting

Values-based goal setting is aligning your goals and aspirations with your core values, beliefs, and principles. It involves identifying what matters to you and using that understanding to guide your decision-making and goal-setting process. This approach emphasizes the impor-tance of pursuing goals that are meaningful and in line with who you are as an individual.

The significance of values-based goal setting lies in its ability to provide direction, motivation, and fulfillment. When your goals are aligned with your values, you are more likely to feel a deep sense of purpose and satisfaction in your pursuit. This alignment creates a harmonious relationship between your goals and your identity, fostering a sense of authenticity and integrity in your actions.

One of the key benefits of values-based goal setting is that it helps you maintain focus on your efforts. By clarifying what matters to you, you can more easily identify which goals are worth pursuing and give your time and resources. This prevents you from chasing after empty achievements or societal expectations that may not align with your values.

Values-based goal setting also enhances decision-making by serving as a compass for navigating various choices and opportunities. When faced with multiple options, you can evaluate them based on their alignment with your core values. This evaluation eliminates the risk of making regretful decisions that may conflict with your beliefs or create internal conflict.

Aligning your goals with your values increases your sense of self-esteem and confidence. When you are pursuing goals rooted in your values, you feel a sense of authenticity and self-assurance. This empowers you to overcome obstacles, take risks, and persist in the face of challenges because you are driven by a deep and genuine desire to achieve some-thing meaningful.

Last, values-based goal setting promotes long-term happiness and fulfillment. When living a life in congruence with your values, you are more likely to experience a profound sense of fulfillment, content-ment, and happiness. This is because your goals are not limited to short-term gratification but are directed towards creating a life that aligns with your deepest values and aspirations.

Recognizing the significance of values-based goal setting is crucial for personal growth and fulfillment. When your goals and values are aligned, you will experience a greater sense of purpose, motivation, and happiness in your pursuit. By incorporating your core values into your goal-setting process, you can create a life that is deeply meaningful, authentic, and in line with your true self.

- Connecting core values to potential professional paths

Connecting core values to potential professional paths involves aligning one's personal values with different occupations or career paths. By identifying and focusing on these core values, individuals can make more informed decisions about their professional pursuits and find fulfillment in their work. Here are a few steps to help connect core values to potential professional paths:

Identify your core values: Start by reflecting on what matters to you. Core values are the fundamental beliefs and principles that guide your decisions and actions. Consider parts like integrity, social impact, personal growth, creativity, teamwork, flexibility, autonomy, diversity, or innovation.

Research potential industries and careers: Look for industries and career paths that align with your core values. For example, if social impact is a core value, roles within non-profit organizations, sustainability, or philanthropy may appeal. If creativity is vital to you, consider fields like design, arts, writing, or marketing.

Evaluate your skills and interests: Assess your existing skills, strengths, and passions. Determine areas where you excel and enjoy working. This evaluation can help identify professional paths that synchronize your core values with your capabilities and interests.

Seek advice and network: Connect with professionals already working in industries or roles that interest you. Reach out for informational interviews or go to relevant networking events or industry conferences. Engage in conversations about their work, core values, and how they align with yours. Their insights and experiences can provide invaluable guidance.

Volunteer or intern: Consider volunteering or interning in fields that resonate with your core values. This firsthand experience can offer a glimpse into the day-to-day parts of different professions, helping you better assess if they align with your interests and values.

Focus on your core values: Once you've gathered information and insights from your research, focus on your core values. Determine which values hold greater importance for you and how they can guide your decision-making process.

Explore overlapping options: Look for professional paths that align with multiple core values. Finding opportunities where multiple values converge increases the likelihood of job satisfaction and fulfillment.

Continuously evaluate and adjust: As you progress in your career, regularly assess whether your core values remain aligned with your chosen path. Reflect on your experiences and adjust your professional trajectory if necessary. Career growth may involve seeking new opportunities that better align with your evolving values.

By connecting core values to potential professional paths, individuals can embark on careers that offer meaning, purpose, and satisfaction. This alignment enhances motivation, personal fulfillment, and overall happiness in professional endeavors.

Section 2: Unleashing Innate Strengths

2.1 Understanding Personal Strengths:

- Defining strengths and their role in achieving success

Strengths are inherent qualities or talents possessed by an individual that enable them to perform certain tasks or activities exceptionally well. These strengths play a crucial role in achieving success as they provide a competitive advantage, boost motivation and confidence, and let individuals maximize their potential.

First, defining and understanding one's strengths is essential for personal and professional growth. By recognizing what we excel at, we can focus our efforts and energy on activities that align with our abilities. This enables us to work more efficiently and effectively, leading to higher levels of productivity and performance. Identifying strengths also lets individuals make informed decisions about their career path or areas of specialization where they can have the most impact.

Strengths provide a competitive advantage in the pursuit of success. When individuals leverage their strengths, they stand out among their peers, making them more sought after by employers, clients, or collaborators. For example, an individual with strong communication skills can effectively convey their ideas, build relationships, and influence others, giving them an edge in various professional settings.

Strengths contribute to higher levels of motivation and confidence. When individuals engage in activities that use their strengths, they experience a sense of fulfillment, accomplishment, and satisfaction. This positive feedback loop enhances their motivation to continue working towards their goals, even when faced with challenges or setbacks. Additionally, leveraging strengths lets individuals build confidence in their abilities, leading to increased self-assurance and belief in their capacity to achieve success.

Last, maximizing strengths enables individuals to reach their full potential. By focusing on what they are naturally good at, individuals can continually refine and enhance their skills, leading to mastery in specific areas. This enables them to perform at their best, tap into their creativity and innovation, and become experts in their chosen fields. Maximizing strengths also lets individuals contribute unique perspectives, ideas, and solutions, making them valuable assets in their personal and professional endeavors.

Strengths play a vital role in achieving success. Defining and leveraging these inherent qualities lets individuals work more efficiently and stand out among their peers. Strengths also motivate individuals, boost confidence, and enable them to reach their full potential. So, recognizing and using strengths is crucial for personal and professional growth, satisfaction, and ultimate success.

- Differentiating between innate strengths and learned skills

Innate strengths and learned skills are two parts of an individual's abilities and features. While both contribute to a person's overall capabilities, they originate from different sources and are developed through different processes. Below, we will discuss the differences between innate strengths and learned skills:

Definition:

Innate strengths: These are natural talents or features that a person is born with. They are often present from a young age and do not require formal training or education to develop.

Learned skills: These are abilities or knowledge that individuals acquire through intentional effort, practice, and training. They are gained through education, experience, and dedicated practice.

Origin:

Innate strengths: These are inherent qualities that individuals have from birth. They are often influenced by genetics and personal traits embedded in their DNA.

Learned skills: These are acquired through external factors such as education, training, mentoring, or observation. They are developed through conscious effort and practice.

Development:

Innate strengths: Although natural talents are present from an early age, they still need to be nurtured and honed through practice and experience. While they may come more easily to the individual, they still require active engagement to reach their full potential.

Learned skills: These abilities are developed through deliberate learning and training. They may involve systematic instruction, repetition, and progressive refinement. With time and practice, individuals can improve and master these skills.

Flexibility:

Innate strengths: Since these strengths are part of an individual's inherent nature, they are less flexible and challenging to change. While they can be further developed, they are essentially fixed qualities that individuals have throughout their lives.

Learned skills: Skills can be continually improved, changed, or even completely changed. They have a higher degree of flexibility as they are acquired and can be adapted to different contexts or specialized areas.

Application:

Innate strengths: These often align with an individual's natural inclinations or preferences. They can be applied in various scenarios and can be beneficial in roles or activities that leverage those specific strengths.

Learned skills: As these abilities are acquired deliberately, they are usually developed for specific purposes or tasks. They are applied in contexts where the acquired knowledge or ability is required.

Innate strengths and learned skills are distinct yet complementary parts of an individual's abilities. While innate strengths are naturally embedded and require development, learned skills are acquired through education and training. Recognizing the differences between the two can help individuals better understand their unique features and make choices regarding their personal and professional development.

2.2 Assessing Individual Strengths:

- Utilizing various tools and techniques to pinpoint strengths

There are many tools and techniques available to help identify strengths in individuals. Here are a few strategies to use:

Self-assessment tests: Encourage individuals to take self-assessment tests such as the StrengthsFinder or the VIA Character Strengths Survey. These tests provide insights into an individual's unique strengths and abilities and can be valuable tools in the self-discovery process.

360-degree feedback: Gather feedback from a variety of sources such as colleagues, supervisors, and subordinates. This comprehensive feedback lets individuals gain a holistic view of their strengths from different perspectives.

SWOT analysis: Use a SWOT (Strengths, Weaknesses, Opportunities, and Threats) analysis to identify and analyze individual strengths. By examining strengths alongside weaknesses, individuals can develop a better understanding of their unique abilities.

Reflection and self-reflection: Encourage individuals to engage in self-reflection and journaling exercises to uncover their strengths. Reflective questioning techniques, such as "What activities make you feel energized?" or "What do others compliment you on?" can aid in identifying areas of strength.

Performance reviews: Regular performance reviews can be an avenue to discuss strengths. By analyzing past achievements and success stories, individuals can identify patterns and recurring strengths crucial in those endeavors.

Observations and feedback from mentors: Engage mentors or coaches who can provide valuable insights and observations about an individual's strengths. Mentors often have a broader perspective and can pinpoint strengths that individuals may not be aware of.

Goal-setting exercises: When setting goals, encourage individuals to align them with their strengths. By focusing on leveraging strengths, individuals are more likely to achieve success and fulfillment.

Peer assessments: Conduct assessments where individuals provide feedback to their peers about their strengths. This peer-to-peer feedback can help uncover strengths that others recognize but individuals may not be aware of.

Using these tools and techniques, individuals can pinpoint their strengths, which can lead to increased self-awareness, personal growth, and the ability to leverage those strengths effectively.

- Recognizing strengths in different contexts: personal and professional

Recognizing our strengths is an essential part of personal and professional growth. Identifying and using our strengths can help us thrive both in our personal lives and in our careers. However, understand that strengths may differ in various contexts. What may be considered a strength in one area of life may not necessarily be useful in another.

In the personal context, strengths often revolve around traits and qualities that contribute to our overall well-being and happiness. For example, being empathetic, compassionate, or a good listener can be considered personal strengths as they foster positive relationships and enhance our social connections. Other personal strengths may include being organized, disciplined, or having a strong work ethic, enabling us to accomplish personal goals and maintain a healthy lifestyle.

But professional strengths refer to the skills, knowledge, and abilities valuable in the workplace or specific industries. These strengths can vary depending on one's job or profession. Some common professional strengths include effective communication, leadership skills, problem-solving abilities, adaptability, and teamwork. These strengths are often sought after by employers as they can contribute to individual and organizational success.

While some strengths may overlap between personal and professional contexts, it's important to recognize that certain attributes may be more useful in one area than the other. For example, being highly detail-oriented and organized may be a valuable professional strength, particularly in roles that demand precision and attention to detail. However, this same attribute might not hold the same significance in personal relationships, where flexibility and spontaneity could be more valuable traits.

Recognizing strengths in different contexts allows individuals to leverage their unique qualities in diverse situations. It helps them highlight the specific skills and characteristics that are most relevant and valued in a particular context, leading to improved performance, confidence, and overall satisfaction. Moreover, understanding the differences between personal and professional strengths allows individuals to adapt and develop new skills according to the demands of each context. This flexibility and self-awareness contribute to personal growth and the ability to excel in various areas of life.

Recognizing and harnessing our strengths is crucial for personal and professional success. However, it is important to acknowledge that strengths can vary in different contexts. Identifying personal strengths helps us enhance our relationships and well-being, while recognizing professional strengths allows us to excel in the workplace and achieve our career goals. By understanding these distinctions, individuals can effectively utilize their strengths to thrive in various aspects of life.

2.3 Leveraging Strengths for Career Development:

- Identifying potential career paths based on individual strengths

Identifying potential career paths is an important process that requires self-reflection and assessment. When determining career paths, it is crucial to consider an individual's strengths, as they play a vital role in finding a fulfilling and successful career. Here are some steps to help identify potential career paths based on individual strengths:

Self-assessment: Begin by understanding your own strengths, skills, interests, and values. Reflect on what activities or tasks energize you and what you excel at. Consider your past accomplishments, hobbies, and areas where you receive positive feedback.

Skill evaluation: Identify your core skills, both hard and soft. Hard skills are specific technical skills, such as coding or accounting, while soft skills include communication, leadership, problem-solving, and teamwork. Evaluate which skills you have and enjoy using.

Research career options: Once you clearly understand your strengths and skills, research various career paths that align with those attributes. Use online resources, career exploration websites, and networking to explore different industries, job titles, and roles available.

Seek guidance: Reach out to career counselors, mentors, or professionals working in industries that interest you. Discuss your strengths and aspirations with them and gather insights on potential career paths that match your strengths.

Consider transferable skills: Identify the transferable skills you have. These are skills that can be applied across various industries or job roles, such as critical thinking, problem-solving, or project management. Consider how these skills can be used in different fields.

Explore job descriptions: Read job descriptions of positions that interest you. Look for requirements, responsibilities, and qualifications that align with your strengths and skills. This will give you a better understanding of the work you may enjoy and excel at.

Volunteer or intern: Gain practical experience in fields that interest you to see how well your strengths align with the day-to-day tasks. This can be done through volunteer work or internships. Note tasks that energize you and offer a sense of fulfillment.

Networking: Talk to professionals in fields that match your strengths to gain insights into the industry. Go to industry events, join professional organizations, and build connections with individuals who can provide guidance on potential career paths.

Experiment: Take the opportunity to dabble in different areas. Take on side projects, freelance work, or temporary assignments to gain exposure to different industries or roles. Experimentation can help you discover new career paths you had not considered before.

Evaluate and refine: Continually assess your progress and experiences. Reflect on what parts of different career paths align with your strengths and values. Use this information to refine and narrow down your potential career paths until you find the best fit.

Career paths can evolve. Regularly reassess your strengths, interests, and aspirations. By focusing on your individual strengths, you can increase your chances of finding a career that brings you satisfaction and success.

- Maximizing professional potential through strengths-based strategies

Maximizing professional potential through strengths-based strategies involves identifying and leveraging individual strengths to achieve success and personal growth in the workplace. Rather than focusing on weaknesses or areas for improvement, this approach centers on developing and using one's innate abilities and talents.

Here are strategies for maximizing professional potential through a strengths-based approach:

Identify your strengths: Begin by identifying your unique strengths and skills. Reflect on your past achievements and tasks where you excelled. Consider feedback from colleagues, mentors, and supervisors to gain a better understanding of your strengths. Tools like the Clifton-Strengths assessment can also provide valuable insights.

Set clear goals: Once you have identified your strengths, set clear goals aligned with those strengths. Consider how you can apply and develop them in your current role or future career path. Establishing goals that use your strengths will help you stay motivated and engaged in your professional journey.

Seek opportunities for growth: Look for opportunities to further enhance and develop your strengths. Go to workshops, training sessions, or industry events that focus on specific areas related to your strengths. Seek mentors or coaches who can provide guidance and support in maximizing your potential.

Build strong networks: Connect with individuals who share similar strengths or have complementary ones. Collaborating with others with different skill sets can lead to innovative solutions and personal growth. Engaging in professional communities and networking events can also provide valuable insights and opportunities.

Choose roles aligned with strengths: When considering career paths or job opportunities, focus on roles that align with your strengths. Look for positions that let you apply and leverage your abilities to achieve success. Assessing the job description and aligning it with your strengths can help you make informed decisions.

Showcase your strengths: Find opportunities to showcase your strengths within your current role. Volunteer for projects or tasks that align with your abilities, take the lead on initiatives that bring out your strengths, and share success stories that highlight your unique talents. This will not only help you gain recognition but also increase job satisfaction.

Practice self-awareness: Regularly reflect on your progress in maximizing your professional potential through your strengths. Assess how your strengths are benefiting your career and overall growth. Continuously seek feedback and adapt your strategies to maximize your potential further.

Maximizing your professional potential through strengths-based strategies is an ongoing process. It requires self-reflection, continuous learning, and a willingness to adapt. With a focus on strengths, you can build a fulfilling and successful career that lets you thrive based on your unique abilities.

Section 3: Aligning Values and Strengths with Career Goals

3.1 Connecting Values and Strengths: The Synergy:

- Recognizing how values and strengths complement one another

Recognizing how values and strengths complement one another is essential to personal and professional development. Understanding this synergy lets individuals leverage their strengths while staying true to their values, which leads to a more fulfilling and successful life.

Values are the guiding principles that shape our beliefs, attitudes, and behaviors. They are what we hold dear and what we focus on in life. Strengths are the inherent qualities and abilities we have, which make us effective and efficient in various areas.

When values and strengths align, individuals experience a sense of authenticity, fulfillment, and flow. They can use their strengths in a way that aligns with their values, enhancing their overall performance and satisfaction. For example, a person who values kindness and empathy may find their strength in effectively listening to others and providing support. Using these strengths while staying true to their values, they can make a positive impact on the people around them, leading to a more meaningful and purposeful life.

Recognizing how values and strengths complement one another helps individuals make better decisions and navigate through challenges. When faced with a difficult situation, knowing one's values can serve as a compass, guiding them towards the right course of action. By leveraging their strengths in alignment with their values, individuals can make well-informed choices consistent with their beliefs and goals.

Recognizing the interplay between values and strengths lets individuals cultivate their personal and professional relationships more effectively. By understanding their own values and strengths, they can identify individuals who share similar values or have complementary strengths. Collaborating with people who share similar values fosters a sense of unity, trust, and cohesiveness. Similarly, working with individuals with complementary strengths can lead to a more synergistic and productive team dynamic.

Recognizing how values and strengths complement one another is crucial for personal and professional success. When individuals leverage their strengths in alignment with their values, they experience a sense of authenticity, fulfillment, and flow. They can make better decisions, navigate challenges effectively, and cultivate meaningful relationships. Understanding this synergy lets individuals lead more balanced, purposeful, and successful lives.

- Understanding how their alignment increases satisfaction and productivity

Alignment refers to the extent to which an individual's values, beliefs, and goals follow an organization's mission, vision, and strategy. When employees are aligned with their organization, it leads to increased satisfaction and productivity. Here's why:

Clear purpose and meaning: When employees understand and align with the organization's mission and vision, their work becomes meaningful. They have a sense of purpose, knowing that their efforts contribute to something larger. This alignment motivates employees to go above and beyond their responsibilities, leading to increased satisfaction and productivity.

Increased engagement: Alignment enhances employee engagement, which refers to the level of emotional commitment an employee has towards their work and the organization. Engaged employees are passionate, dedicated, and actively involved in their tasks. They feel a sense of ownership, which leads to higher job satisfaction and a willingness to put in discretionary effort. Engaged employees are also more likely to stay with the organization, reducing turnover and increasing productivity in the long run.

Improved decision-making: When employees are aligned with the organization's goals, they can make decisions in line with the broader strategy. As employees understand the organization's direction, they can align their choices and actions, which leads to better decision-making. This alignment makes sure employees focus on tasks and projects that contribute to the organization's success, leading to increased productivity.

Enhanced teamwork and collaboration: Alignment fosters a sense of unity and shared goals among employees. When everyone is committed to a common purpose, collaboration and teamwork flourish. Employees work together towards a common vision, leveraging each other's strengths and perspectives. This alignment fosters a positive work environment where communication is open, conflicts are resolved effectively, and collective efforts lead to higher productivity.

Personal growth and development: Organizations that emphasize alignment often provide opportunities for employee growth and development. By aligning employees' personal goals and aspirations with the organization's goals, employees feel valued and supported. When employees have access to training, mentoring, and career advancement opportunities, they are more satisfied and motivated to contribute their best efforts, leading to increased productivity.

Alignment between employees and their organization is crucial for both employee satisfaction and productivity. When employees understand how their values, beliefs, and goals align with the organization's mission and strategy, it leads to increased engagement, improved decision-making, enhanced teamwork, and personal growth. Creating a culture of alignment is a win-win situation where employees find fulfillment, and organizations benefit from higher levels of satisfaction and productivity.

3.2 Identifying Career Opportunities:

- Exploring various industries and professions that align with personal values and strengths

Exploring various industries and professions that align with personal values and strengths is an important process that can help individuals find fulfilling and rewarding career paths. By considering these factors, individuals can identify industries and professions that resonate with their beliefs, values, and talents, leading to greater job satisfaction and overall success.

Here are steps to begin exploring different industries and professions aligning with personal values and strengths:

Reflect on personal values: Take a moment to identify your core values and what is important to you. Consider factors such as work-life balance, social impact, creativity, autonomy, leadership, continuous learning, or any other values that resonate with you.

Assess strengths and skills: Evaluate your strengths and skills. Identify areas where you excel, whether they are technical, analytical, interpersonal, problem-solving, or creative skills. List your strengths and think about how they can be applied in various professional settings.

Research industries: Start researching different industries that interest you. Look into industries that align with your values and strengths. Consider sectors such as non-profit and social services, healthcare, technology, education, finance, sustainability, arts, or any other areas you find fascinating.

Explore professions: Within your chosen industries, explore different professions that match your values and strengths. Get to know the day-to-day responsibilities, required qualifications, and growth opportunities for each profession. Consider job titles like project manager, social worker, software engineer, teacher, financial analyst, psychologist, marketing specialist, or any other positions that appeal to you.

Networking and informational interviews: Reach out to professionals working in industries or professions that interest you. Engage in networking activities, go to industry events, and seek informational interviews to gain insights about their experiences. Learn about the pros and cons of their career paths and gather valuable advice.

Gain relevant experience: To further explore industries and professions, gain hands-on experience through internships, volunteer work, or part-time jobs. This will enable you to test your interests, learn more about the work environment, and develop skills required in your chosen fields.

Evaluate the alignment: Assess how well the industries and professions you have researched align with your values and strengths. Consider which ones resonate most with you and make a shortlist of potential career paths you feel passionate about.

Seek guidance and mentorship: Seek guidance from career counselors, mentors, or professionals who can provide valuable advice based on their knowledge. Their insights can help you make informed decisions and guide you in exploring the best options for your personal and professional growth.

Career exploration is an ongoing process. Stay open-minded, adapt to changing circumstances, and continue learning about new industries and professions. By aligning your values and strengths with your career choices, you are more likely to find fulfillment and enjoy a successful and rewarding professional journey.

- Evaluating potential career options based on alignment

When evaluating potential career options, it is important to consider your personal alignment with each option. Alignment refers to the extent to which a particular career aligns with your values, interests, skills, and long-term goals. By assessing alignment, you can make a more informed decision about which career paths are most likely to lead to personal fulfillment and success. Here are factors to consider when evaluating alignment:

Values: Start by identifying your core values. These are the principles and beliefs that are most important. Evaluate how each potential career option aligns with your values. For example, if environmental sustainability is a core value, you might focus on career paths that contribute to conservation or renewable energy.

Interests: Consider your passions and hobbies. What activities do you enjoy the most? Look for careers that align with your interests, as they are more likely to bring you joy and satisfaction. For example, if you are interested in technology and enjoy problem-solving, a career in software engineering might be a good fit.

Skills: Assess your skills, both technical and soft. Identify the skills you have or would like to develop further. Then, match those skills with career options that would let you utilize and enhance them. For example, if you have strong communication and leadership skills, a management or sales career may suit you well.

Long-term goals: Consider your long-term career goals. Where do you see yourself in 5, 10, or 20 years? Evaluate how each potential career option aligns with your desired trajectory. If your goal is to make a positive social impact, you might consider careers in non-profit organizations or social entrepreneurship.

Work-life balance: Assess how each career option aligns with your desired work-life balance. Some careers may require long working hours or extensive travel, while others may offer more flexibility. Consider how each option fits into your lifestyle and priorities.

Personal growth and learning: Determine the potential for personal growth and learning in each career option. Consider whether the field offers opportunities for skill development, advancement, and a continuously challenging environment. This will make sure you are engaged and motivated in your chosen career path.

Financial considerations: While not the sole determining factor, financial parts can also play a role in evaluating alignment. Consider the earning potential, stability, and benefits associated with each career option. Make sure your financial goals are not in conflict with your desired career path.

By evaluating potential career options based on alignment, you increase the likelihood of finding a fulfilling and successful career that matches your values, interests, skills, and long-term goals. Careful consideration of these factors will help you make a well-informed decision about which path to pursue. Remember, alignment is subjective and may evolve over time, so regularly reassess your choices to ensure continued alignment with your personal aspirations.

3.3 Nurturing a Sustainable Career:

- Developing a long-term plan based on values and strengths

Developing a long-term plan based on values and strengths is crucial for achieving personal and professional success. It involves assessing one's core values and identifying individual strengths to create a sustainable and fulfilling vision for the future. Here is an outline of steps to develop an effective long-term plan:

Reflection and self-assessment:

- Take time to reflect on personal values and beliefs. Identify the principles that guide your decision-making and what matters to you.

- Evaluate your strengths, skills, and talents. Reflect on what you enjoy doing, what comes naturally to you, and what others perceive as your strengths.

Set clear goals:

- Define specific and measurable long-term goals that align with your values and strengths. These goals should challenge yet be attainable and should contribute to your overall vision.

- Prioritize your goals based on their importance and relevance to you.

Create a timeline:

- Establish a realistic timeline for meeting your long-term goals. Break them down into smaller milestones or goals that can be achieved within specific time frames.

- Assign deadlines and regularly review and update your timeline as needed.

Identify resources and support:

- Determine the resources, skills, knowledge, and experiences needed to meet your long-term goals.

- Seek mentors, professionals, or other individuals who can support and guide you throughout your journey. Network with like-minded individuals who share similar values and interests.

Develop strategies and action plans:

- Brainstorm and develop strategies to reach your goals. Identify the necessary steps, actions, and initiatives that will lead you towards your long-term vision.

- Break down each goal into smaller, manageable tasks to make progress more achievable. Determine the order and sequence of these tasks.

Stay adaptable and flexible:

- Understand that long-term planning is not set in stone. Expect and embrace changes or unforeseen circumstances that may occur along the way.

- Continuously re-evaluate your long-term plan, adjusting it when necessary while keeping your core values and strengths in mind.

Review and measure progress:

- Regularly review your long-term plan and assess your progress towards each goal. Reflect on achievements, challenges, and lessons learned.

- Measure your success based on personal growth, fulfillment of values, and progress towards your long-term vision rather than only focusing on external factors.

Seek feedback and reassess:

- Seek feedback from trusted individuals who can provide objective perspectives on your progress and help you reassess your long-term plan.

- Consider adjustments or revisions to your goals, strategies, and action plans based on this feedback and self-reflection.

Developing a long-term plan based on your values and strengths is a dynamic process. It requires self-awareness, dedication, and adaptability. By aligning your actions with your core values and capitalizing on your strengths, you can create a meaningful and fulfilling path towards success.

- Establishing strategies to maintain synchronization as career goals evolve

Regularly assess and evaluate your career goals: As career goals evolve, it is essential to regularly assess and evaluate them to ensure they are aligned with your values, interests, and aspirations. Take the time to reflect on your current goals and determine if they still resonate with you as you grow and develop.

Stay up-to-date with industry trends and changes: The professional landscape is constantly evolving, and it is crucial to stay informed about the latest industry trends and changes. This will let you adapt your career goals, making sure they remain relevant and synchronized with the industry's demands.

Seek continuous learning and development opportunities: Keep acquiring new skills and knowledge in line with your evolving career goals. This can be done through attending workshops, training programs, seminars, or pursuing further education. The aim is to equip yourself with the expertise to stay synchronized with your evolving career aspirations.

Regularly reassess your values and priorities: As your career evolves, it is important to reflect on your values and priorities to ensure they align with your professional goals. Take the time to reassess what is important to you and adjust your career trajectory ensuring a synchronized pursuit of your goals.

Maintain a flexible and open mindset: Career goals are not set in stone. As your interests and passions evolve, be open to adjusting your plans. Embrace opportunities that arise in unexpected areas and be willing to shift your focus if it aligns better with your evolving aspirations.

Seek mentorship and guidance: Connect with mentors or professionals with expertise in your desired career field. They can provide guidance and support as you navigate the changes in your career goals. Their insights and experience can help you stay synchronized and provide valuable advice on aligning your aspirations with industry demands.

Remain adaptable and embrace change: Embracing change is crucial to maintaining synchronization as career goals evolve. Be open to new career paths, industries, or opportunities that may arise. Remaining adaptable will let you pivot when necessary and navigate the changes that come with evolving goals.

Establishing strategies to maintain synchronization as career goals evolve requires regular assessment, staying informed about industry changes, continuous learning, reassessing values, maintaining flexibility, seeking guidance, and embracing change. By starting these strategies, you can make sure your career goals remain aligned with your evolving aspirations.

Discovering personal values and strengths provides a solid foundation for bringing meaning and fulfillment into one's career. By undertaking the journey of self-discovery in this chapter, readers will gain valuable insights into their authentic selves, enabling them to navigate the professional world with purpose and determination. The alignment of intrinsic motivations and abilities with career aspirations will propel readers toward a future filled with both achievement and personal gratification.

GOAL SETTING STRATEGIES:

Goal setting is an essential skill for anyone striving to achieve success in their career. Whether you are starting out or looking to make significant progress in your current position, effective goal setting strategies can provide the direction and motivation you need to reach your goals. In this section, readers will learn about various techniques for setting assertive career goals, with a focus on the SMART framework, visualization, and positive affirmations.

The first strategy readers will explore is the SMART framework. This widely recognized method for setting goals makes sure they are Specific, Measurable, Achievable, Relevant, and Time-bound. By following this framework, individuals can create goals that are clear, quantifiable, realistic, aligned with their aspirations, and set within a specific timeframe. Whether it is aiming for a promotion, learning a new skill, or increasing productivity, the SMART framework provides a structured approach to goal setting that increases the likelihood of success.

Visualization is another powerful technique that can greatly enhance goal setting. When individuals visualize their desired outcomes, they form a mental image of what they want to achieve. This practice can help clarify goals and provide motivation, as the mind has a powerful effect on behavior. By visualizing the successful accomplishment of their career goals, individuals can reinforce positive beliefs and create a sense of determination, improving their chances of realizing their aspirations.

Positive affirmations are closely related to visualization and can significantly affect goal setting. By adopting a positive mindset and using affirmations, individuals can reaffirm their belief in their abilities and stay focused on their goals. These affirmations can be simple statements, such as "I am capable of achieving great things in my career" or "I am consistently progressing toward my goals." By repeating these affirmations regularly, readers can cultivate a positive mindset that aligns with their career aspirations, ultimately enhancing their goal-setting efforts.

Setting assertive career goals requires effective strategies that provide direction and motivation. The SMART framework, visualization, and positive affirmations are techniques that readers can adopt to enhance their goal-setting process. Using these strategies, individuals can create clear, achievable goals aligned with their aspirations, stay focused and motivated, and increase their chances of success in their career endeavors.

EMBRACING CHALLENGES: OVERCOMING OBSTACLES AND SETBACKS:

In our journey toward pursuing our career goals, we often encounter obstacles and setbacks. These challenges may discourage us, make us question our capabilities, and sometimes even push us to the brink of giving up. However, mastering the art of overcoming obstacles is crucial to achieving long-term success. In this chapter, we will explore practical advice on how to overcome these hurdles, manage setbacks effectively, and stay motivated despite the difficulties we encounter along the way.

Recognizing and Accepting Challenges:

The first step toward overcoming obstacles is acknowledging their existence. Often, individuals ignore or deny challenges, which only amplifies their impact. By recognizing the hurdles, we face, we empower ourselves to find solutions and develop resilience. Embrace these challenges as steppingstones toward personal growth and development.

Shifting Perspectives:

Changing our perspective is vital when faced with obstacles. Instead of viewing them as roadblocks, consider them as opportunities for growth. Understand that setbacks are inevitable in any journey and that they provide valuable lessons and experience. By reframing our mindset, we unlock the potential to transform setbacks into stepping-stones toward our ultimate success.

Planning and Strategizing:

Once we recognize challenges, we should create a realistic and actionable plan to overcome them. Break down the problem into smaller, manageable tasks and set achievable short-term goals. Devise a strategy that aligns with your strengths, skill sets, and available resources. A well-thought-out plan will provide direction and serve as a roadmap to navigate through difficulties.

Developing Resilience:

Resilience is the ability to bounce back from setbacks and learn from failures. It involves developing a positive mindset, staying focused on long-term goals, and adapting to changes. Cultivate resilience by seeking support from mentors, surrounding yourself with positive influences, and practicing self-care and self-compassion. Remember, setbacks are temporary, but resilience is enduring.

Seeking Support:

Overcoming obstacles becomes easier when we have a support system. Seek advice from mentors, colleagues, or professionals who have faced similar challenges successfully. They can provide guidance, share valuable insights, and offer emotional support during tough times. Additionally, consider joining networking groups or communities where individuals can share their experiences and provide encouragement.

Learning from Setbacks:

Setbacks are opportunities for growth. Take the time to reflect on what went wrong and what could have been done differently. Understanding the lessons learned will help you develop new strategies and approaches, making you better prepared to face future obstacles. Embrace setbacks as valuable feedback and use them to fuel your determination and motivation.

Maintaining Motivation:

Staying motivated during difficult times is crucial for overcoming obstacles and setbacks. Remind yourself of your long-term goals and celebrate small victories along the way. Setbacks are part of the journey, but they do not define your ultimate success. Engage in self-reflection, visualize your desired outcome, and cultivate a positive mindset to maintain motivation even when faced with major challenges.

While pursuing our career goals, obstacles and setbacks are bound to occur. However, by recognizing challenges, changing our perspective, planning strategically, developing resilience, seeking support, learning from setbacks, and maintaining motivation, we can overcome these hurdles. Embrace challenges as opportunities for growth and remember that setbacks are temporary, but the lessons learned and the resilience gained will last a lifetime.

DEVELOPING AN ASSERTIVE MINDSET:

Developing an assertive mindset is essential for achieving career goals. Being assertive means confidently expressing your thoughts, feelings, and opinions while respecting the rights and boundaries of others. By cultivating assertiveness, you can effectively communicate your needs, assert your boundaries, and handle conflicts constructively. This section will outline the key steps to building self-confidence, improving communication skills, and developing a resilient attitude.

Building self-confidence:

To become assertive, it is imperative to build self-confidence. Start by identifying and acknowledging your strengths, achievements, and qualities. Celebrate your successes and remind yourself of your capabilities. Practicing self-care, such as maintaining a healthy work-life balance, exercising regularly, and adopting a positive mindset, can also contribute to enhancing self-confidence. Set realistic goals and achieve them, as this will help boost your self-belief.

Improving communication skills:

Effective communication is crucial for assertiveness. Develop active listening skills, which involve focusing on the speaker, maintaining eye contact, and understanding their perspective. Pay attention not only to verbal cues but also to non-verbal signals like body language and facial expressions. Express your thoughts and opinions clearly and concisely. Use "I" statements to express yourself, such as "I feel," "I think," or "I believe," which assert your individuality without sounding aggressive. Practice assertive body language, maintaining an open and confident posture.

Developing a resilient attitude:

A resilient attitude helps you overcome obstacles and setbacks on your career journey. Cultivating resilience involves reframing setbacks as learning opportunities and being open to change. Develop problem-solving skills to find solutions and turn challenges into steppingstones. Build a support network by seeking guidance from mentors and connecting with like-minded professionals. Embrace a growth mindset, recognizing that failures and setbacks are temporary and stepping-stones to success.

Embracing assertiveness in professional settings:

Apply these skills in your professional interactions. Express your expectations and needs to your colleagues or superiors. Set boundaries and learn to say 'no' when necessary, without feeling guilty. Practice assertive communication during meetings or presentations by speaking confidently, listening actively, and handling disagreements respectfully. Recognize your worth and advocate for yourself when negotiating salary, workload, or work-life balance.

Consistency and practice:

Developing an assertive mindset requires consistency and practice. Continuously challenge yourself to step outside your comfort zone and assert your opinions. Seek feedback from trusted colleagues and integrate their advice into your assertiveness development. Acknowledge and celebrate your progress, focusing on continuous improvement.

· · ·

Developing an assertive mindset is vital for achieving career goals. Building self-confidence, improving communication skills, and developing a resilient attitude are key parts of assertiveness. By cultivating these qualities, you will be better equipped to express yourself, handle conflicts, overcome setbacks, and succeed in your career.

CREATING AN ACTION PLAN:

Creating an action plan is essential for individuals determined to achieve assertive career goals. This plan serves as a roadmap, outlining the steps to reach those goals, and helps individuals stay focused, organized, and motivated. In this section, we will explore the key elements required to create a comprehensive action plan and highlight the importance of breaking down goals into manageable tasks with realistic deadlines.

Define your goals: Start by clearly defining your assertive career goals. These goals should be specific, measurable, attainable, relevant, and time-bound (SMART). For example, instead of stating, "I want to advance in my career," specify, "I want to be promoted to a team leader position within the next two years."

Break down your goals: Once you have identified your goals, break them down into smaller, manageable tasks. This step is crucial as it lets you create a clear path toward meeting your overall goal. For example, if your goal is to become a team leader, break it down into tasks such as enhancing your leadership skills, improving your communication abilities, and expanding your professional network.

Set realistic deadlines: Assign realistic deadlines to each task. Be honest with yourself about the time and effort required to accomplish each step. Setting unrealistic deadlines can lead to frustration and a lack of motivation. Consider external factors such as work commitments, personal life, and potential obstacles that may affect your timeline. Remember, it's better to give more time than necessary than to rush through tasks.

Focus on tasks: After assigning deadlines, focus on your tasks based on their importance and urgency. Determine which tasks are critical for meeting your overall goal and focus on those first. By focusing efficiently, you make sure you tackle the most significant tasks early on, increasing your chances of success.

Seek guidance and support: Don't hesitate to seek guidance and support from mentors, colleagues, or professionals in your field. Discussing your action plan with them can provide valuable insights, advice, and suggestions for improvement. They can also hold you accountable, making sure you stay on track.

Reassess and adjust: Your action plan should not be set in stone. It's essential to periodically reassess your progress, reevaluate the effectiveness of your tasks, and adjust your plan. As circumstances change or new opportunities arise, be willing to change your action plan to ensure it remains relevant and aligned with your goals.

By creating a comprehensive action plan that breaks down your goals into manageable tasks with realistic deadlines, you will significantly increase your chances of achieving your assertive career goals. This plan will serve as a constant reminder of what needs to be done and will guide you throughout your journey, helping you stay focused, motivated, and in control of your professional growth.

TRACKING PROGRESS AND ADJUSTING GOALS:

Achieving assertive career goals requires not only setting them but also regularly tracking progress and adjusting them along the way. This final section will delve into the importance of tracking progress and reassessing goals periodically. Readers will discover how to evaluate their progress, make necessary changes, and stay committed to achieving their assertive career goals.

Evaluating Progress: Regularly evaluating one's progress is crucial in determining whether goals are being met or if changes need to be made. This evaluation involves looking back at the initial career goals and assessing how far one has come in achieving them. By examining milestones, accomplishments, and skill development, individuals can gain insights into their progress.

Making Necessary Adjustments: Monitoring progress enables individuals to identify areas where changes are required. Sometimes, external factors like changing market needs or personal circumstances may require reevaluating and changing goals. It is essential to adapt goals as circumstances change to ensure they remain realistic and relevant.

Staying Committed: Adjusting goals may be challenging, as it can make one feel as though they are veering off course. However, staying committed to the overarching vision and remaining flexible are key to achieving assertive career goals. This involves accepting that circumstances may change and that changes are necessary to maintain progress.

Seeking Feedback: Seeking feedback from mentors, supervisors, or trusted confidantes can provide valuable insights into one's progress and help identify areas for improvement. Constructive feedback helps in aligning goals with organizational or industry expectations, thus increasing the chances of success.

Celebrating Milestones: Acknowledging milestone achievements along the way can boost motivation and enhance commitment toward career goals. By taking the time to celebrate successes, individuals reinforce their determination and perseverance, providing the momentum required to continue working toward assertive career goals.

Maintaining Focus: It is easy to get sidetracked or lose focus amidst the constant demands of professional life. Regularly reviewing and reassessing goals helps individuals keep their priorities in check and reminds them of the vision they are working toward. This focus enables individuals to realign their efforts, fostering productivity and efficiency.

Monitoring progress and adjusting goals periodically is crucial to achieving assertive career goals. By consistently evaluating progress, making necessary changes, staying committed, seeking feedback, celebrating milestones, and maintaining focus, individuals can ensure they are on the right path and remain dedicated to their aspirations. Boldly pursuing these goals requires adaptability and a willingness to change course when circumstances dictate, ultimately leading to long-term career success.

CHAPTER TWELVE SUMMARY: SETTING AND ACHIEVING ASSERTIVE CAREER GOALS

Chapter Twelve explores the importance of setting assertive career goals and provides guidance on how to achieve them. It emphasizes the significance of goals in providing direction, motivation, and a clear roadmap for success.

The chapter highlights the role of assertiveness in meeting career goals by advocating for oneself, seizing opportunities, and overcoming obstacles. It also discusses how personal values and strengths contribute to shaping a fulfilling professional journey.

The chapter introduces strategies for effective goal setting, including the SMART framework, visualization, and positive affirmations. Additionally, it addresses the need to embrace challenges, overcome setbacks, develop an assertive mindset, and create a comprehensive action plan.

The chapter concludes by emphasizing the importance of tracking progress, adjusting goals when necessary, and staying committed to achieving assertive career goals.

CHAPTER 13

NETWORKING WITH CONFIDENCE: BUILDING CONNECTIONS TO ADVANCE YOUR CAREER

UNDERSTANDING THE IMPORTANCE OF NETWORKING IN TODAY'S PROFESSIONAL LANDSCAPE:

In today's fast-paced and competitive professional landscape, networking has become an indispensable tool for career growth. Building connections and nurturing relationships with individuals in your industry can open doors to new opportunities, expand your knowledge base, and enhance your professional reputation. This chapter will delve into the critical role that networking plays and underscore the significance of confidence when forming and maintaining connections.

1. Networking as the Catalyst for Career Advancement:

1.1 Expanding professional circles:

Networking provides a way to expand your professional circles beyond your immediate workplace or industry. By connecting with individuals from diverse backgrounds, you gain access to a wider range of perspectives, ideas, and potential collaborations that can lead to career advancement.

1.2 Accessing hidden opportunities:

Building a network lets you tap into hidden job opportunities that may not be advertised publicly. Through informal conversations and connections with industry professionals, you may gain access to unadvertised positions or be recommended for upcoming opportunities, giving you a competitive edge in your career progression.

1.3 Developing a support system:

Networking not only opens doors for new opportunities but also helps in developing a support system in your professional journey. By establishing meaningful relationships with mentors, peers, and industry experts, you can seek guidance, advice, and support during challenging times, aiding in personal and professional growth.

2. The Confidence Factor in Networking:

2.1 Building a positive first impression:

Confidence plays a crucial role in building effective connections. By projecting self-assurance in social and professional settings, you create a positive first impression. This impression opens the door for further engagement, leading to fruitful networking opportunities.

2.2 Breaking the ice:

Confidence is essential for overcoming first shyness or fear when approaching new individuals. Having faith in your abilities and knowing your worth can propel you to step out of your comfort zone, start conversations, and establish connections with ease.

2.3 Engaging in meaningful conversations:

Confidence enables you to engage in meaningful conversations and convey your thoughts and ideas articulately. It lets you present your skills, knowledge, and experiences effectively, making you memorable and building credibility within your network.

2.4 Fostering lasting connections:

Confidence plays a pivotal role in nurturing lasting connections. Building trust and maintaining relationships in the professional world requires assertiveness and self-assuredness. Being confident makes sure you can actively participate in conversations, establish rapport, and show your commitment to building genuine connections.

3. Strategies for Building Confidence in Networking:

3.1 Awareness of your strengths:

Recognizing your unique skills, experiences, and strengths lets you approach networking with confidence. Understanding and appreciating what you bring to the table will empower you to showcase your abilities effectively.

3.2 Preparation for networking events:

Preparation is key to boosting confidence in networking situations. Researching potential attendees, understanding industry trends, and practicing elevator pitches can equip you with the knowledge and assurance to engage in meaningful conversations.

3.3 Embracing a growth mindset:

Adopting a growth mindset and viewing networking as an opportunity for learning and growth can bolster your confidence. Embrace challenges, seek feedback, and navigate networking situations with a positive outlook, as this will enable you to refine your networking skills and build meaningful connections.

Networking holds immense importance in today's professional landscape. It is much more than exchanging business cards or attending events; it is a gateway to career advancement, hidden opportunities, and a strong support system. Understanding the role of confidence in networking is crucial for successfully building connections. By recognizing your worth, preparing adequately, and embracing a growth mindset, you can approach networking situations with confidence, leading to fruitful connections and a thriving professional network.

OVERCOMING THE FEAR OF NETWORKING: BUILDING CONFIDENCE AND ALLEVIATING ANXIETY

Networking plays a crucial role in professional development, providing opportunities for career growth, expanding knowledge, and fostering collaborations. However, for many, the mere thought of networking can evoke feelings of fear and anxiety. In this chapter, we will delve into common fears and apprehensions associated with networking and provide practical tips and guidance on building confidence and overcoming anxiety when making potential professional contacts.

1. Understanding the Fear:

a. Fear of Rejection: One of the most significant fears individuals have when networking is the fear of rejection. The thought of approaching someone and being turned down can be daunting. However, it is essential to acknowledge that rejection is a natural part of the process, and it should not be taken personally.

b. Fear of Inadequacy: Many people fear they are not skilled or knowledgeable enough to engage in meaningful conversations. This fear can stem from imposter syndrome or the belief that others are more experienced or competent than they are. It is crucial to remember that networking is not about proving oneself, but rather about building relationships and learning from others.

c. Fear of the Unknown: Networking often involves stepping out of one's comfort zone, meeting new people, and navigating unfamiliar environments. Fear of the unknown and fear of social situations can make individuals anxious. By addressing these fears head-on, it is possible to cultivate the confidence needed to overcome them.

2. Building Confidence:

a. Preparation: Being prepared before attending networking events can significantly boost confidence. Research the event or individual you plan to connect with, be knowledgeable about industry trends, and have a concise elevator pitch ready. Feeling prepared brings confidence, ensuring smoother and more engaging conversations.

b. Start with Familiar Faces: Networking does not always have to involve approaching complete strangers. Begin by connecting with individuals you already know, such as colleagues, classmates, or friends. Leverage these existing relationships to expand your network and gradually ease into approaching new connections.

c. Positive Self-Talk: Negative self-talk can exacerbate fears and anxiety. Counteract it by practicing positive self-talk, focusing on strengths, and acknowledging past accomplishments. Remind yourself that you have value to offer and are deserving of building professional relationships.

3. Alleviating Anxiety:

a. Set Realistic Goals: Instead of pressuring yourself to meet everyone at an event, set small, achievable goals. Aim to have meaningful conversations with a few individuals or establish connections with professionals from specific industries or fields of interest.

b. Active Listening: Engaging in active listening during networking interactions helps alleviate anxiety. By focusing on the conversation and showing genuine interest in the other person, you can divert attention from your anxiety and create more meaningful connections.

c. Practice, Practice, Practice: The more you practice networking, the easier it becomes. Consider joining groups or organizations centered on professional development, attending workshops or webinars, or participating in mock networking sessions. Regularly putting yourself in networking situations will gradually reduce anxiety levels.

Networking can be a valuable tool for professional growth, but it is understandable that fear and apprehension can hinder one's ability to make connections. By understanding common fears, building confidence through preparation and positive self-talk, and actively working to alleviate anxiety, individuals can overcome their fear of networking. Embracing networking as an opportunity for growth and relationship building will open doors to a fulfilling professional journey.

DEVELOPING A NETWORKING STRATEGY:

In today's interconnected world, building and nurturing professional relationships has become more crucial than ever. A robust networking strategy can significantly enhance career prospects and open doors to new opportunities. This section will highlight the importance of developing a well-thought-out networking strategy, including aligning it with career goals and using key events and platforms for making valuable connections.

Importance of a Networking Strategy:

Creating a networking strategy ensures a proactive and organized approach to building professional relationships. It lets individuals leverage their connections effectively and provides a platform for mutual support and growth. A well-executed networking strategy can yield many benefits, such as job referrals, mentorship opportunities, business partnerships, and access to industry insights and trends.

Aligning with Career Goals:

To develop an effective networking strategy, it is essential to align it with specific career goals. Identifying the desired outcomes and direction can help individuals focus their efforts on making connections that will drive professional growth. For example, someone seeking career advancement in marketing may focus on attending industry conferences or joining relevant online communities to connect with potential employers, mentors, or collaborators.

Identifying Key Events:

Attending key events is an excellent way to expand one's professional network. Key events include industry conferences, trade shows, seminars, workshops, or webinars in one's field of interest. Such events provide a conducive environment for meeting like-minded individuals, industry experts, and potential employers. Researching and focusing on events that attract individuals who can contribute to one's career growth is an integral part of a networking strategy.

Using Online Platforms:

In today's digital age, leveraging online platforms is crucial to complement traditional networking efforts. Social media platforms like LinkedIn, Twitter, and professional forums provide opportunities to reach a wide audience and engage with professionals from around the world. Building a strong online presence, sharing industry insights, and actively participating in discussions can help establish credibility and attract valuable connections.

Creating a Systematic Approach:

Networking should be approached strategically and systematically. Setting measurable goals, such as attending a specific number of events per quarter or connecting with some industry professionals each month, can provide a real roadmap for success. Developing a calendar and establishing routines for networking activities ensures consistent efforts toward expanding one's network.

Nurturing Relationships:

Networking is not just about making initial connections, but also about cultivating and nurturing relationships. Maintaining regular contact with connections through emails, occasional phone calls, or attending industry-related social events helps solidify these relationships. Offering help, providing value, and staying engaged in their professional journeys can lead to a mutually beneficial networking ecosystem.

Developing a networking strategy is pivotal in today's professional landscape. It provides individuals with a structured approach to building meaningful relationships that align with their career goals. By identifying key events and using online platforms, individuals can expand their networks, gain valuable insights, and potentially unlock many professional opportunities. A well-executed networking strategy acts as a catalyst for career growth and a valuable asset in today's inter-connected world.

In today's interconnected and competitive world, the ability to effectively introduce oneself and leave a lasting impression is essential. This is true when attending networking events, where the first impression can make all the difference. Crafting a compelling elevator pitch is a crucial tool to confidently portray one's skills, interests, and aspirations in a concise and memorable manner. In this chapter, we will delve deeper into the art of crafting an elevator pitch that elevates your personal brand and captivates your audience.

1. Understanding the Elevator Pitch:

1. What is an elevator pitch?

An elevator pitch is a concise and compelling pitch or summary of an idea, product, or service that can be delivered in a short elevator ride. It is typically around 30 seconds to 2 minutes long, capturing the attention of the listener quickly and leaving a lasting impression.

The purpose of an elevator pitch is to effectively communicate the key points, benefits, and uniqueness of what you are offering, leaving the listener wanting to know more.

It should engage, be persuasive, and tailored to the specific audience. An elevator pitch is often used when networking, seeking job opportunities, or when pitching a business idea to potential investors or customers. It is a valuable tool to make a strong first impression and generate interest in a concise and memorable manner.

1. Why is an elevator pitch important?

An elevator pitch is important for several reasons:

Capturing attention: In today's fast-paced world, people have limited time and attention spans. An elevator pitch allows you to communicate your key message quickly and succinctly, capturing the listener's attention within a few seconds.

Making a memorable impression: A well-crafted elevator pitch enables you to leave a lasting impact on others. It helps you communicate your unique selling proposition, knowledge, or project in a way that sticks in people's minds, making them remember you and what you offer.

Effective networking: Elevator pitches are especially useful where you often have limited time to introduce yourself and make an impression. Having a clear and concise elevator pitch can significantly increase the chances of making valuable connections and opportunities.

Building credibility: An elevator pitch shows your expertise, knowledge, and passion about your subject matter. It helps establish credibility and trust with your audience, making them more likely to take you seriously and consider your ideas or proposals.

Generating interest and opportunities: A compelling elevator pitch can generate interest, spark curiosity, and attract potential collaborations, partnerships, or investors. It can open doors to new opportunities, whether it's securing funding, landing a job interview, or getting media coverage.

Clarifying your own goals and ideas: Crafting an elevator pitch forces you to clarify your goals, key messages, and value proposition. It helps you articulate your thoughts concisely, which leads to a deeper understanding of your own project or venture. This clarity can be beneficial when communicating with others or refining your overall strategy.

Overall, an elevator pitch is crucial for effectively communicating your message, making a memorable impression, and opening doors to new opportunities. It is a powerful tool that can help you stand out in a crowded marketplace and make a lasting impact on others.

1. **How to tailor your elevator pitch to specific situations and audiences?**

Tailoring your elevator pitch to specific situations and audiences can greatly increase its effectiveness in connecting with your listeners. Here are steps you can follow to tailor your elevator pitch:

Understand Your Audience: Before crafting your elevator pitch, take time to research and understand your target audience. Consider their needs, interests, and background. This will help you create a pitch that resonates with them.

Define Your Objective: Determine the specific goal or objective you want to achieve with your elevator pitch. For example, are you trying to gain clients, attract investors, or secure partnerships? Clarity about your goal will guide the content and tone of your pitch.

Customize the Content: Once you comprehend your audience and goal, customize the content of your elevator pitch. Highlight the parts of your products, services, or skills that are most relevant to the specific audience's needs. Use language they can easily grasp and relate to.

Adapt Your Tone and Style: Consider the proper tone and style that matches the situation and audience. For a more formal and professional setting, maintain a polished and composed tone. Conversely, for a casual or networking event, you might adopt a friendlier and conversational tone to connect on a personal level.

Incorporate Relevant Examples or Stories: People often remember stories better than facts or figures. Include examples or stories in your pitch that illustrate how your offering has benefited others in a similar situation. This helps the audience visualize the potential value and impact of what you are presenting.

Be Concise and Memorable: Keep your elevator pitch focused and concise. Aim to deliver a clear and compelling message within 30-60 seconds. Use simple and memorable language that captivates your audience and leaves a lasting impression.

Practice and Seek Feedback: Practice your tailored elevator pitch repeatedly to gain confidence and fluency. Evaluate its effectiveness by seeking feedback from trusted colleagues, mentors, or friends. Incorporate their suggestions and refine your pitch.

Test and Adapt: Test your tailored elevator pitch in various situations and observe how different audiences respond. Be adaptable, and if necessary, make changes based on their reactions and feedback. Continuously refining your pitch will help you create an effective and versatile tool.

The key to tailoring your elevator pitch is to understand your audience, their needs, and the environment in which you will deliver the pitch. By customizing your content, adapting your tone and style, and incorporating relevant examples, you can create a compelling and impactful elevator pitch for any situation or audience.

2. The Components of a Compelling Elevator Pitch:

2.1 Identifying your unique selling proposition (USP)

Your Unique Selling Proposition (USP) is a crucial element in the success of your business. It differentiates you from your competitors and communicates your unique value to your target audience. Here are steps to identify your USP:

Define your target audience: Understand who your ideal customers are, their needs, desires, and pain points. This will help you tailor your USP to address their specific concerns.

Research your competitors: Analyze your competitors to identify what they offer, their strengths, weaknesses, and how they position themselves in the market. This will help you find a unique angle to differentiate yourself.

Identify your strengths and weaknesses: Assess your business objectively to determine what you do better than anyone else. Identify your unique capabilities, knowledge, or resources that can set you apart from the competition.

Determine your customer value: Consider the benefits your customers can gain by choosing your product or service. What problems can you solve for them? How can you provide more value than your competitors?

Conduct market research: Engage with your target audience through surveys, interviews, or online forums to gather insights and feedback. This will help you understand their perceptions, preferences, and what they find appealing.

Analyze customer feedback: Review your existing customer testimonials, reviews, or feedback to identify the parts they appreciate most about your business. Look for patterns or common themes that reflect the unique value you provide.

Identify your differentiators: Based on the previous steps, determine what sets you apart from your competitors. It could be your exceptional customer service, innovative product features, personalized approach, affordable pricing, or any other part that makes you stand out.

Craft your USP statement: Once you've identified your differentiators, create a concise and compelling statement that summarizes your unique value proposition. Make sure it is clear, concise, and easily understood by your target audience.

Test and refine: Share your USP statement with your existing customers, industry experts, or people in your target market to gather feedback. Refine your USP based on their suggestions or insights to make it resonate even more with your audience.

Integrate your USP into your marketing: Incorporate your USP into your branding, messaging, website, marketing materials, and customer communications. Consistently communicate your unique value proposition to establish a strong brand identity and attract your target audience.

As your business evolves, your USP may need to be adjusted to stay relevant and competitive. Continually evaluate and refine your USP to ensure it accurately reflects your unique value and resonates with your target audience.

2.2 Showcasing your skills and achievements:

As a professional, it is crucial to showcase your skills and achievements to potential employers, clients, or colleagues. Here are effective ways to do so:

Portfolio: Create an online portfolio or a physical document that highlights your best work. Include not only the outcome but also the process, challenges overcome, and any positive feedback received. Keep it updated with your most recent projects to show ongoing growth and development.

Professional Website: Build a personal website that showcases your skills, experience, and achievements. Include sections such as a detailed resume, your portfolio, a list of certifications or relevant courses, and testimonials from clients or employers. This digital presence allows others to learn more about you and your work in one central location.

LinkedIn Profile: optimize your LinkedIn profile to highlight your skills, experience, and accomplishments. Use the summary section to effectively communicate your knowledge and include links to your portfolio or personal website. Connect with colleagues and industry professionals to expand your network and improve your visibility.

Certifications and Credentials: Display any certifications, degrees, and other professional credentials you have obtained over the years. These give credibility to your skills and show your commitment to continuous learning. Mention them in your resume, on your website, and in professional profiles.

Awards and Honors: If you have received any awards or honors related to your field, make sure to showcase them. Include them in your resume, on your website, or in your portfolio to distinguish yourself from others and highlight your exceptional abilities.

Testimonials: Collect testimonials from satisfied clients, employers, or colleagues who can vouch for your skills and work ethic. Display these endorsements on your website or LinkedIn profile to build trust and credibility with potential employers or clients.

Volunteer Work: Highlight any volunteer work or pro bono projects you have participated in. This showcases your dedication to your field and your willingness to contribute to meaningful causes. Include these experiences in your resume, portfolio, or personal website to show your versatility and commitment.

Consistent Self-improvement: Continuously work on developing your skills and keep up to date with industry trends. Regularly go to workshops, seminars, or take relevant courses to expand your knowledge and stay ahead of the curve. Mention these efforts in your resume or professional profiles to highlight your dedication to personal growth.

Tailor your showcasing techniques to the specific audience or industry you are targeting. By effectively highlighting your skills and achievements, you can increase your chances of landing new opportunities and standing out in a competitive job market.

2.3 Conveying your passion and interest:

When conveying your passion and interest in your elevator pitch, it is important to focus on effective communication and concise storytelling. Craft your pitch with care, combining your enthusiasm and expertise into a captivating message that can be delivered within the span of an elevator ride.

Approach crafting your elevator pitch as if you are solving a puzzle. Choose your words and structure carefully to leave a lasting impact on your audience. Condense the essence of your idea into a few memorable sentences that grab attention, generate curiosity, and make the listener want to learn more.

Strive for a balance between being concise and impactful. Deliver a clear and compelling message that showcases your passion and interest while effectively conveying the value you bring to the table. Tap into your creativity and storytelling skills to make your pitch memorable and relatable.

Remember that adaptability is key. Tailor your elevator pitch to the specific audience or situation, showcasing your ability to adapt your message. Flex your communication skills and confidently convey why your idea or project stands out from the rest.

Embrace the challenge and satisfaction that comes from crafting an elevator pitch. View it as an opportunity to channel your passion, showcase your abilities, and make a lasting impression. Believe in the power of a well-crafted elevator pitch to open doors, spark conversations, and create countless opportunities.

Keep honing this skill, as it continues to fascinate and excite you. Embrace the journey you take on, both personally and professionally. With a well-crafted elevator pitch, you can effectively convey your passion and interest, leaving a lasting impact on those you connect with.

2.4 Aligning your pitch with your audience's needs and interests:

3. Crafting an Engaging Elevator Pitch:

Aligning your pitch with your audience's needs and interests is essential to persuade and engage them. By understanding what drives and motivates your audience, you can tailor your pitch to effectively connect with them and address their specific concerns. Here are a few key steps to help you align your pitch with your audience's needs and interests:

Research your audience: Before creating your pitch, gather information about your audience. Understand their demographics, backgrounds, interests, values, and any specific challenges they may face. This will give you a deeper understanding of what resonates with them.

Identify their pain points: During your research, identify the pain points or problems your audience is experiencing. This lets you empathize with their struggles and position your pitch as a solution to their challenges. By addressing their pain points, you can capture their attention and show them you understand their needs.

Highlight benefits and outcomes: Once you have identified your audience's pain points, emphasize how your pitch will specifically solve their problems and generate positive outcomes for them. Focus on the benefits they will gain from your proposal, whether its financial returns, increased efficiency, timesaving, or enhanced productivity. This will help them visualize the value they can receive by accepting your pitch.

Use relatable language and examples: Tailor your pitch to fit your audience's level of knowledge and industry knowledge. Avoid jargon or technical terms that may confuse or alienate them. Instead, use relatable language and practical examples they can easily understand and connect with. Frame your pitch in their world and speak their language to establish a sense of familiarity and credibility.

Show social proof: Incorporate testimonials, case studies, or success stories that show how others, particularly those who share similar features or face similar challenges as your audience, have benefited from your product, service, or idea. Social proof adds credibility to your pitch and helps alleviate any skepticism or doubts your audience may have.

Address objections preemptively: Anticipate possible objections or concerns your audience may raise and proactively address them in your pitch. By providing thoughtful answers or solutions in advance, you will increase your audience's confidence in your pitch and show them you have taken their concerns into consideration.

Maintain a conversational tone: Last, deliver your pitch in a conversational tone rather than a salesy or overly formal manner. Engage your audience by actively listening to their feedback and questions. Encourage their participation and adapt your pitch in real-time to better suit their needs. By maintaining a conversational approach, you can build trust and rapport with your audience, making them more receptive to your message.

Aligning your pitch with your audience's needs and interests requires thorough research, empathy, and effective communication. By understanding their pain points, showcasing benefits, using relatable language, providing social proof, addressing objections, and maintaining a conversational tone, you can create a persuasive and compelling pitch that resonates with your audience and increases your chances of success.

3.1 Start with a captivating hook:

The power of a well-crafted elevator pitch lies in its ability to captivate and engage the listener right from the start. Like a captivating hook instantly grabs someone's interest and keeps them wanting to know more. When done effectively, an elevator pitch can create a strong and memorable impression that lingers long after the initial conversation.

The first few seconds of your elevator pitch are crucial. This is your opportunity to hook the listener, to pique their curiosity, and compel them to lean in and pay attention. A captivating hook can be a thought-provoking question, a compelling statistic, a surprising fact, or even a brief story that resonates with your audience. It should be tailored to the specific context and audience, aiming to immediately capture their attention and make them eager to hear more.

Once you have successfully grabbed their interest, it is important to maintain their attention by delivering a concise yet impactful message. Your elevator pitch should clearly communicate the unique value you offer, whether it is a groundbreaking idea, a product or service that solves a specific problem, or a compelling story that sparks intrigue. Keep it focused, compelling, and relevant to the listener's needs or interests.

To maximize the power of your elevator pitch, it is crucial to make it relatable and memorable. Connect with your audience on an emotional level by highlighting the benefits or positive impact your idea, product, or service can bring to their lives. Use language that resonates with them, and weave in storytelling elements to make your pitch more engaging and relatable.

A well-crafted elevator pitch not only sparks interest but also invites further conversation. It should invite questions, curiosity, and a desire to delve deeper into the topic. By leaving the listener wanting to know more, you open the door for meaningful discussions, potential partnerships, or even opportunities for collaboration.

The power of a well-crafted elevator pitch extends beyond the initial encounter. It can serve as a valuable tool for networking, job interviews, or even securing funding for a project or venture. An effective pitch can leave a lasting impression on your audience, positioning you as a confident and compelling communicator who is worth paying attention to.

The power of a well-crafted elevator pitch lies in its ability to instantly grab someone's interest and keep them wanting to know more. By using a captivating hook, delivering a concise yet impactful message, making it relatable and memorable, and leaving room for further conversation, you can harness the full potential of your elevator pitch. Embrace the opportunity to captivate, engage, and create meaningful connections with those you encounter, and let your well-crafted elevator pitch pave the way for exciting opportunities and collaborations.

3.2 Use clear and concise language:

When crafting your elevator pitch, using clear and concise language is essential to effectively communicate your message and make a strong impact in a short amount of time. Here are reasons why clear and concise language is important in your elevator pitch:

Grabbing attention: In today's fast-paced world, people have limited time and attention spans. Using clear and concise language helps you quickly capture the listener's interest and ensure they understand your message within the limited time of an elevator ride. By avoiding jargon, complex terminology, or unnecessary details, you can deliver a succinct pitch that immediately grabs attention and leaves a lasting impression.

Communicating key points effectively: A concise elevator pitch lets you focus on the most important parts of your idea, product, or service. By using clear language, you can effectively convey the unique value proposition, benefits, or impact of what you're offering. Clarity eliminates ambiguity and makes sure your audience understands the essence of your pitch without confusion or misunderstandings.

Creating understanding: Clear and concise language enhances comprehension. By avoiding long-winded explanations or unnecessary technical terms, you make it easier for the listener to grasp and process your message. When your pitch is clear, it lets the listener connect the dots and understand the value you bring without having to sift through unnecessary details.

Maximizing memorability: Concise language aids in making your elevator pitch memorable. By distilling your message to its essence, you create a pitch easier to remember and recall. Conciseness helps your key points stick in the listener's mind, making it more likely for them to remember and share your pitch with others.

Adaptability and versatility: A clear and concise elevator pitch is adaptable to various contexts and situations. It can be easily changed or tailored to fit different audiences, whether it's a potential investor, a potential client, or a networking event. Conciseness allows for flexibility, making it easier to adjust your pitch to the specific needs and interests of your listeners.

To ensure clarity and conciseness in your elevator pitch, consider these tips:

- Use simple and straightforward language that your target audience can easily understand.
- Eliminate unnecessary words, jargon, or technical terms that may confuse or overwhelm the listener.
- Focus on the most compelling and relevant information, highlighting the key benefits or unique parts of your idea, product, or service.
- Practice your pitch to make sure it flows smoothly, with no unnecessary repetitions or tangents.
- Seek feedback from others to make sure your message is clear and impactful.

Using clear and concise language in your elevator pitch is crucial for effectively communicating your message, capturing attention, and leaving a lasting impression. By focusing on clarity and eliminating unnecessary details, you can create a pitch that is easy to understand, memorable, and adaptable to different situations. Take the time to craft and refine your elevator pitch, making sure every word counts and resonates with your audience.

3.3 Tell a compelling story:

When crafting your elevator pitch, incorporating a compelling story can greatly enhance its impact and effectiveness. Stories have a unique power to engage and connect with others on an emotional level, making your pitch more memorable and persuasive. Here's why telling a compelling story is important and how to effectively integrate it into your elevator pitch:

Captivating the audience: Stories can capture attention and hold it. By starting your elevator pitch with a captivating story, you immediately draw in your audience and pique their curiosity. A well-crafted story can create an emotional connection, making the listener more receptive to the rest of your pitch.

Making your message relatable: Stories let you present your ideas or experiences in a relatable context. By weaving a narrative that resonates with your audience, you create a bridge between their own experiences and the value you're offering. When listeners can see themselves in the story, they are more likely to connect with your message and be interested in what you must say.

Showing impact and results: A compelling story can showcase the real-life impact or results of your idea, product, or service. By sharing a specific example or case study, you provide physical evidence of the value you bring. Stories that highlight how you have solved a problem, helped a customer achieve success, or made a difference in someone's life can make your pitch more persuasive and compelling.

Engaging emotions: Emotions play a crucial role in decision-making. When you tell a compelling story, you tap into the emotions of your audience, evoking empathy, inspiration, or excitement. Emotionally engaged listeners are more likely to remember and act on your pitch. By connecting your story to the emotional needs or desires of your audience, you create a stronger impact and leave a lasting impression.

Differentiating yourself: Stories can help differentiate you from others in your field. Your unique experiences and perspectives can be showcased through a well-crafted narrative, setting you apart from competitors. A compelling story adds depth and personality to your pitch, making you more memorable and creating a strong personal connection with your audience.

When incorporating a compelling story into your elevator pitch, remember the following tips:

- **Start with a strong hook:** Begin your pitch with an attention-grabbing opening line or scenario that immediately engages the listener.
- **Keep it concise:** While storytelling is important, remember to keep your story brief and focused. Avoid unnecessary details that may distract from your main message.
- **Highlight the problem and solution:** Clearly communicate the problem or challenge you encountered and how your idea, product, or service offers a solution or addresses the issue.
- **Show the impact:** Emphasize the results, benefits, or transformation that your solution brings, using specific examples or anecdotes to illustrate the positive outcomes.
- **Practice and refine:** Rehearse your story to ensure it flows smoothly and effectively conveys your message. Seek feedback from others to make necessary changes and improvements.

Telling a compelling story in your elevator pitch can significantly enhance its effectiveness. By captivating your audience, making your message relatable, showing impact, engaging emotions, and differentiating yourself, a well-crafted story can make your pitch more memorable and persuasive. Take the time to develop and refine your story, ensuring it aligns with your message and resonates with your audience. A compelling story has the power to leave a lasting impression and increase the chances of meeting your goals with your elevator pitch.

3.4 Incorporate real examples and accomplishments:

Incorporating real examples and accomplishments in your elevator pitch can significantly strengthen its impact and credibility. By showcasing tangible evidence of your past successes and accomplishments, you provide concrete proof of your capabilities and build trust with your audience. Here's why incorporating real examples and accomplishments is important and how to effectively integrate them into your elevator pitch:

Establishing credibility: Sharing real examples and accomplishments helps establish your credibility and expertise in your field. It shows you have practical experience and a track record of success. When you can back up your claims with specific achievements, it instills confidence in your audience and increases their trust in you and what you offer.

Providing social proof: Including real examples and accomplishments lets you provide social proof, showing that others have benefited from your knowledge or solutions. Testimonials, case studies, or success stories from satisfied clients or customers can be powerful tools in convincing your audience of the value you bring. When others have experienced positive outcomes, it adds credibility to your pitch and increases the likelihood that your audience will perceive you as a reliable and trusted resource.

Showing knowledge and problem-solving abilities: Real examples and accomplishments enable you to showcase your expertise and problem-solving abilities. By highlighting specific challenges, you have overcome and the outcomes you have achieved, you illustrate your ability to provide solutions and deliver results. This helps your audience understand how you can address their own challenges and adds weight to your pitch.

Making your pitch relatable and tangible: Real examples and accomplishments make your pitch more relatable and real for your audience. Instead of presenting abstract ideas or vague promises, you provide concrete evidence of what you have achieved. This makes your pitch more memorable and helps your audience visualize the potential benefits of working with you or your product/service.

Tailoring to your audience: Incorporating real examples and accomplishments lets you tailor your pitch to the specific needs and interests of your audience. By selecting examples that resonate with their challenges or goals, you can show how your knowledge and solutions are relevant and valuable to them. This customization enhances the relevance and impact of your pitch, increasing the likelihood of capturing their interest and generating a positive response.

When incorporating real examples and accomplishments into your elevator pitch, remember the following tips:

- **Choose relevant and recent examples:** Select examples directly related to your audience's needs and are recent enough to be seen as current and applicable.
- **Quantify results:** Whenever possible, use specific metrics or data to measure the results or impact you have achieved. This adds credibility and lets your audience grasp the real benefits you offer.
- **Keep it concise:** While it's important to include real examples and accomplishments, be mindful of keeping your pitch concise and focused. Highlight the most impactful and relevant achievements to maintain the attention of your audience.
- **Practice and refine:** Rehearse your pitch to make sure you can smoothly and confidently articulate your examples and accomplishments. Practice communicating with them in a concise and compelling manner, so they effectively support your overall message.

Incorporating real examples and accomplishments into your elevator pitch provides compelling evidence of your capabilities, builds credibility, and makes your pitch more relatable and tangible. By selecting relevant examples, measuring results, and tailoring to your audience, you can enhance the impact of your pitch and increase the likelihood of meeting your goals. Take the time to carefully select and refine your examples to ensure they effectively support your message and resonate with your audience.

3.5 Highlight your aspirations and future goals:

Highlighting your aspirations and future goals in your elevator pitch adds a layer of inspiration and motivation to your message. It helps you paint a vivid picture of your vision for the future and shows your drive and ambition. Incorporating your aspirations and future goals can effectively engage your audience and create a sense of shared purpose. Here's why it's important to highlight your aspirations and future goals in crafting an elevator pitch and how to effectively integrate them:

Showing ambition and motivation: By sharing your aspirations and future goals, you showcase your ambition and motivation. This communicates to your audience that you are driven and have a clear direction for where you want to go. It adds depth to your pitch and helps you stand out from others who may only focus on their current achievements.

Creating a compelling vision: Sharing your aspirations and future goals lets you create a compelling vision of what you want to achieve. It helps your audience see the bigger picture and understand how your work or ideas fit into a broader context. This vision can inspire and ignite curiosity and interest in your audience.

Showing alignment with your audience: When you highlight your aspirations and future goals, you can align them with the needs and interests of your audience. By emphasizing how your goals align with their challenges or aspirations, you create a sense of shared purpose and foster a deeper connection. This can make your pitch more relatable and increase the likelihood of engaging your audience on an emotional level.

Communicating growth potential: Sharing your aspirations and future goals also communicates your growth potential. It shows you are constantly evolving, learning, and striving for improvement. This can be important when you are pitching yourself or your ideas for future opportunities, such as career advancement or business partnerships. It signals to your audience that you are open to new challenges and are committed to continuous development.

Inspiring collaboration and support: By highlighting your aspirations and future goals, you invite collaboration and support from your audience. When others see the passion and ambition you have for your work or ideas, they may be more inclined to offer help, provide guidance, or ask about being part of your journey. This can open doors to valuable connections, partnerships, or opportunities.

When highlighting your aspirations and future goals in your elevator pitch, consider these tips:

- **Be specific and focused:** Clearly articulate your aspirations and future goals in a specific and focused manner. This helps your audience grasp your vision and understand your direction.
- **Connect to your current work or achievements:** Link your aspirations and future goals to your current work or achievements. Show how they build on your experiences and align with your knowledge.
- **Use inspiring and descriptive language:** Use language inspiring, descriptive, and evokes emotion. Paint a vivid picture of what you want to achieve and why it matters.
- **Keep it relevant:** Ensure that your aspirations and future goals relate to the context of your elevator pitch. Tailor them to the needs and interests of your audience.
- **Practice delivery:** Practice delivering your aspirations and future goals with confidence and enthusiasm. Make sure your passion and motivation shine through in your tone and body language.

By highlighting your aspirations and future goals in your elevator pitch, you can create a compelling vision, show ambition, and foster a sense of shared purpose. When effectively integrated, this can engage your audience, inspire collaboration, and open doors to new opportunities. Remember to be specific, connect to your current work, use inspiring language, and keep it relevant. Craft your pitch in a way that showcases your aspirations and future goals as an integral part of your personal or professional journey.

4. Perfecting Delivery and Building Confidence:

4.1 Mastering non-verbal communication:

Mastering non-verbal communication is a crucial part of delivering an effective elevator pitch. While the words you choose are important, your body language, facial expressions, and overall demeanor can significantly affect how your message is received. Non-verbal cues can convey confidence, credibility, and authenticity, enhancing the overall impact of your pitch. Here's why mastering non-verbal communication is essential and how to effectively incorporate it into your elevator pitch:

Establishing credibility and confidence: Non-verbal cues such as maintaining eye contact, standing tall, and using confident gestures help establish credibility and convey confidence. When you seem self-assured and composed, your audience is more likely to trust and believe in what you're saying. By mastering non-verbal communication, you project an image of competence and professionalism.

Engaging and capturing attention: Non-verbal cues can be powerful tools for capturing your audience's attention and engaging them in your pitch. Expressive facial expressions, dynamic hand gestures, and varying your tone of voice can add emphasis and energy to your message. These cues help you create a connection with your audience and keep them engaged throughout your pitch.

Conveying enthusiasm and passion: Non-verbal communication helps to express your enthusiasm and passion for your topic or idea. When you speak with energy, use animated gestures, and smile genuinely, your audience can feel your excitement. These non-verbal cues help create an emotional connection, making your pitch more memorable and impactful.

Showing active listening: Non-verbal cues play a vital role in showing active listening during interactions. Nodding your head, maintaining an open posture, and making appropriate facial expressions indicate that you are attentive and receptive to feedback or questions. By showing you value your audience's input, you foster a sense of collaboration and create a positive impression.

Adapting to cultural norms: Non-verbal communication is highly influenced by cultural norms and can vary across different cultures. Understanding cultural cues and adapting your non-verbal communication is essential, especially in cross-cultural interactions. It shows respect, adaptability, and sensitivity toward your audience's cultural background.

To effectively incorporate non-verbal communication into your elevator pitch, consider these tips:

- **Practice body language and gestures:** Be conscious of your body language and practice using gestures that complement your message. Avoid fidgeting or crossing your arms, as these can convey defensiveness or disinterest.
- **Maintain eye contact:** Make direct eye contact with your audience to establish rapport and connection. Be mindful of cultural differences in eye contact norms and adjust in diverse settings.
- **Use facial expressions strategically:** Use facial expressions to reflect your emotions and add emphasis to key points. Smile genuinely when appropriate to create a positive and approachable impression.
- **Control your voice tone and pace:** Vary your voice tone and pace to match the content and emotions of your pitch. Use pauses strategically to highlight important points and give your audience time to absorb the information.

- **Be aware of your posture:** Stand or sit tall with good posture to project confidence and professionalism. Avoid slouching or seeming tense, as this can undermine your credibility.
- **Practice active listening:** Show active listening skills by responding appropriately to your audience's cues, maintaining an open and receptive demeanor, and asking thoughtful questions. This shows your engagement and willingness to connect with others.
- **Seek feedback and self-evaluate:** Record or observe yourself delivering your pitch to assess your non-verbal communication. Solicit feedback from trusted colleagues or mentors to identify areas for improvement and refine your non-verbal cues.

Mastering non-verbal communication enhances the impact of your elevator pitch, helping you establish credibility, engage your audience, and convey your enthusiasm effectively. By practicing and being aware of your non-verbal cues, you can create a powerful and compelling impression that complements your words and leaves a lasting impact. Remember to adapt your non-verbal communication to cultural norms, maintain eye contact, use expressive facial expressions and gestures strategically, and show active listening.

4.2 Practicing your pitch with confidence:

Practicing your elevator pitch with confidence is a key factor in delivering a compelling and impactful message. Confidence not only helps you feel more comfortable and in control during your pitch but also leaves a lasting impression on your audience. Here are reasons why practicing with confidence is important and tips to help you build and exude confidence in your elevator pitch:

Establishing credibility: Confidence is closely linked to credibility. When you speak with confidence, your audience is more likely to perceive you as knowledgeable and trustworthy. It conveys that you believe in what you're saying, which instills confidence in your listeners. By practicing your elevator pitch with confidence, you project an image of competence and knowledge.

Capturing attention and engaging your audience: Confidence grabs attention and creates a positive energy in the room. When you deliver your pitch with assurance and self-assurance, you naturally draw people in and keep them engaged. Confident body language, a steady voice, and strong delivery help you establish a connection with your audience and make them more receptive to your message.

Overcoming nervousness and anxiety: Practicing your elevator pitch with confidence helps you overcome nervousness and anxiety. By rehearsing your pitch repeatedly, you become more familiar with the content and structure, which boosts your confidence. Additionally, practicing in front of a mirror, with a friend, or recording yourself lets you identify areas where you may lack confidence and work on improving them.

Making a lasting impression: Confidence has a lasting impact on your audience. When you exude confidence, people are more likely to remember you and your pitch. It creates a sense of assurance and trust, making your message more memorable. A confident delivery leaves a positive impression, which can lead to further opportunities and connections.

To practice your elevator pitch with confidence, consider these tips:

- **Prepare and rehearse:** Thoroughly prepare your pitch by outlining the key points, structuring your message, and practicing the delivery. Rehearse your pitch multiple times until you feel comfortable with the content and flow. The more you practice, the more confident you will become.
- **Visualize success:** Before delivering your pitch, take a moment to visualize yourself delivering it confidently and successfully. Imagine the positive reactions from your audience and the impact of your message. Visualizing success can boost your confidence and help you approach your pitch with a positive mindset.

- **Focus on your strengths and accomplishments:** Remind yourself of your strengths, accomplishments, and expertise related to your pitch. Reflecting on your past successes can help boost your confidence and reinforce your belief in yourself and your abilities.
- **Maintain a strong and open body posture:** Your body language plays a crucial role in projecting confidence. Stand tall, maintain an open posture, and avoid fidgeting or slouching. These cues convey self-assurance and professionalism, which contribute to your overall confidence.
- **Practice active and positive self-talk:** Replace self-doubt and negative thoughts with positive and affirming statements. Encourage yourself, remind yourself of your preparation, and reinforce your belief in your abilities. Positive self-talk can help you maintain a confident mindset during your pitch.
- **Seek feedback and learn from each practice:** Practice in front of trusted colleagues, mentors, or friends and ask for their feedback. Pay attention to their observations and suggestions and use them to refine and improve your pitch. Constructive feedback can help boost your confidence and identify areas for further development.

Confidence is a skill that can be developed and honed. By consistently practicing your elevator pitch with confidence, you can effectively showcase your expertise, captivate your audience, and leave a lasting impression. Embrace opportunities for practice, visualize success, and focus on your strengths and accomplishments. With each practice, your confidence will grow, letting you deliver your elevator pitch with poise and conviction.

4.3 Handling questions and objections gracefully:

Handling questions and objections gracefully in an elevator pitch is a crucial skill that can greatly enhance your ability to communicate effectively and leave a positive impression on your audience. When faced with questions or objections, it is important to respond in a calm, confident, and respectful manner. Here are tips to help you handle questions and objections gracefully during your elevator pitch:

Active listening: When someone asks a question or raises an objection, actively listen to their concerns, and understand their viewpoint. Give them your full attention, maintain eye contact, and avoid interrupting. This shows respect and shows you value their input.

Clarify and restate: Before responding, take a moment to clarify the question or objection to ensure you fully understand it. Restate the question or objection in your own words to show you have listened attentively and to confirm your understanding. This also lets the other person confirm that you have captured their point accurately.

Remain calm and composed: It is natural to feel defensive when faced with a challenging question or objection, but it is important to remain calm and composed. Take a deep breath, maintain a relaxed posture, and respond in a measured and confident manner. Avoid becoming defensive or argumentative, as it can create tension and hinder effective communication.

Respond with empathy and respect: Show empathy and respect for the person's perspective, even if you disagree with their question or objection. Acknowledge their concerns and address them in a thoughtful and respectful manner. Avoid dismissing or belittling their viewpoint, as this can escalate the situation and create a negative impression.

Provide evidence and examples: Support your response with evidence, data, or examples that illustrate your point. Providing tangible evidence can help alleviate concerns and strengthen your position. Share relevant success stories, case studies, or testimonials that show the value or effectiveness of your idea, product, or service.

Offer alternative perspectives or solutions: If the question or objection highlights a valid concern, offer alternative perspectives or solutions that address those concerns. Show your ability to think critically and adapt your pitch to different perspectives. This shows that you are open-minded, flexible, and willing to consider different viewpoints.

Stay focused and concise: When addressing questions or objections, stay focused on the main message of your elevator pitch. Avoid going off on tangents or getting too detailed in your response. Keep your answers concise, clear, and to the point. This makes sure you maintain the interest and attention of your audience.

Express gratitude: Thank the person for their question or objection, even if you agree or not. Expressing gratitude shows you value their engagement and input, and it helps maintain a positive and respectful atmosphere. A genuine expression of gratitude can leave a lasting impression and foster further dialogue.

Practice active problem-solving: Approach questions and objections as opportunities for problem-solving and collaboration. Instead of becoming defensive, focus on finding common ground and exploring potential solutions. Engage in a constructive dialogue and show your willingness to work together toward a resolution.

Handling questions and objections gracefully shows your ability to think on your feet, adapt to different perspectives, and maintain professionalism under pressure. By actively listening, responding with empathy and respect, providing evidence, and offering alternative perspectives or solutions, you can navigate challenging moments in your elevator pitch with confidence and grace. Remember, handling questions and objections gracefully can leave a lasting impression and reinforce your credibility as a knowledgeable and skilled communicator.

4.4 Tailoring your pitch in different networking scenarios:

Tailoring your elevator pitch for different networking scenarios is a strategic approach that lets you effectively connect with individuals from diverse backgrounds and contexts. By customizing your pitch to suit the specific networking situation, you can maximize your impact and create meaningful connections. Here are key considerations for tailoring your elevator pitch:

Research the event or audience: Before attending a networking event or engaging in a networking opportunity, take the time to research the event, organization, or individuals you expect to meet. Understand their interests, needs, and goals to tailor your pitch. This knowledge will help you position yourself and your pitch in a way that resonates with the specific audience.

Identify common interests or goals: Look for commonalities between yourself and the individuals you will network with. Find shared interests, industry affiliations, or professional goals that can serve as the foundation of your pitch. Highlighting these connections can help establish rapport and build a stronger first connection.

Customize your value proposition: Adapt your elevator pitch to emphasize the parts of your background, skills, or experiences that are most relevant to the networking situation. Consider the specific needs or challenges that the audience may have and position yourself as someone who can provide value or solutions. Tailoring your value proposition to address their specific interests and goals can make your pitch more compelling.

Use industry-specific language: When networking within a particular industry or professional field, it is important to speak the language of that industry. Use industry-specific terms, acronyms, or buzzwords familiar to the audience. This shows your knowledge and understanding of the industry, instantly establishing credibility and helping with a deeper conversation.

Adjust the tone and level of detail: Depending on the networking scenario, you may need to adjust the tone and level of detail in your pitch. For informal networking events, a more conversational and relaxed tone may be appropriate, while for formal or professional settings, a more polished and concise approach may be necessary. Gauge the atmosphere and adapt your pitch.

Focus on their needs and interests: Rather than only focusing on yourself, shift the emphasis of your pitch toward addressing the needs, challenges, or goals of the individuals you are networking with. Show how your skills, experiences, or resources can benefit them. By showing genuine interest in their needs and actively listening to their concerns, you can create a more engaging and mutually beneficial conversation.

Prepare multiple versions of your pitch: it's helpful to have multiple versions of your elevator pitch prepared to suit different networking scenarios. Consider creating variations that highlight different parts of your background or knowledge. This flexibility lets you tailor your pitch on the spot based on the specific interests and priorities of the individuals you are engaging with.

Practice and refine: As with any elevator pitch, practice is key. Rehearse your tailored pitches to ensure they flow smoothly and effectively convey your message. Seek feedback from trusted peers or mentors to refine your pitch and make necessary changes based on their insights.

By tailoring your elevator pitch for different networking scenarios, you show your adaptability, attentiveness, and genuine interest in building connections. This customization lets you connect more deeply with your audience, establish rapport, and increase the chances of meaningful follow-up conversations. Remember, networking is about building relationships, and tailoring your elevator pitch shows your commitment to understanding and meeting the needs of the individuals you engage with.

5. Elevating Your Elevator Pitch in the Digital Age:

Adapting your elevator pitch for online platforms is crucial in the digital age, where virtual interactions have become a norm. Online platforms offer unique opportunities and challenges, requiring you to tailor your pitch to effectively engage and connect with your audience. Here are strategies for adapting your elevator pitch for online platforms:

Grab attention quickly: In online platforms, attention spans are shorter, and distractions are abundant. Start your pitch with a captivating hook or a concise value proposition to capture your audience's attention right from the beginning. Use engaging visuals, compelling headlines, or a short video introduction to make a strong first impression and entice your audience to continue listening.

Be concise and clear: Online platforms often demand brevity, so it is essential to deliver your elevator pitch in a concise and clear manner. Strip away unnecessary details and focus on the most impactful and relevant information. Craft a pitch that can be delivered within a short time frame, whether it's in a video call, social media post, or email. Make every word count to ensure your message is easily understood and remembered.

Leverage visual and multimedia elements: Online platforms offer opportunities to enhance your elevator pitch with visual and multimedia elements. Incorporate relevant images, infographics, or videos to support and reinforce your message. Visuals not only help break up text but also make your pitch more engaging and memorable. Use visual storytelling techniques to convey your message effectively and create a lasting impact.

Customize for the platform: Different online platforms have their own unique formats and requirements. Tailor your elevator pitch to fit the specific platform you are using. For example, on social media platforms like LinkedIn or Twitter, you may need to condense your pitch to fit within character limits. In a video conference, you can leverage body language and gestures to enhance your delivery. Customize your pitch to make the most of the platform's capabilities and ensure it resonates with the target audience.

Highlight key accomplishments and social proof: Online platforms offer opportunities to showcase your achievements and social proof. Include relevant accomplishments, testimonials, or examples of successful projects to establish credibility and build trust. Social proof plays a significant role in online interactions, so leverage it to reinforce the value you bring and differentiate yourself from the competition.

Foster engagement and interaction: Online platforms enable interactive communication, so actively engage with your audience, and encourage interaction. Ask questions, seek feedback, and respond to comments or inquiries promptly. Engaging in two-way conversations helps build relationships and establishes a connection beyond your first pitch. Use polls, surveys, or interactive content to create opportunities for your audience to participate and engage with your pitch.

Optimize for mobile devices: With the increasing use of mobile devices, it is crucial to optimize your elevator pitch for mobile viewing. Ensure your content is responsive and displays well on different screen sizes. Use concise and impactful visuals, easily readable text, and mobile-friendly formats to make your pitch accessible and engaging on smartphones and tablets.

Practice for online delivery: Adapting your elevator pitch for online platforms requires practice and preparation. Familiarize yourself with the technology and tools you will use, such as video conferencing platforms or presentation software. Test your pitch in advance to ensure a smooth and confident delivery. Consider the lighting, background, and audio quality to present yourself professionally in an online setting.

Adapting your elevator pitch for online platforms is essential to effectively communicate and connect with your audience. By leveraging the unique features and opportunities of online platforms, you can tailor your pitch for maximum impact. Be concise, visually appealing, and interactive to capture attention and make a lasting impression in the digital landscape.

5.1 Adapting your elevator pitch for online platforms:

Adapting your elevator pitch for online platforms is crucial in today's digital world, where virtual interactions have become increasingly common. Whether you're participating in online networking events, video conferences, or connecting with potential clients or employers through digital platforms, effectively adapting your elevator pitch can help you stand out and make a memorable impression. Here are key strategies for adapting your elevator pitch for online platforms:

Be concise and clear: Online platforms often require brevity and conciseness. Craft a pitch that can be delivered within a short time frame, capturing the essence of your message quickly and clearly. Avoid long explanations or unnecessary details. Focus on the most compelling and relevant parts of your pitch to grab attention and maintain engagement.

Optimize for virtual delivery: When delivering your elevator pitch online, pay attention to your virtual presence. Make sure your audio and video quality are clear and reliable. Position yourself in a well-lit area with a clutter-free background. Consider using a high-quality external microphone and camera to enhance the professionalism of your presentation. Practice your pitch beforehand to become comfortable with the virtual delivery format.

Leverage visuals and multimedia: Online platforms offer opportunities to incorporate visuals and multimedia elements into your elevator pitch. Consider creating a visually appealing slide deck, video, or infographic that complements and reinforces your message. Use engaging visuals and concise text to convey key points effectively. Visual aids can help keep your audience engaged and make your pitch more memorable.

Engage with storytelling: Storytelling is a powerful technique to capture attention and create an emotional connection. Incorporate storytelling elements into your elevator pitch by sharing relevant anecdotes or examples that highlight your expertise or the value you bring. Craft a narrative that engages your audience and makes your pitch more compelling and relatable.

Customize for the platform: Different online platforms have unique formats and requirements. Tailor your elevator pitch to fit the specific platform you are using. For example, on social media platforms like LinkedIn or Twitter, you may need to condense your pitch to fit within character limits. In a video conference, adapt your pitch to the allotted time and consider the level of formality required. Customize your pitch to align with the platform's culture and audience expectations.

Show enthusiasm and energy: When delivering your elevator pitch online, it's important to convey your passion and energy through the screen. Since non-verbal cues can be harder to interpret online, amplify your body language, facial expressions, and vocal tone to compensate. Use gestures and facial expressions to emphasize key points and display enthusiasm for what you're sharing. Engage with eye contact by looking directly into the camera, simulating a sense of connection with your audience.

Foster engagement and interaction: Online platforms offer opportunities for engagement and interaction. Encourage your audience to ask questions, provide comments, or share their thoughts. Incorporate interactive elements such as polls, surveys, or live chat to encourage participation and create a sense of connection. Engaging in two-way conversations helps build relationships and establishes a memorable connection beyond your first pitch.

Be adaptable and flexible: Online platforms can vary in terms of format and functionality. Be ready to adapt your elevator pitch to different scenarios and platforms. Familiarize yourself with the technology and tools you'll be using, such as video conferencing platforms or presentation software. Test your pitch in advance to ensure a seamless and confident delivery. Be adaptable and ready to pivot if technical issues arise during your presentation.

Adapting your elevator pitch for online platforms is essential for making a strong impression and effectively conveying your message in a digital environment. By being concise, visually appealing, and engaging, you can capture attention and leave a lasting impact. With practice and preparation, you can master the art of adapting your elevator pitch for online platforms, enhancing your networking opportunities and professional interactions in the virtual realm.

5.2 Leveraging social media and networking platforms:

Leveraging social media and networking platforms for your elevator pitch can significantly expand your reach and visibility, letting you connect with a broader audience and make a lasting impression. Here are strategies to effectively use social media and networking platforms for your elevator pitch:

Define your target audience: Before crafting your elevator pitch for social media and networking platforms, identify your target audience. Understand who you want to reach and tailor your message. Consider the demographics, interests, and needs of your target audience to ensure your pitch resonates with them.

Choose the right platforms: Research and select the social media and networking platforms that align with your goals and target audience. LinkedIn, Twitter, Facebook, Instagram, and industry-specific platforms are popular choices for professional networking. Determine which platforms are most relevant to your industry or the audience you want to reach and focus your efforts there.

Optimize your profiles: Update your social media profiles to reflect your elevator pitch effectively. Use clear and concise language in your bio or summary section to communicate your value proposition and expertise. Include keywords relevant to your industry or niche to make it easier for others to find you. Add a professional photo and ensure your profiles are complete and up to date.

Create engaging content: Use social media platforms to showcase your knowledge and engage with your target audience. Share valuable content such as blog posts, chapters, infographics, or videos that align with your elevator pitch and show your knowledge and skills. Incorporate storytelling elements to make your content more compelling and relatable.

Craft attention-grabbing headlines: Social media platforms are crowded with content, so it's crucial to create attention-grabbing headlines or captions for your elevator pitch. Craft concise and impactful statements that instantly capture attention and entice people to engage with your content. Use compelling language, ask thought-provoking questions, or share intriguing statistics to pique curiosity.

Engage with relevant communities and groups: Join professional groups, forums, or communities related to your industry or areas of interest on social media platforms. Engage in conversations, offer valuable insights, and share your elevator pitch. Actively participate in discussions, answer questions, and prove yourself to be a knowledgeable and valuable contributor.

Use video and live streaming: Video content is highly engaging and can help you effectively deliver your elevator pitch on social media platforms. Consider creating short videos or going live to introduce yourself, share your expertise, or provide insights into your industry. Visual elements and your passion expressed through video can have a strong impact on your audience.

Foster relationships through networking: Networking platforms like LinkedIn provide opportunities to connect with professionals in your industry. Actively contact individuals who align with your target audience or who can help you further your career goals. Personalize your connection requests and use your elevator pitch to express your interest in connecting and collaborating.

Track and respond to feedback: Keep an eye on comments, messages, and mentions related to your elevator pitch on social media. Respond promptly and professionally to engage with your audience and build relationships. Actively track any feedback or inquiries you receive and use them to refine and improve your elevator pitch.

Analyze and adapt: Take advantage of the analytics and insights provided by social media platforms to measure the effectiveness of your elevator pitch. Monitor engagement, reach, and audience demographics to assess the impact of your pitch and make necessary changes. Continuously analyze the data to refine your strategy and maximize your results.

By leveraging social media and networking platforms for your elevator pitch, you can amplify your message, connect with a wider audience, and build valuable professional relationships. Through engaging content, thoughtful engagement, and targeted networking efforts, you can establish a strong online presence and create opportunities for career growth and success.

5.3 Using multimedia tools to enhance your elevator pitch:

Using multimedia tools can greatly enhance your elevator pitch, adding a dynamic and engaging element to your message. Incorporating multimedia elements can capture attention, leave a lasting impression, and effectively convey your key points. Here are ways you can leverage multimedia tools to enhance your elevator pitch:

Visual presentations: Create visually appealing slides or presentations to support your elevator pitch. Use platforms like Microsoft PowerPoint, Google Slides, or Prezi to design professional and captivating visuals. Include key information, graphics, images, and charts that complement your message and help reinforce your main points. Visual presentations can add clarity, structure, and visual interest to your pitch.

Infographics: Condense complex information into visually appealing and easy to understand infographics. Tools like Canva or Piktochart provide user-friendly interfaces with pre-designed templates to create eye-catching infographics. Incorporate relevant statistics, key facts, and visuals to convey your message in a concise and visually appealing manner. Infographics can help simplify complex ideas and make your elevator pitch more memorable.

Videos and animations: Create short videos or animations to deliver your elevator pitch in a visually engaging format. Use platforms like Adobe Spark, Powtoon, or Biteable to produce professional-looking videos. Introduce yourself, share your story, and highlight your key points through animated characters, text, and visuals. Videos and animations let you convey your passion, personality, and expertise effectively, making your pitch more captivating and memorable.

Audio recordings: Consider creating audio recordings to complement your elevator pitch. You can record your pitch using tools like

Audacity or online voice recorders. Audio recordings are especially useful for platforms that focus on audio content, such as podcasts or audio-sharing platforms. Delivering your pitch in audio format lets your audience focus only on your message, without visual distractions.

Interactive media: Explore interactive media formats to engage your audience in a more immersive way. Platforms like Genially or ThingLink enable you to create interactive presentations or images. Incorporate clickable elements, hotspots, or quizzes to encourage audience interaction and participation. Interactive media adds an element of interactivity, making your elevator pitch more engaging and memorable.

Website or landing page: Develop a dedicated website or landing page that serves as a multimedia platform to showcase your elevator pitch. Use website builders like WordPress, Wix, or Squarespace to create a visually appealing and user-friendly platform. Include multimedia elements such as videos, images, infographics, and testimonials to create a comprehensive and impactful presentation of your pitch. A dedicated website or landing page lets you provide more context, resources, and contact information to interested parties.

Social media platforms: Leverage social media platforms that support multimedia content to enhance your elevator pitch. Share videos, images, infographics, or slideshows on platforms like LinkedIn, Twitter, Instagram, or Facebook to engage with your target audience. Tailor your multimedia content to the specific platform and audience, ensuring it aligns with your elevator pitch and conveys your message effectively.

Virtual presentations: In the age of remote work and virtual events, consider leveraging virtual presentation tools like Zoom, Microsoft Teams, or Google Meet to deliver your elevator pitch. Use features like screen sharing, virtual backgrounds, and interactive elements to enhance your pitch and engage your audience. Practice your virtual presentation skills to ensure a smooth and impactful delivery.

When incorporating multimedia tools into your elevator pitch, remember to balance visual appeal and the clarity of your message.

Make sure the multimedia elements support and enhance your pitch rather than distract from it. Practice your pitch with the multimedia tools to ensure smooth transitions and a cohesive overall presentation. By leveraging multimedia tools effectively, you can create a memorable and impactful elevator pitch that stands out in the minds of your audience.

5.4 Creating a memorable personal brand online:

Creating a memorable personal brand online is closely linked to crafting an elevator pitch that effectively represents who you are and what you offer. Your personal brand is how you present yourself to the world, both personally and professionally, and it plays a crucial role in establishing your reputation and attracting opportunities. Here are key considerations for creating a memorable personal brand online in relation to crafting your elevator pitch:

Define your unique value proposition: Before you can effectively craft your elevator pitch and establish your personal brand, you need to clearly understand your unique value proposition. Identify your strengths, skills, experiences, and passions that set you apart from others. This will form the foundation of your personal brand and inform how you communicate your value in your elevator pitch.

Consistent messaging: Ensure that your elevator pitch aligns with your personal brand message. Consistency in your messaging across different platforms and interactions helps to reinforce your brand and build recognition. Craft a concise and compelling elevator pitch that succinctly communicates your unique value proposition and resonates with your target audience.

Authenticity and storytelling: Authenticity is key in building a memorable personal brand. Share your authentic story, experiences, and perspectives in your elevator pitch and online presence. Incorporate storytelling techniques to make your brand relatable and engaging. People connect with stories, so use your elevator pitch as an opportunity to showcase your journey, achievements, and aspirations in a genuine and compelling way.

Visual identity: Establish a consistent visual identity that represents your personal brand. Choose a set of colors, fonts, and graphics that reflect your personality and align with your brand message. Use these visual elements consistently across your online presence, including your website, social media profiles, and any other platforms you engage with. Visual coherence helps to create a memorable and recognizable brand.

Professional online presence: Ensure that your online presence reflects a professional image that aligns with your personal brand. Use high-quality professional headshots for your profiles and maintain a polished and up-to-date online presence. Regularly review and update your profiles to showcase your skills, experiences, and achievements. Engage in thought leadership activities, such as writing blog posts or sharing valuable insights, to prove yourself to be an authority in your field.

Engage with your audience: Building a memorable personal brand requires active engagement with your audience. Respond to comments and messages promptly, participate in relevant online communities, and contribute valuable content to establish yourself as a trusted resource. Engaging with your audience helps to build relationships, increase your visibility, and strengthen your personal brand.

Consistent online platforms: Identify the online platforms that are most relevant to your personal brand and focus on maintaining a consistent presence on those platforms. Whether it's LinkedIn, Twitter, Instagram, or a personal blog, choose platforms where your target audience is most active and engage with them consistently. By being present and active on these platforms, you can amplify your elevator pitch and extend your personal brand's reach.

Seek feedback and iterate: Continuously seek feedback from your audience and peers to refine and improve your personal brand and elevator pitch. Be open to constructive criticism and use it as an opportunity for growth and refinement. Regularly evaluate your online presence, track your brand's performance, and make necessary changes to make sure your personal brand continues to align with your goals and resonate with your audience.

Crafting a memorable personal brand online is an ongoing process that requires consistent effort and refinement. By aligning your elevator pitch with your personal brand message, showcasing authenticity and storytelling, maintaining a professional online presence, and engaging with your audience, you can create a personal brand that is memorable, impactful, and resonates with your target audience.

6. Case Studies: Elevator Pitches That Left a Lasting Impression:

6.1 Successful elevator pitches and their key elements:

Example 1:

Elevator Pitch: "Hi, I'm Jane. I'm a digital marketing specialist with a passion for helping businesses grow their online presence. I have a track record of creating successful digital campaigns that drive traffic, increase engagement, and generate leads. I specialize in social media strategy and content marketing, and I'm skilled in data analysis to optimize campaign performance. I'm excited to connect with businesses looking to take their digital marketing efforts to the next level."

Key Elements:

- **Clear introduction:** The pitch starts with a clear introduction, stating the person's name and professional role.
- **Unique value proposition:** It highlights the person's knowledge and passion for helping businesses grow their online presence.
- **Specific achievements:** It mentions the person's track record of creating successful digital campaigns and their specialization in social media strategy and content marketing.

- **Results-oriented:** It emphasizes the outcomes of their work, such as driving traffic, increasing engagement, and generating leads.
- **Call to action:** It expresses the person's eagerness to connect with businesses looking to enhance their digital marketing efforts

.

Example 2:

Elevator Pitch: "Hello, I'm John, and I'm a software engineer with a focus on developing innovative solutions for complex problems. I have experience working on diverse projects, ranging from mobile app development to machine learning algorithms. I thrive in collaborative environments, where I can contribute my expertise in coding, problem-solving, and creating scalable software solutions. I'm passionate about leveraging technology to improve people's lives and I'm currently seeking new opportunities to apply my skills and make an impact."

Key Elements:

- **Introduction and role:** The pitch starts with a simple introduction and states the person's role as a software engineer.
- **Unique value proposition:** It highlights the person's focus on developing innovative solutions for complex problems and their broad experience in different areas.
- **Key skills:** It mentions the person's knowledge in coding, problem-solving, and creating scalable software solutions.
- **Passion and mission:** It conveys the person's passion for leveraging technology to improve people's lives.
- **Open to opportunities:** It says the person is seeking new opportunities to apply their skills and make an impact.

Example 3:

Elevator Pitch: "Hi, I'm Sarah, a project manager with a proven track record of delivering successful projects on time and within budget. I excel at coordinating cross-functional teams, managing resources effectively, and ensuring clear communication throughout the project lifecycle. My attention to detail, strong organizational skills, and ability to handle multiple priorities make me an asset in fast-paced environments. I'm passionate about driving project success and fostering collaboration, and I'm currently seeking challenging projects to contribute to."

Key Elements:

- **Introduction and role:** The pitch starts with a friendly greeting and introduces the person as a project manager.
- **Unique value proposition:** It emphasizes the person's track record of delivering successful projects and their key strengths in coordination, resource management, and communication.
- **Key skills:** It highlights attention to detail, strong organizational skills, and the ability to handle multiple priorities.
- **Passion and mission:** It conveys the person's passion for driving project success and fostering collaboration.
- **Seeking opportunities:** It says the person is seeking challenging projects to contribute to.

In each example, the elevator pitches are concise, focused, and high-light the individual's unique value proposition. They provide a clear introduction, emphasize relevant skills and accomplishments, convey passion and mission, and express openness to new opportunities. These key elements help to make the elevator pitches effective and memorable.

6.2 Learning from real-life examples:

Learning from real-life examples is an excellent way to enhance your elevator pitch crafting skills. By studying and analyzing successful elevator pitches, you can gain valuable insights and inspiration for crafting your own pitch. Here are ways to learn from real-life examples:

Research successful elevator pitches: Look for examples of elevator pitches in your industry or field of interest. Study the pitches of successful professionals or entrepreneurs and observe how they effectively communicate their value proposition, achievements, and goals. Note the language, structure, and key elements that make their pitches compelling.

Go to networking events and pitch competitions: Participate in networking events or pitch competitions where individuals present their elevator pitches. Listen to a variety of pitches and observe how different individuals showcase their unique strengths and aspirations. Pay attention to the pitches that stand out and capture your attention. Consider what makes them memorable and how they effectively convey their message in a short span of time.

Seek feedback from mentors or peers: Share your elevator pitch with mentors or peers and ask for their feedback. They can provide valuable insights and suggestions to improve your pitch. Additionally, if you have the opportunity to observe others delivering their elevator pitches, pay attention to the audience's reactions and consider how you would respond to their pitches.

Study elevator pitch templates and frameworks: Explore different templates or frameworks for crafting elevator pitches. These resources often provide guidance on structuring your pitch, choosing impactful words, and highlighting key elements. By studying these templates, you can understand the parts that make a pitch successful and adapt them to your own style and goals.

Practice active listening during elevator pitch presentations: When at conferences, workshops, or seminars, actively listen to the elevator pitches of speakers or presenters. Pay attention to how they engage the audience, effectively convey their message, and respond to questions or objections. Reflect on what parts of their pitches resonate with you and how they can inspire your own pitch.

Join professional networking groups or communities: Engage with professional networking groups or communities both online and offline. Participate in discussions and observe how members introduce themselves and share their elevator pitches. Note the pitches that capture your attention and spark your interest. Analyze what makes them compelling and consider how you can incorporate similar elements into your own pitch.

Learning from real-life examples is not about copying someone else's pitch, but rather understanding the strategies and techniques that make them successful. Adapt and personalize these insights to showcase your unique strengths, accomplishments, and aspirations. By learning from real-life examples and continuously refining your pitch, you can develop a compelling and impactful elevator pitch that effectively communicates your value and leaves a lasting impression.

6.3 Analyzing the impact of powerful elevator pitches:

Analyzing the impact of powerful elevator pitches is an exercise that can provide valuable insights into what makes a pitch effective and influential. By examining the impact of successful pitches, you can uncover key elements and strategies that contribute to their success. Here are aspects to consider when analyzing the impact of powerful elevator pitches:

Attention-Grabbing Opening: Powerful elevator pitches often start with a captivating hook that instantly grabs the listener's attention. Analyze the opening lines of successful pitches and observe how they effectively pique interest and create curiosity. Look for unique and compelling ways to start your pitch and capture the attention of your audience from the beginning.

Clear and Concise Messaging: Effective elevator pitches convey a clear and concise message. Analyze how successful pitches effectively communicate their value proposition, goals, or unique selling points within a short timeframe. Look for clarity in the language used, simplicity in the message conveyed, and the ability to distill complex ideas into easily understandable ideas.

Compelling Storytelling: Stories have a powerful impact on the listener. Analyze how successful elevator pitches incorporate storytelling techniques to engage the audience and create an emotional connection. Look for narratives that resonate with the audience and effectively communicate the speaker's passion, journey, or vision. Consider incorporating storytelling elements into your own pitch to make it more memorable and relatable.

Showing Credibility and Expertise: Powerful elevator pitches establish credibility and expertise early on. Analyze how successful pitches communicate the speaker's qualifications, achievements, or track record. Look for ways to effectively show your knowledge and build trust with your audience. Highlighting relevant accomplishments, credentials, or industry experience can strengthen your pitch and enhance its impact.

Audience-Centric Approach: Analyze how successful pitches tailor their message to the needs and interests of the audience. Look for pitches that show an understanding of the listener's pain points, challenges, or goals. Consider how you can adapt your pitch to address the specific needs of your audience and show how your offering can provide value or solve their problems.

Engaging Delivery: The delivery of an elevator pitch plays a significant role in its impact. Analyze successful pitches and observe how the speakers use their voice, body language, and enthusiasm to engage the audience. Look for confident and compelling delivery styles that effectively convey passion and enthusiasm. Practice and refine your own delivery to ensure it is engaging and impactful.

Call to Action: Powerful elevator pitches often include a clear call to action that prompts the listener to take the next step. Analyze how successful pitches incorporate a compelling call to action that encourages further engagement or follow-up. Consider what specific action you want your audience to take after hearing your pitch and craft a clear and compelling call to action.

By analyzing the impact of powerful elevator pitches, you can gain valuable insights into what elements and strategies contribute to their success. Use these insights as inspiration and guidance to refine your own pitch, adapt it to your unique strengths and goals, and create a pitch that leaves a lasting impact on your audience.

Crafting a compelling elevator pitch is a skill that can significantly affect your networking success. By effectively articulating your skills, interests, and aspirations, you can confidently introduce yourself, make lasting impressions, and open doors to exciting opportunities. This chapter has provided valuable insights and tools to help you develop an elevator pitch that elevates your personal brand and sets you apart from the crowd. Now, armed with this knowledge, it's time to step onto the elevator of success and make your pitch with confidence.

CHAPTER 14

ESTABLISHING AND NURTURING PROFESSIONAL RELATIONSHIPS: PRACTICAL ADVICE FOR BUILDING VALUABLE CONNECTIONS

Building and maintaining professional relationships is crucial for career growth and personal development. Networking and forming connections within your industry can lead to job opportunities, collaborations, and knowledge exchanges. Here are practical tips to help you start conversations, ask meaningful questions, and sustain rapport with your contacts:

Reach out: Take the initiative and introduce yourself to industry professionals at events, conferences, or through mutual connections. Make a positive first impression by being well-prepared, confident, and approachable.

Show genuine interest: Engage in meaningful conversations by actively listening and showing curiosity about the other person. Take the time to understand their interests, challenges, and goals. People appreciate being heard and understood.

Master the art of asking questions: Thoughtful questions inspire insightful discussions and show your genuine interest. Avoid simple yes/no questions and instead ask open-ended inquiries that encourage the person to share their experiences and insights. This fosters a deeper connection and enables you to learn from their expertise.

Be a resource: Networking is not just about taking; it's also about giving. Offer your assistance, knowledge, or resources to others. Providing value without expecting immediate returns helps establish you as a reliable and generous professional, making people more willing to invest in the relationship.

Follow up and maintain contact: After initial conversations, follow up with a thank-you email or a LinkedIn connection request. A brief message acknowledging the positive interaction and expressing a desire to stay in touch shows your commitment to nurturing the relationship. Regularly engage with your professional network through social media, attending industry events, or reaching out for catch-up meetings.

Be reliable and responsive: Consistency and reliability are vital in any professional relationship. Respond to emails and requests in a timely manner, show your reliability by meeting deadlines, and maintain your commitments. This enhances trust and respect, ensuring your connections feel valued and appreciated.

Seek opportunities for collaboration: Look for ways to collaborate or help your professional contacts. A joint project, knowledge sharing, or sharing relevant resources can lead to meaningful connections. When you collaborate, you not only strengthen your bond but also potentially create value for both parties.

Show gratitude: Express your appreciation for the support and guidance you receive from your contacts. Gratitude goes a long way in building and sustaining strong professional relationships. Sending a quick note of thanks or acknowledging their contributions publicly helps reinforce the connection and leaves a positive impression.

Building and nurturing professional relationships takes time and effort. Be patient, proactive, and sincere in your interactions. By following these practical tips, you can establish and maintain valuable connections that will contribute to your personal and professional growth.

CHAPTER FOURTEEN SUMMARY:

Chapter Fourteen focuses on the crucial part of establishing and nurturing professional relationships for career growth and personal development. The chapter offers practical advice and tips to help individuals effectively build and maintain connections within their respective industries.

The chapter begins by highlighting the significance of taking the initiative in contacting industry professionals. It encourages readers to introduce themselves at events, conferences, or through mutual connections. The importance of making a positive first impression is emphasized, suggesting that being well-prepared, confident, and approachable is key.

Genuine interest is emphasized as a vital part of successful professional relationships. The chapter stresses the importance of engaging in meaningful conversations by listening and displaying curiosity about the other person. By understanding their interests, challenges, and goals, individuals can establish rapport and foster a deeper connection.

Another crucial skill discussed is the art of asking thoughtful questions. Readers are encouraged to ask open-ended inquiries that inspire insightful discussions and show genuine interest. This approach not only strengthens connections but also lets individuals learn from the knowledge and experiences of others.

The chapter highlights the importance of being a resource rather than a taker in networking. It recommends that readers offer help, knowledge, or resources to others, positioning themselves as reliable and generous professionals. By providing value without immediate expectations of returns, individuals can prove themselves to be trustworthy and valuable contacts.

Following up and maintaining contact is another key aspect covered in the chapter. It stresses the importance of expressing gratitude and staying connected. After initial conversations, readers are advised to send thank-you emails or LinkedIn connection requests. Regular engagement with professional networks through social media, industry events, or catch-up meetings is also recommended.

Reliability and responsiveness are highlighted as essential qualities in professional relationships. Consistency and meeting commitments, such as responding to emails and requests in a timely manner and honoring deadlines, are vital for building trust and respect.

Seeking opportunities for collaboration is encouraged to strengthen connections. Joint projects, knowledge sharing, and resource sharing are mentioned as potential avenues for creating meaningful connections and mutual value.

Finally, the chapter emphasizes the significance of showing gratitude. Expressing appreciation for the support and guidance received from professional contacts is considered essential. The chapter suggests sending thank-you notes or publicly acknowledging contributions as ways to reinforce connections and leave a positive impression.

The chapter underscores the importance of patience, proactivity, and sincerity in building and nurturing professional relationships. By implementing the practical tips provided, readers can establish and maintain valuable connections that contribute to their personal and professional growth.

LEVERAGING ONLINE NETWORKING PLATFORMS: EXPLORING THE POWER OF PROFESSIONAL NETWORKS

Building a supportive network is crucial for career growth and development. A diverse network that includes mentors, sponsors, and peers can provide valuable support, guidance, and opportunities. In this chapter, we will explore the benefits of having a diverse network and provide practical advice on how to consciously diversify your connections.

The Benefits of a Diverse Network:

Exposure to Different Perspectives: When you interact with people from diverse backgrounds and industries, you gain access to a wide range of perspectives. This exposure can broaden your horizons, challenge your assumptions, and stimulate creative thinking.

Access to Opportunities: A diverse network increases your chances of learning about job openings, projects, and collaborations. People with different backgrounds and experiences may know opportunities you would not have come across otherwise.

Personal Growth and Learning: Engaging with a diverse network lets you learn from others' experiences, knowledge, and skills. This continuous learning fosters personal growth, enabling you to develop new competencies and expand your knowledge.

Building Cultural Competence: Interacting with individuals from different cultural backgrounds enhances your cultural competency. This skill is becoming increasingly important in today's globalized and multicultural workplaces.

Increased Resilience: A diverse network can provide emotional support during challenging times. Having a variety of individuals who understand your experiences and can offer guidance and encouragement can bolster your resilience and help you overcome obstacles.

Consciously Diversifying your Connections:

Identify the Gaps: Start by reflecting on your existing network and identifying any gaps in terms of diversity. Consider factors such as industry, ethnicity, gender, age, and geographic location.

Be Proactive: Actively seek individuals who have different perspectives and experiences. Go to industry events, seminars, and conferences where you can meet professionals from various backgrounds.

Join Professional Associations and Online Communities: Participate in professional associations and online communities relevant to your field of interest. These platforms provide opportunities to connect with individuals who share your professional passions but come from diverse backgrounds.

Seek Mentors and Sponsors: Look for mentors and sponsors who can guide you in your career journey. Mentors offer advice and support, while sponsors advocate for your professional advancement.

Engage in Cross-Functional Collaborations: Seek opportunities to collaborate with individuals from different departments or areas of knowledge within your organization. This will help you build relationships outside your immediate team and expand your network within the organization.

Participate in Diversity and Inclusion Initiatives: Get involved in diversity and inclusion initiatives in your workplace or community.

These initiatives often bring together individuals from various backgrounds, fostering connections and helping with networking.

Building a supportive and diverse network is essential for career growth and personal development. By consciously diversifying your connections, seeking mentors, sponsors, and peers who can provide support and guidance, you open a world of opportunities. Remember to focus on building relationships, being genuine, and fostering an inclusive professional community that values diversity.

CHAPTER FIFTEEN LEVERAGING ONLINE NETWORKING PLATFORMS SUMMARY:

Chapter Fifteen explores the importance of building a diverse network for career growth. It emphasizes the benefits of exposure to different perspectives, access to opportunities, personal growth, cultural competence, and increased resilience.

The chapter provides practical advice on consciously diversifying connections by identifying gaps, being proactive, joining professional associations and online communities, seeking mentors and sponsors, engaging in cross-functional collaborations, and participating in diversity and inclusion initiatives.

Building a diverse network is essential for personal and professional development, and readers are encouraged to foster genuine relationships within an inclusive professional community.

CHAPTER 16

ASSERTIVE DECISION-MAKING: MAKING SOUND CHOICES AND TAKING ACTION

UNDERSTANDING THE IMPORTANCE OF ASSERTIVE DECISION-MAKING IN PERSONAL AND PROFESSIONAL AREAS OF LIFE

Assertive decision-making is a crucial skill that can have a profound impact on both personal and professional areas of life. It involves making confident and proactive choices while considering different perspectives, needs, and constraints. Understanding the importance of assertive decision-making can lead to many benefits and positive outcomes in various parts of life.

In personal life, making assertive decisions empowers individuals to effectively communicate their needs, preferences, and boundaries. Without assertiveness, people may become passive and let others decide on their behalf, leading to feelings of dissatisfaction and resentment. But being excessively aggressive can strain relationships and cause conflicts. By adopting an assertive approach, individuals can express their thoughts, desires, and concerns assertively and respectfully, leading to healthier and more fulfilling personal relationships.

Additionally, assertive decision-making enables personal growth and achievement of personal goals. When individuals are assertive in setting and pursuing their goals, they have a higher likelihood of realizing their aspirations. By making clear and confident choices, individuals can create a roadmap for their personal development, making sure their decisions align with their values, interests, and long-term goals.

Similarly, assertive decision-making plays a crucial role in professional settings. In the workplace, assertiveness lets individuals voice their ideas, suggestions, and concerns effectively. It enables them to actively participate in discussions, contribute to decision-making processes, and assert their knowledge. By being assertive, professionals can enhance their credibility, gain respect from colleagues and superiors, and increase their chances of career advancement.

Assertive decision-making also helps professionals establish healthy boundaries and manage their workload effectively. By confidently saying "no" to unrealistic demands or setting realistic expectations, individuals can avoid burnout and preserve their well-being. This promotes a healthy work-life balance and makes sure professionals have the necessary resources and energy to perform at their best.

Assertive decision-making can positively affect problem-solving and conflict resolution. People who are assertive are more likely to address conflicts directly, express their needs, and seek mutually beneficial solutions. This approach fosters open communication, cooperation, and collaboration, allowing for the resolution of issues in a fair and efficient manner.

Understanding the importance of assertive decision-making in personal and professional areas of life is essential for various reasons. It empowers individuals to communicate effectively, achieve personal goals, enhance professional success, establish boundaries, manage workload, and resolve conflicts. By embracing assertiveness, individuals can take control of their lives and make decisions that align with their values, resulting in a more fulfilled, balanced, and successful life.

EXPLORING THE DIFFERENCE BETWEEN PASSIVE, AGGRESSIVE, AND ASSERTIVE DECISION-MAKING STYLES

Passive, aggressive, and assertive decision-making styles represent different approaches to making choices and expressing oneself in various situations. Understanding the differences between these styles is crucial for effective communication and conflict resolution.

Passive Decision-Making Style:

Passive decision-making is characterized by a lack of initiative and avoidance of conflict. Individuals with this style prioritize the desires and opinions of others over their own. They often struggle in expressing their needs and are inclined to go along with the majority to maintain harmony. Passive decision-makers often feel powerless and do not speak up when they disagree with others.

For example, in a group discussion about a project, a passive individual may silently agree to a plan even if they have concerns or alternative ideas. They may fear rejection or confrontation and may feel resentful or dissatisfied with the outcome.

Aggressive Decision-Making Style:

Aggressive decision-making is characterized by imposing one's opinion and desires on others without considering their needs or opinions. Individuals with this style tend to be forceful, confrontational, and often disregard the perspectives of others. They may resort to intimidation, manipulation, or verbal attacks to get their way. Aggressive individuals often focus on winning over finding mutual satisfaction or compromise.

For example, in the same group project discussion, an aggressive individual may dominate the conversation, dismiss others' ideas, and use harsh language to belittle their teammates' input. This approach can lead to a hostile environment and hinder collaboration and cooperation.

Assertive Decision-Making Style:

Assertive decision-making is characterized by confident communication of thoughts, feelings, and needs while respecting the rights and opinions of others. Individuals with this style express themselves openly and honestly, yet tactfully, without resorting to aggression or passiveness. They actively listen to others' viewpoints, consider alternatives, and strive for win-win outcomes. Assertive decision-makers focus on effective communication, mutual respect, and problem-solving.

For example, in the group project discussion, an assertive individual would actively contribute to the conversation, actively listen to others, present their ideas and concerns, and seek collaboration and compromise from the other members. This approach encourages open dialogue, enables problem-solving, and enhances cooperation within the group.

Passive decision-making lacks initiative and fails to express one's needs, aggressive decision-making disregards others' opinions and focuses on forceful imposition, while assertive decision-making promotes open and honest communication while respecting others' rights and perspectives. Developing an assertive decision-making style promotes effective communication, conflict resolution, and healthier interpersonal relationships.

IDENTIFYING BARRIERS THAT MAY HINDER ASSERTIVE DECISION-MAKING, SUCH AS FEAR OF REJECTION OR CONFLICT

Several barriers may hinder assertive decision-making, and these barriers often stem from internal fears and concerns. Some of the common barriers include:

Fear of rejection: Many individuals fear being rejected or disapproved of by others. This fear can prevent them from asserting their opinions or making decisions that might differ from the majority. The fear of not being liked or accepted can lead to conformity and compromise, impeding assertive decision-making.

Fear of conflict: Conflict is inevitable in decision-making processes, as differing opinions and perspectives collide. However, some individuals have a strong aversion to conflict and will go to great lengths to avoid it. This fear of confrontation can hinder assertive decision-making, as people may opt for compromise or silence rather than expressing their true opinions.

Lack of self-confidence: Many people lack confidence in their abilities, knowledge, or contribution. This lack of self-assurance can hinder assertive decision-making, as individuals may hesitate to voice their opinions or take decisive action. They may doubt their ability to contribute, which can lead to self-silencing and passivity.

Perceived power dynamics: Hierarchical structures or power imbalances within a team or organization can create barriers to assertive decision-making. People may feel intimidated or subordinate to those in positions of authority, causing them to withhold their opinions or ideas. The perceived consequences for going against authority can deter individuals from making assertive decisions.

Groupthink mentality: Groupthink occurs when individuals focus on harmony and conformity within a group over critical thinking and independent decision-making. In such situations, members may suppress their own dissenting views or suppress their assertiveness to maintain a united front. This pressure for consensus can limit innovative and assertive decision-making.

Cultural and societal expectations: Cultural norms, social expectations, and cultural conditioning can also act as barriers to assertive decision-making. For example, certain cultures may value deference to authority or consensus building, which can discourage individual assertiveness. Societal expectations regarding gender roles or expressive behaviors can also discourage assertiveness in decision-making.

Overcoming these barriers requires self-awareness, skill-building, and a supportive environment. Developing assertiveness skills, building self-confidence, and promoting a culture of open communication and respect are necessary steps toward enabling assertive decision-making in individuals and groups.

LEARNING EFFECTIVE COMMUNICATION TECHNIQUES TO EXPRESS OPINIONS AND NEEDS CONFIDENTLY

Learning effective communication techniques to express opinions and needs confidently is crucial for assertive decision-making. However, various barriers can hinder this process, such as fear of rejection or conflict. By identifying these barriers, individuals can overcome them and improve their assertiveness in decision-making situations.

One barrier that hinders assertive decision-making is the fear of rejection. Many individuals are afraid that expressing their opinions or needs may lead to disapproval or rejection from others. This fear often stems from a lack of self-confidence or past negative experiences. To overcome this barrier, it is crucial to build self-esteem and develop a positive self-image. This can be achieved through self-reflection, setting realistic expectations, and focusing on personal strengths. Additionally, practicing assertive communication through role-playing or seeking support from a trusted friend or mentor can help individuals gain confidence in expressing themselves without the fear of rejection.

Another barrier is the fear of conflict. Many people avoid assertive decision-making because they fear potential conflicts that may arise from expressing their opinions or needs. Conflict can be uncomfortable, and the fear of it often leads individuals to adopt passive or aggressive communication styles instead of being assertive. Conflict is a normal part of life and can sometimes be necessary for growth and positive outcomes. Learning conflict resolution techniques, such as active listening, empathy, and compromise, can help individuals navigate conflicts more effectively. By viewing conflict as an opportunity for understanding and growth, individuals can overcome fear and become more assertive in decision-making processes.

Other barriers to assertive decision-making may include a lack of assertiveness skills, ineffective communication styles, or cultural and social norms that discourage assertive behavior. Recognizing these barriers is the first step toward overcoming them. Seeking professional training or guidance in assertiveness skills can help individuals develop effective communication techniques and break free from societal or cultural constraints. Building awareness of one's communication style and recognizing its impact on decision-making can also be beneficial. Additionally, creating a supportive environment that encourages assertiveness and open dialogue can help individuals feel more comfortable expressing their opinions and needs confidently.

Learning effective communication techniques to express opinions and needs confidently is essential for assertive decision-making. Identifying barriers such as the fear of rejection or conflict is crucial in over-coming them. By building self-confidence, developing conflict resolution skills, and understanding cultural and social norms, individuals can enhance their assertiveness and make decisions confidently.

DEVELOPING STRATEGIES TO EVALUATE OPTIONS AND GATHER INFORMATION TO MAKE INFORMED DECISIONS

Developing strategies to evaluate options and gather information to make informed decisions involves a systematic approach that considers various factors and potential barriers. One common barrier to assertive decision-making is the fear of rejection or conflict. To overcome this barrier, it is essential to develop strategies that address these fears and enable individuals to make decisions confidently. Here are strategies to consider:

Self-awareness: Begin by understanding your own fears and anxieties related to rejection or conflict. Recognize how these fears may hinder your decision-making process. Being self-aware will help you identify when these fears are influencing your choices.

Identify the root cause: Analyze the underlying reasons for your fear of rejection or conflict. Are there specific past experiences or beliefs that contribute to these fears? Understanding their origins will help you address them more effectively.

Challenge negative thoughts: Often, fear is fueled by negative thoughts and self-doubt. Challenge and reframe these thoughts by focusing on your strengths and past successes. Remind yourself that rejection or conflict are normal parts of life and should not hinder your decision-making abilities.

Seek support: Discuss your concerns and fears with trusted friends, mentors, or colleagues. Sharing your thoughts and receiving objective feedback can provide valuable perspectives and reassurance, helping you make more assertive decisions.

Gather information: To make informed decisions, it is crucial to collect relevant information. Conduct research, consult experts or reliable sources, and gather data about the options you are considering. Having comprehensive information can boost your confidence and decrease fears.

Weigh pros and cons: Create a list of advantages and disadvantages for each option. Evaluate the potential outcomes, risks, benefits, and long-term implications. By objectively assessing the pros and cons, you can make more informed decisions and reduce the fear of making the wrong choice.

Practice assertiveness: Develop assertiveness skills by engaging in situations that require decision-making and assertive communication. Gradually expose yourself to situations that involve potential rejection or conflict. This will help build your confidence over time and reduce fear.

Accept imperfections: Understand that not all decisions will result in a perfect outcome. Accept that making assertive decisions involves risk-taking and the possibility of facing challenges. Embrace the learning opportunities and growth that come with making decisions, even if they lead to rejection or conflict.

Reflect and learn: After making decisions, evaluate the outcomes and learn from the experience. Reflect on the lessons gained, even if the decision succeeded or not. This ongoing learning process will build resilience and confidence in your decision-making abilities.

. . .

By using these strategies, you can overcome fear of rejection or conflict when making assertive decisions. Assertiveness and confident decision-making are skills that can be developed and refined over time with practice and self-reflection.

OVERCOMING SELF-DOUBT AND BUILDING SELF-CONFIDENCE TO TAKE ACTION ON DECISIONS

Overcoming self-doubt and building self-confidence to act on decisions can be a transformative journey that requires dedication and persistence. Here are steps to help you on this process:

Acknowledge your self-doubt: The first step toward building confidence is to recognize and accept your self-doubts. Understand that self-doubt is a natural part of being human and everyone experiences it at some point. Give yourself permission to feel uncertain, but also make a commitment to work on overcoming it.

Challenge negative thoughts: Self-doubt often stems from negative thoughts and beliefs about ourselves. Start by identifying these negative thoughts and consciously challenge them with positive and affirming statements. Remind yourself of your strengths, accomplishments, and the times you successfully handled similar situations.

Set realistic goals: Break down your decisions or goals into smaller, achievable tasks. By setting realistic goals, you create opportunities for small wins, which can strengthen your belief in yourself. Each accomplishment will fuel your self-confidence and provide evidence you can make decisions and act.

Surround yourself with positivity: Surrounding yourself with positive and supportive people who believe in you can have a tremendous impact on your self-confidence. Seek individuals who uplift and encourage you. Share your goals and decisions with them and listen to their feedback and support.

Celebrate small victories: It's essential to acknowledge and celebrate your achievements, no matter how small they may seem. Reinforce positive behavior by rewarding yourself for acting and making decisions. This positive reinforcement will help you build momentum and fuel your self-confidence.

Embrace failure as a learning opportunity: Fear of failure often fuels self-doubt. However, it's important to reframe failure as a valuable learning opportunity. Understand that setbacks and mistakes are part of the growth process and allow yourself to learn from them. Reflect on what you could have done differently and use that knowledge to make better decisions.

Practice self-care: Taking care of yourself physically and mentally is crucial for building self-confidence. Focus on self-care activities that help you relax, recharge, and maintain a positive mindset. Exercise regularly, eat nutritious meals, get enough sleep, and engage in activities that bring you joy and fulfillment.

Embrace discomfort and take calculated risks: Often, self-doubt holds us back from acting. Start by stepping out of your comfort zone and taking calculated risks. Each decision and action you take, no matter the outcome, strengthens your belief in your abilities and builds resilience.

Building self-confidence is a continuous process. Be patient with yourself, and even on days when doubt creeps in, remind yourself of your progress and the steps you are taking to overcome it. With time, consistent effort, and a positive mindset, you can overcome self-doubt and build the self-confidence needed to act on decisions.

IMPLEMENTING ASSERTIVE DECISION-MAKING IN VARIOUS REAL-LIFE SCENARIOS, INCLUDING WORK, RELATIONSHIPS, AND PERSONAL DEVELOPMENT

Implementing assertive decision-making in various real-life scenarios, including work, relationships, and personal development, can greatly enhance one's effectiveness and overall satisfaction in life. Assertive decision-making involves making choices that align with one's values, needs, and goals while considering the impact on oneself and others. It involves expressing oneself honestly, confidently, and respectfully, which allows for open communication, collaboration, and growth. Here are examples of how assertive decision-making can be applied in different areas of life:

Work:

- When faced with a new project or task at work, assertive decision-making involves gathering all the necessary information, considering one's own capabilities and workload, and then communicating with colleagues or supervisors to negotiate possible timelines and expectations.
- In a team setting, assertive decision-making includes voicing one's opinions, ideas, and concerns constructively during meetings and discussions while being open to others' perspectives. It also means taking ownership of one's responsibilities and setting boundaries when needed to maintain a healthy work-life balance.
- If faced with a challenging situation such as disagreements or conflicts, assertive decision-making involves addressing the issues directly, expressing oneself assertively without being aggressive or passive, and seeking mutual understanding and resolution.

Relationships:

- In romantic relationships, assertive decision-making requires open and honest communication about desires, boundaries, and expectations. It means expressing one's feelings and needs without fearing rejection or conflict, while also actively listening and respecting the partner's perspective.
- In friendships, assertive decision-making involves setting boundaries, saying "no" when needed, and expressing concerns or opinions honestly. It means being true to oneself while also considering the other person's feelings and needs.

- With family members, assertive decision-making means expressing oneself respectfully despite differing opinions or conflicts. It involves seeking compromises, finding common ground, and maintaining healthy boundaries to foster positive relationships.

Personal Development:

- In personal development, assertive decision-making entails setting clear goals and priorities based on one's own values and aspirations. It means taking ownership of one's choices and actions, and making decisions that align with personal growth and self-care.
- Assertive decision-making also involves saying "no" to opportunities or commitments that do not align with one's goals or values. It means being assertive in protecting one's time, energy, and resources to focus on personal growth and well-being.
- When faced with challenges or setbacks, assertive decision-making involves assessing the situation honestly, seeking support or guidance when needed, and taking proactive steps to overcome obstacles while remaining true to one's values and goals.

Starting assertive decision-making in these scenarios requires self-awareness, effective communication skills, and the willingness to focus on one's well-being and values. It can lead to improved self-confidence, stronger relationships, and a greater sense of fulfillment in various parts of life.

CHAPTER SIXTEEN SUMMARY: ASSERTIVE DECISION-MAKING: MAKING SOUND CHOICES AND TAKING ACTION

Chapter Sixteen delves into the importance of assertive decision-making in both personal and professional parts of life. The chapter emphasizes the significance of making confident and proactive choices while considering different perspectives, needs, and constraints. It explores the benefits of assertive decision-making and provides practical guidance for starting it in various real-life scenarios.

In personal life, assertive decision-making empowers individuals to effectively communicate their needs, preferences, and boundaries. By adopting an assertive approach, individuals can express their thoughts, desires, and concerns assertively and respectfully, leading to healthier and more fulfilling personal relationships. Assertive decision-making also promotes personal growth and achievement of personal goals by aligning decisions with one's values, interests, and long-term aspirations.

Similarly, in professional settings, assertive decision-making enables individuals to voice their ideas, suggestions, and concerns effectively. It enhances credibility, gains respect, and increases the chances of career advancement. Assertiveness also helps professionals establish healthy boundaries, manage their workload effectively, and engage in problem-solving and conflict resolution.

The chapter emphasizes the need to overcome barriers that hinder assertive decision-making, such as the fear of rejection or conflict. Strategies for overcoming these barriers are provided, including self-awareness, challenging negative thoughts, seeking support, gathering information, weighing pros and cons, and practicing assertiveness. The chapter also highlights the importance of self-confidence and offers strategies for overcoming self-doubt and building the confidence needed to act on decisions.

The chapter explores the implementation of assertive decision-making in real-life scenarios, including work, relationships, and personal development. It provides examples of how assertiveness can be applied, such as negotiating timelines and expectations at work, expressing needs and boundaries in relationships, and setting goals aligned with personal growth and values.

By adopting assertive decision-making, individuals can enhance their effectiveness, satisfaction, and overall well-being in various areas of life. The chapter concludes by emphasizing the transformative impact of assertive decision-making and the potential for personal growth, improved relationships, and a greater sense of fulfillment.

CHAPTER 17

MAINTAINING WORK-LIFE BALANCE: ASSERTIVENESS FOR A FULFILLING CAREER AND PERSONAL LIFE

RECOGNIZING THE IMPORTANCE OF WORK-LIFE BALANCE:

Recognizing the importance of work-life balance is crucial in today's fast-paced and demanding world. An imbalance between work and personal life can have harmful effects on both our mental and physical well-being. It not only impacts our relationships with family and friends but also hampers our overall quality of life.

When we focus on our career over our personal life, we neglect our own needs, such as relaxation, hobbies, and self-care. Stress and burnout can quickly creep in, leading to decreased productivity, compromised mental health, and even physical illnesses. Constant work-related stress can strain our relationships with loved ones, causing isolation and a sense of disconnect.

A healthy work-life balance promotes a fulfilling career alongside a rich personal life. It lets us maintain strong relationships, pursue personal interests, and take care of ourselves. A balanced lifestyle helps in mitigating stress, improving mental health, and enhancing overall well-being.

A fulfilling career is not only defined by working long hours or achieving professional milestones. Rather, it encompasses finding true satisfaction and purpose in what we do, while still dedicating ample time to our personal lives. When we balance work and personal life, we become more motivated, engaged, and creative in our professional endeavors. We can also fully enjoy and appreciate our personal moments, which contribute to our overall happiness.

Achieving work-life balance is a dynamic process that requires conscious effort and effective time management. Focusing on tasks, setting boundaries, and learning to detach from work during personal time are essential strategies for establishing a healthier balance. Effective communication with colleagues, supervisors, and loved ones is crucial to ensure understanding and support from all parties involved.

Ultimately, recognizing the importance of work-life balance means acknowledging that a fulfilling career and a rich personal life are not mutually exclusive. Both parts are equally important and contribute to our overall happiness and well-being. By striving for balance, we can achieve personal fulfillment, have strong relationships, and lead a more gratifying life.

SETTING CLEAR BOUNDARIES:

Setting clear boundaries is essential for maintaining a healthy work-life balance and overall well-being. It involves developing assertiveness skills to effectively communicate personal limits and preferences, making sure work does not encroach on personal time and vice versa.

To begin, it's important to assess your own needs and priorities. Take the time to understand how much personal time you need and what activities or relationships are important to you outside of work. This will help you establish clear boundaries that align with your values and goals.

Next, communicate your boundaries and preferences assertively and directly. Express your needs to your colleagues, supervisors, and clients. For example, let your colleagues know that you will not be available for work-related tasks during certain hours or on specific days. Use "I" statements to express how certain actions or requests affect you personally, rather than placing blame or being confrontational.

Maintain consistency in enforcing your boundaries. Follow through and reinforce your limits. If you consistently let work encroach on your personal time, others may develop the expectation that it's acceptable. Be firm and assertive when protecting your personal time and space.

Establish routines and rituals to separate work from personal life. Create clear boundaries between these two parts by starting practices that help you transition from one to the other. For example, you could establish a daily wind-down routine that includes activities like exercise, reading, or spending time with loved ones to mark the end of the workday.

Practice self-care and focus on your well-being. Set aside time for activities that help you relax and rejuvenate. This could include hobbies, exercise, spending time in nature, or pursuing personal interests. By focusing on self-care, you send a clear message that you value your personal time and well-being.

Last, be open to compromise and negotiation. Sometimes, certain work situations may require flexibility and changes. However, this does not mean your boundaries should be consistently compromised. Assess each situation individually and find a middle ground that respects your personal limits while being mindful of work demands.

Developing assertiveness skills and setting clear boundaries are crucial for maintaining a healthy work-life balance. By effectively communicating personal limits and preferences, and enforcing them consistently, you make sure work does not encroach on personal time and vice versa. Remember, protecting your personal well-being is essential for long-term satisfaction and success in all areas of life.

EFFECTIVE TIME MANAGEMENT:

Effective time management is an essential skill for success in both personal and professional life. Learning strategies to focus on tasks, delegate responsibilities, and maximize productivity can greatly enhance one's ability to handle multiple commitments and responsibilities, ultimately leading to more time being available for personal pursuits and maintaining healthy relationships. Here are key strategies to effectively manage time and achieve a better work-life balance:

1. Focus on tasks: Start by examining your to-do list and identifying the most important and urgent tasks. Use techniques such as the Eisenhower Matrix to categorize tasks based on their importance and urgency. Focus your energy on completing high-priority tasks first, as they have a greater impact on your goals.

2. Set clear goals and deadlines: Define specific, measurable, achievable, relevant, and time-bound (SMART) goals for each task. Establishing deadlines for yourself keeps you accountable and helps you stay motivated. Break down larger goals into smaller, actionable steps that can be easily managed.

3. Avoid multitasking: Contrary to popular belief, multitasking is not an efficient way to manage time. It decreases productivity and increases the likelihood of errors. Instead, practice single tasking, dedicating your full attention to one task at a time until completion before moving on to the next.

4. Delegate responsibilities: Learn to trust and rely on others by delegating tasks that can be handled by someone else. Identify team members or colleagues with the skills and willingness to help you. Delegating not only reduces your workload but also allows others to develop their skills and feel valued.

5. Organize and schedule: Maintain an organized work environment by decluttering your workspace and implementing effective filing systems. Use digital tools like calendars, task management apps, or project management software to schedule and track tasks. Create a daily or weekly schedule that includes dedicated blocks of time for specific activities.

6. Avoid procrastination: Procrastination is a major time management killer. Identify the reasons behind your procrastination and overcome them. Break down tasks into smaller, manageable parts and tackle them gradually. Use techniques like the Pomodoro Technique, where you work in focused bursts with short breaks between, to enhance productivity.

7. Practice self-care and focus on personal time: Recognize the importance of self-care and giving time for personal pursuits. Set aside time for activities you enjoy, such as exercise, hobbies, spending quality time with loved ones, or simply relaxing. Taking breaks and nurturing yourself helps maintain a healthy work-life balance and increases overall productivity.

8. Learn to say no: Avoid overcommitting yourself and learn to say no when necessary. Assess your workload and commitments realistically before taking on more responsibilities. Setting boundaries and managing your workload is crucial for effective time management.

By starting these strategies, you can develop effective time management habits that focus on tasks, delegate responsibilities, and maximize productivity. Ultimately, this lets you create more time for personal pursuits and nurturing relationships, leading to a more fulfilling and balanced life.

SETTING REALISTIC GOALS:

Setting realistic goals is crucial for achieving success in both professional and personal parts of our lives. It lets us establish achievable expectations, avoid burnout, and ultimately foster a sense of accomplishment and satisfaction. Here are key strategies to help you in this process:

Reflect on your values and priorities: Before setting any goals, take the time to reflect on your values and priorities. Understand what truly matters to you in both your professional and personal life. This will help you align your goals with what is most meaningful to you, increasing your motivation and dedication.

Break down bigger goals into smaller, actionable steps: Big goals can be overwhelming and may lead to burnout if not managed properly. Instead, break them down into smaller, actionable steps that can be done incrementally. This approach not only makes your goals more attainable but also gives you a sense of progress along the way.

Set specific and measurable goals: Make sure your goals are specific and measurable. Vague or abstract goals are much harder to achieve and assess progress. By setting clear targets, you can objectively measure your accomplishments and adjust your approach as needed.

Be realistic and consider your limitations: While it's important to challenge yourself, it's equally important to be realistic and consider your limitations. Assess your skills, resources, and time constraints before setting your goals. This will help you avoid setting expectations that are too high, which can lead to frustration and burnout.

Focus on self-care and maintain a healthy work-life balance: Burnout can hinder your ability to achieve any goals, so focus on self-care and nurture a healthy work-life balance. Take breaks, engage in activities you enjoy, and make time for relaxation. This will help you recharge and maintain a sustained level of motivation.

Celebrate accomplishments, no matter how small: Acknowledge and celebrate your accomplishments, no matter how small they may seem. Recognizing your progress reinforces a sense of satisfaction and motivates you to keep moving forward. It also helps you appreciate the journey rather than only focusing on the result.

Reevaluate and adjust goals when necessary: As circumstances change or new opportunities arise, be willing to reevaluate and adjust your goals. This flexibility lets you adapt and make sure your goals remain relevant and attainable.

By following these strategies, you can establish realistic goals in both your professional and personal life. Doing so will not only help you avoid burnout but also foster a sense of accomplishment and satisfaction as you progress toward your aspirations.

COMMUNICATING EFFECTIVELY:

Effective communication is a crucial skill that enables individuals to express their needs, concerns, and desires in both professional and personal relationships. It plays a significant role in fostering understanding, collaboration, and building healthy connections. To enhance communication skills, these strategies can be employed:

Active Listening: Actively listening to others shows respect and empathy. It involves giving full attention, maintaining eye contact, and providing verbal and nonverbal cues to show understanding. Paraphrasing or summarizing the speaker's message helps ensure clarity and avoid misinterpretation.

Clarity and Conciseness: Expressing thoughts and ideas in a clear and concise manner helps prevent confusion and misunderstanding. Using simple language, avoiding jargon, and organizing thoughts before speaking or writing ensures a coherent message.

Nonverbal Communication: Nonverbal cues, such as facial expressions, body language, and tone of voice, often carry more meaning than words alone. Being aware of one's nonverbal signals and noting others' cues enhances understanding and reinforces the intended message.

Empathy: Understanding others' perspectives and emotions is key to effective communication. Empathy involves actively acknowledging the other person's feelings and confirming their experiences, even if one does not agree. This fosters a safe environment for open dialogue and mutual understanding.

Open and Honest Communication: Being open and honest, while maintaining tact and respect, encourages trust and enables effective communication. Expressing needs, concerns, and desires directly promotes transparency and prevents unnecessary misunderstandings or conflicts.

Feedback and Validation: Providing constructive feedback and acknowledging others' contributions confirms their efforts, encourages growth, and strengthens relationships. Giving feedback in a non-threatening and specific manner makes sure the message is well-received and understood.

Conflict Resolution: Conflict is an inevitable part of any relationship, but effective communication can help navigate through it. Listening to all parties involved, acknowledging differences, and finding a common ground through compromise and understanding are essential for resolving conflicts constructively.

Cultural Sensitivity: In diverse environments, being aware of cultural differences and respecting them fosters effective communication. Learning about others' cultures, communication norms, and etiquette helps avoid misinterpretation and promotes a respectful and inclusive atmosphere.

Practice and Seek Feedback: Communication is a skill that can be improved through practice and seeking feedback. Engaging in conversations, participating in group discussions, and asking for feedback on communication style and effectiveness can help identify areas for improvement.

By consistently using these strategies, individuals can enhance their communication skills, both at work and in personal relationships. Effective communication builds trust, fosters collaboration, and leads to deeper connections and understanding.

PRIORITIZING SELF-CARE:

In our fast-paced and busy lives, it's easy to neglect our own well-being. However, practicing self-care is essential for maintaining overall health, happiness, and resilience. By incorporating activities like physical exercise, hobbies, and relaxation techniques into our daily routines, we can focus on self-care and improve our overall well-being.

Recognize the importance of self-care:

Understanding the significance of self-care is the first step toward making it a priority. Acknowledge that taking care of yourself enables you to better handle stress, boosts confidence, and improves the quality of your life. By recognizing and focusing on self-care, you are committing to your own well-being.

Incorporate physical exercise:

Physical exercise is one of the most effective ways to promote self-care. Engaging in regular physical activity not only enhances physical health but also releases endorphins, which boost mood and reduce stress. Find an exercise routine that suits your preferences, whether it's running, yoga, swimming, or dancing. Make time for exercise each day and ensure it becomes a non-negotiable part of your routine.

Cultivate hobbies and interests:

Engaging in hobbies and activities that bring you joy, and fulfillment is an essential part of self-care. It can be anything from painting, playing a musical instrument, gardening, writing, or cooking. Give time each day or week to indulge in activities that make you happy and stimulate your creativity. Focusing on hobbies helps alleviate stress, provides a sense of purpose, and lets you relax and rejuvenate.

Practice relaxation techniques:

Incorporating relaxation techniques into your daily routine contributes to overall well-being and resilience. These techniques include deep breathing exercises, meditation, mindfulness, or taking a warm bath. Set aside a few minutes each day to engage in these practices, allowing yourself to unwind and alleviate stress. By practicing relaxation techniques consistently, you can build resilience, reduce anxiety, and improve your ability to handle challenges.

Create a self-care schedule or plan:

To ensure self-care becomes a priority, create a schedule or plan that incorporates these activities into your daily routine. Make a list of self-care practices you want to engage in regularly, give specific time slots for each, and commit to sticking to the schedule. By treating self-care as an essential appointment with yourself, you are more likely to focus on it and reap the benefits.

Focusing on self-care is crucial for promoting overall well-being and resilience. By incorporating activities such as physical exercise, hobbies, and relaxation techniques into our daily routines, we can make sure caring for ourselves becomes an essential part of our lives. Remember, self-care is not selfish; it is a necessary investment in our physical, mental, and emotional health. Make self-care a priority and reap the rewards of improved well-being and resilience.

SEEKING SUPPORT AND COLLABORATION: BUILDING A STRONG NETWORK FOR WORK-LIFE BALANCE

In our competitive society, maintaining a healthy work-life balance while pursuing a fulfilling career and personal life can often feel like an arduous task. However, with the right support, collaboration, and accountability, this challenge can be overcome. This chapter aims to discuss the importance of building a support system and developing a network of like-minded individuals who focus on work-life balance. By seeking this support and collaboration, we can foster a conducive environment for personal growth, professional development, and overall well-being.

Recognizing the Need for Support:

- Acknowledging the struggle with work-life balance.
- Understanding the impact on physical and mental health.
- Realizing the advantages of having a strong support system.

Building a Support System:

- Identifying personal values and priorities.
- Seeking friends, family, and mentors who share similar goals.
- Joining organizations or support groups dedicated to maintaining work-life balance.

Nurturing Collaboration:

- Engaging with like-minded professionals in your industry.
- Attending conferences, workshops, and networking events.
- Utilizing online platforms and industry-specific forums for collaboration.

The Power of Accountability:

- Creating accountability partnerships or groups.
- Setting realistic goals and expectations.
- Regular check-ins, feedback, and support to maintain balance.

Benefits of a Supportive Network:

- Sharing experiences, challenges, and success stories.
- Learning from others' strategies for work-life balance.
- Inspiring and motivating each other to overcome obstacles.

Paying It Forward:

- Supporting others in their pursuit of work-life balance.
- Mentoring and sharing experiences.
- Creating a ripple effect of balance throughout your network.

To achieve work-life balance, it is crucial to build a strong support system and collaborate with like-minded individuals who understand the importance of this balance. By seeking support and collaboration, we can foster an environment that focuses on personal growth, well-being, and professional development. Remember, finding the right support and contributing to this network will not only benefit you but also empower others in their journey toward a fulfilling career and personal life.

CHAPTER SEVENTEEN SUMMARY: MAINTAINING WORK-LIFE BALANCE: ASSERTIVENESS FOR A FULFILLING CAREER AND PERSONAL LIFE

Chapter Seventeen emphasizes the significance of work-life balance in today's fast-paced world. It highlights how an imbalance between work and personal life can negatively affect our mental and physical well-being, relationships, and overall quality of life.

The chapter discusses the importance of recognizing work-life balance and how it promotes a fulfilling career and a rich personal life. It emphasizes the need for conscious effort, effective time management, setting clear boundaries, and developing assertiveness skills to establish a healthier balance.

The chapter also provides strategies for effective time management, setting realistic goals, communicating effectively, focusing on self-care, and seeking support and collaboration to build a strong network for work-life balance.

Ultimately, the chapter encourages individuals to strive for balance, leading to personal fulfillment, strong relationships, and a more gratifying life.

CHAPTER 18

COMMON MYTHS ABOUT ASSERTIVENESS

MYTH OF THE GOOD FRIEND:

- assumes any good friend knows our thoughts and feelings without them being said

This myth assumes anyone who is a good friend, or spouse, relative, or neighbor, or boss, or salesperson should be able to expect our needs, our feelings, our thoughts and give us what we would like without clearly saying what those needs are.

How many times have you heard yourself or someone else say "If he really was a friend, he would have known that I don't like... or "If she really loved me she would..." We often expect others to be able to accurately read our thoughts and feelings and then respond accordingly.

Unfortunately, most people are not very good at this, including most therapists. Because you are the only person who knows what is going on inside your head or your guts in time, it becomes your responsibility to let others know what you are feeling and thinking.

For if you do not verbally and specifically communicate what you want, expect, resent, appreciate or feel hurt by, the other person may never respond in a way that satisfies you. Resentment may grow on your part until you either "blow up" at the individual or begin to avoid him more and more.

Part of the myth, and a common incorrect assumption, is that values you hold to be important must be held in equal importance by others. This is not always the case.

MYTH OF ANXIETY:

- it is wrong for others to perceive us as anxious
- if people see I am anxious, I am not a good person

Essentially, people who try to live their lives within this myth are phobic of their own anxiety and phobic of revealing they are anxious in interpersonal situations. They fear others noticing their anxiety because they believe that to be anxious shows others that there is something wrong with them or they are "weak" individuals.

The stereotype of "the Great American Male" who is unafraid and unaffected by anything in his environment is the tragic "hero" of the myth of anxiety. Men who subscribe to this myth often feel prevented from expressing emotions when they are anxious.

One of the harmful effects of this myth is that individuals suffering from its influence often spend a great deal of energy trying to conceal their anxiety from others. However, in many cases, this concern to "look good" actually increases the anxiety level.

MYTH OF OBLIGATION:

- favors must be accepted to keep friendships
- shouldn't ask favors of friends because they can't say no

This myth can be divided into two parts. The first part assumes that if a person asks a friend for a favor, for that friendship to continue the friend must grant the request. Essentially, there seems to be little or no possibility for a refusal in a friendship according to this myth.

Individuals who never seem to say "No" are often seen as happy-go-lucky people always smiling and are always ready to help a friend. Others may often call on them for favors since they never refuse and never express they are feeling imposed on. These individuals often feel imposed on, and they feel resentful that others keep asking them for favors. However, they do not assert themselves and refuse any requests for they fear they will hurt their friend's feelings and their friends will not like them anymore.

The second part of this myth of duty equates making a request of someone with an imposition. The individual feels that the other person could not refuse the request, so rather than imposing on the person and possibly making him angry and resentful, the request is not made. As a result, the individual who avoids making the requests may have many unfulfilled needs.

CHAPTER EIGHTEEN SUMMARY: COMMON MYTHS ABOUT ASSERTIVENESS

Chapter Eighteen addresses common myths about assertiveness: the myth of the good friend, the myth of anxiety, and the myth of obligation. These myths can hinder effective communication and healthy relationships.

The myth of the good friend assumes others should understand our needs without us expressing them. The myth of anxiety suggests that being anxious is a sign of weakness.

The myth of obligation implies that favors must be accepted and making requests is an imposition.

Overcoming these myths promotes assertiveness, clear communication, and fulfilling relationships.

CHAPTER 19

BODY POSTURE, FACIAL EXPRESSIONS & VOICE CHARACTERISTICS (REVISITED)

There are almost an infinite number of body postures and facial expressions that a person can assume. Essentially, we should try to teach the individual to adopt a body posture and facial expressions that correspond with the feeling and the message the person is trying to convey: e.g., if an individual is trying to be tender, this does not correspond with a rigid, stiff posture.

In working with voice features -- not what is said, but how it is said- we deal primarily with volume, tone, and inflection. It has been found that many non-assertive individuals typically talk in a quiet, timid voice-- even if they are trying to be tender or angry.

The pitch of the words, the amount of quavering in the voice, and the stress on different syllables in the words can also be important variables.

TIMING:

A person may have the correct words, body posture, and gestures and still come across inappropriately if the timing of the assertive response is wrong. As the individual must learn what to do, he must also learn when to do it. This is perhaps a more difficult skill to teach, but, yet it is an important factor. For example, asking the boss for a raise right after he knowingly had a fight with another employee could be disastrous.

CHAPTER 20

CONVERSATIONAL AND OTHER RELATIONSHIP SKILLS

There are several component behaviors to establishing, maintaining, and terminating conversations. There are also several more skills which can enhance a new or well-established relationship between two or more individuals. In reality, these different behaviors can overlap and intertwine with one another during any interaction.

An individual possessing conversational skills is often regarded as: "sociable", "fun", "friendly", and sometimes "charismatic." The individual is more likely to have a greater number of acquaintances and friends than a person lacking in the ability to start and sustain conversations. Usually, before you can make a friend, you must first talk to the person and get to know him. Conversely, the "stranger" must learn something about you.

It is felt that being able to comfortably talk with others is a skill that can be important for those individuals who have relegated themselves to the roles of social wall flowers and isolates. With the proper skills and moderately low anxiety, such people can increase the probability of starting friendships and enhancing relationships in a variety of social situations. These skills are applicable whenever people meet people.

Before we describe some behaviorally defined parts of an interaction, there is an important point to consider. Although some of these skills will increase the probability of starting and maintaining a conversation with someone, they will not ensure an extended dialogue or guarantee a resulting friendship. If the person you are trying to talk with does not wish to participate, a conversation will probably not occur. Similarly, if the "stranger" and you cannot find mutual interests, a friendship will probably not develop. So, a risk is taken by a person trying to form a relationship with someone else. The risk is one of rejection or the possible fear of rejection. The risk of being alone and isolated is also present if no socialization attempts are made.

In working with individuals who show a deficit in establishing and maintaining enjoyable conversations, we can break down the process of a conversation into these observable components which can be labeled as conversational skills.

SKILL ONE: OPEN-ENDED QUESTIONS

To find out information about another individual, asking questions is often necessary. However, there are at least two kinds of questions you can ask, the open-ended question and the closed-ended question. A close-ended question can be answered with a simple one-word answer or grunt: "Do you come to the beach here often?", "Do you like that book?" Closed ended-questions such as these often elicit a "Yes," "No," or "uh-huh" response. If the individual does not elaborate on his "Yes," "No," or "uh-huh" response you will only acquire a minimal amount of information about him. Also, if closed-ended questions are asked one after another, the recipient of these questions may feel like they are being interrogated. Consequently, he may begin to back off from the interaction. One or two of these closed-ended questions may be appropriate at the beginning of the conversation to get the conversation started. However, if several questions are to be asked, it is recommended that open-ended questions be asked.

An open-ended question cannot easily be answered by a monosyllabic reply: "What is it about this beach that you enjoy?" or "How do you feel about the movement for equal rights for women in our society?" If you receive a "Yes" or "No" reply from these questions, you will probably think that the person was odd (or did not want to talk to you.) Open-ended questions are usually much more difficult to answer with a simple, short reply; consequently, you are more likely to gain more information about the individual when asking these open-ended questions. Actually, there are two categories of these open-ended questions. The first category includes those questions that begin with the words or ideas of what, who, when, or where: "What is it about sailing that is so exciting?", "Who do you recommend that I go to get my car repaired?" The second type of open-ended question begins with how or why, such as "How did you get into that business in the first place?" How and why questions tend to elicit detailed explanations from the individual; consequently, they give the individual an opportunity to tell you a great deal about themself. As such they are the most useful questions in leading to a comfortable interaction between two or more individuals.

SKILL TWO: ATTENDING TO FREE INFORMATION

Free information is information given by another individual which goes beyond the question being asked or is given without being asked. If, for example, you asked, "How do you like this windy weather we have been having?" and the other person replied by saying, "I'd like it a lot better if I was out sailing my boat rather than painting my house this weekend," you have obtained four bits of free information. The person likes to sail and has a sailboat, he owns a house, and he is presently painting his house. The free information given to you can be on a superficial level: "I don't like to paint." It can also be of a more personal nature: "Since my recent divorce, doing housework has really become depressing." After receiving some free information from an individual, you are at a choice point. You can either continue talking about the topic you were on, or you can begin talking about the free information. For example, with the question asked about the weather, you could continue talking about the weather, or you could branch the conversation onto the topic of sailing, owning a home, or doing housework. Where you go with the information depends on your personal interests and your interests in knowing more about the other person.

The ability to listen for and respond to selected pieces of free information is an important factor in starting and maintaining enjoyable conversations. People rarely volunteer information they do not wish to talk about. If we receive information from the other individual freely, it is usually all right to discuss that topic. We avoid discussing information given by the other individual which we consider embarrassing or of a too personal nature. If the information is too embarrassing or too personal for your comfort, that is one thing. However, if the other person has freely volunteered the information, it likely is not too embarrassing or personal for him.

This does not mean that all free information needs to be discussed. Some individuals may repeatedly volunteer free information you do not want to touch with a ten-foot pole: "Do you want to hear about my fifth sexual conquest of the week?" But one of the basic skills in good conversation is at least listening for the free information given by the other person. If the information is interesting, then talk about it or store it in the back of your mind so you can come back to it later. If the free information is of no interest to you, then skip it and listen for more free information that may interest you. Remember that if you pursue a topic in which you are uninterested or with which you feel uncomfortable, there is greater likelihood of a dead-end conversation, boredom, or high anxiety.

SKILL THREE: GIVING SELF-DISCLOSURE

Self-disclosure is free information you give about yourself during a conversation. To get more information from the other person, you must be willing and able to give information about yourself. To what degree the conversation stays on a superficial level or moves to a personal level depends on the information mutually shared. Typically, conversations between individuals who do not know one another well will move from a superficial to a more personal level, if both individuals contribute increasingly greater amounts of personal information.

It is suggested that the information revealed be gradually increased in intimacy if you are trying to move from a superficial relationship to a more intimate relationship. On each new level of intimacy, it is wise to pause and consider the other individual's response. If he is receptive and responds similarly, then you may want to disclose more intimate information.

As a rule of thumb in giving Self-disclosure, it is suggested that a person give about as much free information as he receives in a conversation. If too little free information is given, the other individual may begin to feel as if they are being interrogated. But if too much free information is provided without giving the other individual the opportunity to respond, the conversation may become too one-sided.

SKILL FOUR: INITIATING A CONVERSATION

You have the right to initiate conversation with other people. Initiating conversation is a skill in which you assertively start and maintain a conversation with friends, acquaintances, or "strangers". Most people enjoy meeting others and usually respond favorably to people who try to initiate contact with them. Occasionally, some people will not welcome such interactions. In these instances, you have the responsibility not to force yourself on them. Unfortunately, it is not immediately clear whether an individual is unwilling to engage in a conversation or whether he/she is initially shy or distrustful. Unwillingness to engage in social interactions is sometimes indicated by lack of smiles, hostile looks or comments, unresponsive nonverbal behavior, curt responses and failure to ask the inquirer questions in return. Conversely, willingness to engage in social interaction is indicated by: frequent smiles and gestures which indicate nonverbal responsiveness, verbal responses which disclose personal information, and/or questions directed to the initiator.

Many people report difficulty in knowing when to initiate a conversation and how to do it. It usually is easier to begin a conversation if you have the other person's attention and if you are not more than a few feet away so you can be heard easily. Once you catch the other person's eye you can smile and say whatever it is you would like to say. In most initial conversations, people search for a topic of common interest to break the ice.

Key: What do you say after you say "hello?" Try open questions, listen for free information, and use self-disclosure. . . try it! Be aware of keeping the conversation a two-way exchange. You can maintain the conversation for as long as desired by using open-ended questions, by listening actively and by giving and being open to free information and self-disclosure. Express a desire for future contact if you so choose --- set a time and place --- initiate! Why use it?

You have the choice of taking an active role in initiating interactions --- you don't miss social contact because of fear (of rejection, of what to say...) or anxiety.

The stress of being in a conversation is decreased -- by applying assertive skills you can relax and enjoy another.

You can expand/maintain your social network by becoming an actively interested partner-- a fun friend!

Counterproductive Beliefs

I don't have the right to impose on or bother other people.

But he/she is so important and someone like me can't go up and start a conversation. It's not right.

I don't know what to say. If I don't say something brilliant, the other person will think that I'm an idiot, and I should be a brilliant conversationalist.

It's risky to start conversations and besides, the other person may not like me.

SKILL FIVE: CHANGING TOPICS

Individuals may often terminate a conversation prematurely when they run out of questions to ask or when the conversation begins to focus on an area which they are not interested in. Most initial conversations, especially those between two strangers, take a while to get started. Before a common topic of interest is found, there may be several silences and several periods where topics are briefly picked up and dropped. Knowing that this is a common occurrence helps to alleviate much of this problem. It is also important to teach people they have some control over the direction the conversation takes, especially if only two people are involved in the conversation. If they are not satisfied with the current topic, asking another open-ended question, following up on some free information stored away, making a self-disclosure statement regarding another topic, or simply stating "I am really interested in hearing more about..." will often move the topic to another area more satisfying for the individual.

SKILL SIX: BREAKING INTO ONGOING CONVERSATION

Another difficulty frequently reported involves becoming part of an ongoing conversation. If the other individuals are open to having another person join in, their body posture and eye contact will convey this: They will look your way, give you eye contact, and they may realign their bodies, so they are facing you. If this seems to be the case, then it is a matter of standing by, listening to the context of the conversation, and then join in with some appropriate statement of self-disclosure, opinion, interest, or free information when appropriate.

SKILL SEVEN: SILENCES (THE PREGNANT PAUSE PHOBIA)

Have you ever become aware of the periods of silence that occur in a conversation? These periods occur and are normal. Sometimes this silence can be uncomfortable, and, at other times, it can feel natural. Some individuals, especially those who are inexperienced in conversational skills, are phobic of pauses or silences in a conversation. These individuals feel they should fill every moment of conversation with words. They irrationally see silence as a "pregnant pause" that will give birth to personal disaster if they cannot end it immediately. However, most conversations, especially those between individuals getting to know one another better, have periods of silence. Giving the individual some relaxation skills and some other things to think about during these silent periods can be useful.

SKILL EIGHT: TELLING STORIES

As the individual becomes more comfortable in talking with others, he will begin to talk in longer sentences and may relate stories, experiences, or jokes. However, in relating these, it is important that each have a beginning, a middle, and especially an end. Some potentially good stories seem to go on forever. Other stories seem to start from nowhere.

SKILL NINE: NONVERBAL CUES

In addition to verbal content skills, it is important to practice nonverbal conversational skills as well. For example, maintaining appropriate eye contact during the conversation rather than looking out the window or staring at the other person is important. Other variables such as body space and posture, smiling and head-nodding, animation, voice features, and so forth are also important additions to a smooth-flowing conversation. As such each variable may be worked on separately or as part of the total procedure in developing more interesting and effective communications.

SKILL TEN: TERMINATING CONVERSATIONS

Simultaneous to learning how to start a conversation, it is also necessary to learn how to terminate one. Can you recall situations where you felt "cornered" by someone talking to you, and you used some excuse such as "I have to go the bathroom" or "Oh, I forgot to make a phone call" to stop the interaction. Many clients do report situations such as this, and they are anxious about entering into any conversation where they may feel later trapped or imposed on. Consequently, some practice is required with things to do and say to terminate a conversation comfortably. Things to say may involve some "canned" types of verbal responses which may be given at the end of a conversation: "I really have enjoyed talking with you" or "I see someone here whom I have not spoken to for a long time; I would like to continue our conversation later if you are free then." Other solutions may involve a change in the verbal content-- less self-disclosure and fewer open-ended questions-- as well some nonverbal cues such as a decrease in eye contact and head-nodding or an increase in body distance from the other person.

SKILL ELEVEN: SELF PRAISE/POSITIVE SELF-TALK

It is important that the individual be able to recognize his strengths, interests, and opinions. Far too often, people can recognize and share their weaknesses and shortcomings rather than their interests.

In assertion training we try to reverse this process, that is, encourage individuals to share information about their hobbies, interests, strengths, and opinions.

With maneuvering, a person should be able to work almost any topic of enjoyable personal interest into a conversation.

We subscribe to the idea that thoughts occur first, then they lead to emotions that trigger behavior. Increasing control of our thoughts increases control of our feelings and actions. Further, we are constantly thinking and engaging in self-talk, which affects self-esteem. What you tell yourself about yourself is what you become.

If you engage in negative self-talk you inadvertently encourage yourself to meet that expectation. If you think "I can't do that procedure." "People don't like me." "I am ugly." "I will never find someone to love.", you unintentionally set yourself up to get what you expect. You can unnecessarily upset yourself and block yourself from reaching your desired goals.

Successful people talk confidently to themselves, boasting their feelings of self-esteem, thus encouraging success: "I know I can learn that procedure", "I am basically a lovable and attractive person."

SKILL TWELVE: GIVING AND RECEIVING COMPLIMENTS

A compliment phobic individual experiences a high rise in his anxiety level when giving or receiving a compliment. When you accept an honest compliment from another, you are listening to important feedback. If you do not accept the compliment or make it difficult for the other person to give it, you are questioning the validity of that judgment or the honesty of the person giving the compliment. A compliment, if accepted rather than rejected, can make both the giver and the receiver feel good. It is a mutually rewarding activity.

For example, assume that a person compliments you on a suit that you are wearing. Your response is "this old thing?" or "You don't really mean that." What your response communicates is that the person giving the compliment has poor taste in clothing or that he/she is an insincere flatterer. There are situations in which a compliment is undeserved, and you assert yourself and say you appreciate the compliment but that it is unjustified (for example someone else did the report for which you are being complimented.)

People often subscribe to counterproductive attitudes that make it difficult for them to accept compliments.

Counterproductive Beliefs

- People really shouldn't compliment me because I rarely deserve it.
- If someone says something nice about me, then I must say something nice back.
- I shouldn't have to compliment others. They should know how I feel from the way I act. Besides, I feel funny complimenting them.
- Why should I compliment him/her? He/she is getting paid for the work.
- If I go around complimenting people and telling them how much I appreciate them, they will think that I want something from them. Also, they may think that I am insincere.

- I don't compliment other people because most people don't know how to take a compliment gracefully; they get all flustered or embarrassed.

Techniques:

Acknowledge the complementor.

"Thank you."

Acknowledge the complementor and the statement.

"Thank you, Jean, for saying so."

Acknowledge the compliment and state your opinion.

"Thank you, Fred. I appreciate the compliment, but I haven't yet decided myself how much I like it."

Agree with the truth.

"Thank you, Lois. I think it looks nice on me too."

Positive Inquiry-- to be used when you have the gut feeling that the flattery is too general and probably manipulative.

"Thank you. But I don't understand. What is it about my personality that you enjoy."

Remember: A person who is independently assertive in his thoughts, feelings and behavior reserves the final judgment on how statements or actions of others, even the positive ones, affect him. You are the ultimate judge of praise.

Why Use It?

- It feels good to accept compliments honestly and comfortably.
- Other people enjoy hearing sincere, positive expressions about how you feel about them.
- Expressing compliments results in deepening and strengthening the relationship between two people.

- As a complementor, you give me positive feedback on my investment in you as a person (i.e., my honest compliment) when you can assertively receive my input.
- When people are complimented, it is less likely that they will feel unappreciated or taken for granted.
- It is an effective method of dealing with and confronting manipulative behavior.

Those instances in which you must express negative feelings or stand up for your legitimate rights with an individual are less likely to result in a high-pitched, emotional confrontation if they occur in a relationship in which you have previously complimented the individual about other parts of his/her behavior. Negative feedback is received more favorably and is less likely to be threatening if a generally positive climate exists between the people involved.

SKILL THIRTEEN: HANDLING CRITICISM (RESPONDING ASSERTIVELY TO CRITICISM FROM OTHERS)

- Relax and allow yourself to listen carefully to what the other person is saying. Breathing deeply may help you to relax.
- Paraphrase the criticism so the person knows you really "heard" and understood their point.
- Decide whether the criticism is fair or unfair. If unfair, bring up your question about unfairness rather than the criticism itself.
- Ask for clarification if the criticism is somewhat vague or unclear, e.g. "You are cold with people." Ask the person to give specific examples.
- If it's fair criticism, ask for specific suggestions or alternatives, such as what you might do to handle the situation or behave differently.
- Do not go into long, self-critical, or rationalizing excuses.
- If you disagree with the criticism, respond with opinion statements -- "I" statements rather than "You" statements, e.g.

"I think you misinterpreted what I said", instead of "Your interpretation is all wrong."

- When responding to someone speaking loudly and at a fast pace keep your voice low and speak softly.
- It's helpful to share your feelings about the criticism, "I'm annoyed that you're bringing up this issue again" or "It's not easy for me to take criticism."

SKILL FOURTEEN: GIVING CRITICISM TO OTHERS

There are several situations in which you are justifiably annoyed or displeased by the behavior of another person.

What you are trying to accomplish is direct, nonaggressive communication of your feelings. Such an expression might result in a change in your circumstances which originally caused your annoyance or displeasure. Sometimes it is too late to change the situation. However, by expressing your feelings you get these feelings off your mind, so you need not stew about them. The purpose of expressing negative feelings is simply to relieve you of them and make the other person aware of them so he/she doesn't repeat the same behavior again. We believe that usually you should express your justified annoyance and displeasure on the spot and hopefully resolve the matter then carry these unpleasant feelings around with you.

If you are bringing up an issue that took place some time ago, ask permission to bring up the issue now, i.e., don't spring it on the person, but set aside a time and place, e.g. "I'd like to discuss something that's been bothering me, do you have time now?" Or "I'd like to talk about what happened last Tuesday, how about some coffee?"

Be specific about feedback, give examples, cite situations and what the person said and/or did. It may help to outline grievances before verbalizing them, i.e., develop a script so what you would like to say so that your anxiety won't hamper your agenda.

Use personal pronouns, express your dissatisfaction, unhappiness, etc., without blaming or scolding the person, e.g. "It bothers me when you say. . .", instead of "You always say that I'm so and so..." Or "I feel uncomfortable when you do..." instead of, "You make me feel uptight when you..." Take responsibility for your own feelings, don't blame the other for making you react in a certain way.

Avoid name calling or otherwise "loaded" words, e.g., "you're so inconsiderate, cold, intolerable, unfair, controlling, paranoid, etc."

Assume an assertive body image, i.e., maintain eye contact, lean forward slightly, stand with your arms at your sides. Be serious--don't giggle or laugh.

Give the person suggestions as to what they could do to alleviate your discomfort etc. Provide ideas to change problematic situations. Again, some thought to these before speaking with the person would be helpful. Ask yourself, "How would I like things to be?", "What do I want?", e.g. "I'd like you to call before coming over, that would eliminate my dissatisfaction about your coming over unannounced."

Don't let negative feelings pile up until you explode at another person. Deal with things as they come up. Don't overload a person with criticism but limit the number of negative remarks you make in any one interaction. Bombarding a person with negative feedback is likely to make him/her become defensive.

Give positive feedback as well as negative if you have positive things to say. Often it is helpful to begin by telling a person several positive aspects of his/her behavior and then telling them what you don't like, e.g. "You have really been making an effort to do your share of the housework, but I noticed you didn't clean the kitchen floor this week as you planned. I'd like you to do it."

Avoid side-tracking. Often when people are uncomfortable giving and receiving criticism, they will avoid the issue by changing the subject or bringing up the past. Stick to the issue.

Again, it's helpful to express your feeling of discomfort in giving criticism. This may help to put the other person at ease, knowing you are honestly struggling with being direct, e.g. "This is difficult for me to say, but I do want to talk to you about it..."

SKILL FIFTEEN: COMMUNICATION OF FEELINGS WITH THE USE OF "I" STATEMENTS (RATHER THAN "YOU" MESSAGES)

Assertion training procedures encourage the use of "I" statements rather than using "You" statements. "I" statements relate specifically to what the person is feeling, thinking, and experiencing. The "I" statements are often avoided because individuals report they feel more vulnerable after making one of these statements. The individual is more vulnerable after using the word "I" however, using "I" statements provides a means of communication whereby individuals can become much closer in their relationship rather than further apart.

An "I" message is just what it sounds like; a direct, clear message about describing my feelings. Sending an "I" message is making room for myself in communication as active listening is a way of making room for the other person.

An "I" message tells the other person clearly how I'm feeling without blaming him: "I really get annoyed when you borrow my book and don't return it" rather than "You're rude and thoughtless about borrowing things" or "You're certainly inconsiderate" which are both "You" messages.

"You" messages, as their name implies, start off with the pronoun you are often blaming or judging, and hold the other person responsible for what I am feeling. (Actually, it is by choice to feel hurt, angry, bored, or good about whatever happens; I choose to feel what I feel, another person might feel differently under the same circumstances.)

Since I, rather than you, are responsible for my feelings, an "I" message is a more congruent statement about the source of my feelings. "You" messages are incongruent because they usually mask or distort feelings.

"You never listen to me!"verses"I don't feel heard."

"Your jokes are boring."verses"I feel impatient hearing the same jokes."

In an "I" message I own and describe my feelings; in a "you" statement I blame and judge you for my feelings.

An "I" message is easier to hear because there is no blame; without blame the listener is more likely to remain open and even offer to change. By contrast "You" messages cause defensiveness, resentment and resistance.

Your "I" message can be a powerful influence over the behavior of others. Your openness and willingness to risk sharing your feelings in an "I" message can encourage others to risk being more open and direct as well.

A simple formula for an 'I' message is: When you_____, I feel_____, because -_____.

SKILL SIXTEEN: STATEMENTS INSTEAD OF QUESTIONS.

Closely related to the more frequent use of "I" statements, we encourage clients to make statements of their feelings rather than hiding behind a dishonest question. A dishonest question is one in which we are not willing to equally accept a "Yes" or "No" answer or is a question we ask when we should really make a statement of self-disclosure.

For example, if you wanted to go out and play cards one evening, a statement like "I would really like to play cards tonight" is more appropriate than "Is it all right if I play cards tonight?"-- especially if you would sit at home and pout or start an argument if you received a "No" answer.

Likewise, the question, "Do you love me?" may be a cover- up for "I really miss you and would like you to spend some more time with me." The point we are trying to make here is that some questions are truly questions (Do you want tea or coffee with your dinner?) Whereas other questions are coded messages for hidden feelings. Rather than assume that the other person can decipher the coded message (remember the myth of the good friend) or will respond with the "correct " answer by chance alone, we encourage clients to state their feelings and wishes directly, with a direct "I" statement.

SKILL SEVENTEEN: SAYING "NO" OR REFUSING REQUESTS

What is it?

A skill in which you can comfortably and calmly refuse a request, demand, or manipulative statement. You can say no.

When or where to use it?

When you choose, for your own reasons, to refuse a request.

How to use it.

- You have the right to say no.
- You deny your own importance, your self-worth, if you say yes when you meant to say no.
- Saying no does not imply that you reject another. . . you are simply refusing a request.
- Say no assertively. Be direct, concise and to the point.
- When you say no, don't be influenced by pleading, begging, cajoling, criticism, flattery, or manipulative statements.
- You may choose to offer the reason for your refusal, but don't get carried away with never-ending excuses.
- Do not become overly apologetic ("I'm sorry... I feel badly...")
- Show assertive body language.:
- direct eye contact
- erect body posture
- clear and audible speech
- don't whine or sound apologetic
- use gestures and facial expressions for emphasis

- Saying "no" is a learned skill. First the behavior then the feeling.
- Saying "no" and not feeling guilty about it feels good and can easily become a habit.

Why use it?

- It feels good to consider your own needs and desires when considering others' requests and demands.
- You lose part of yourself when you place another's request or demands ahead of your own.

SKILL EIGHTEEN: EXPRESSING YOUR OPINION

What is it?

A skill in which you share with another your honest opinion, or how you feel on a subject or happening.

Key: I feel... I think...I believe...My opinion is...

When or where to use it?

When you choose, in a conversation, to assertively reveal how you feel about something or what you believe in.

How to use it?

- You have the right to express your opinion.
- You do not have the right to force your opinion on others; they need not accept your viewpoint, i.e., "My opinion is the right one. Agree or else!"
- State your opinion and support it. Conclude your opinion with a restatement. Then pass the conversation on to the other person.

"I believe...because..."

"In conclusion, I really feel..."

"What do you think?"

- Listen attentively. Don't be judgmental about another's opinion.

"Because you believe that, you're a rotten person."

- Remember-- you have the right to change your mind.

"You have an excellent point..."

- If you do not agree, or do not wish to continue the discussion, state this assertively.

"We'll agree to disagree."

Why Use It?

- Let's you take an active role in an interaction; you can carry half the weight of the conversation by being the leader for a while.
- Shows your personal interest in the conversant and/or the topic.
- Shows your very human willingness to take a risk and be vulnerable by saying how you honestly feel.

Limitations:

If you feel threatened by the topic and/or conversant, perhaps you cannot comfortably and calmly reveal how you feel. Remember it's your choice to decide when and where to express your opinion.

SKILL NINETEEN: STANDING UP FOR YOUR LEGITIMATE RIGHTS

This category, expressing your legitimate rights, relates to a variety of situations in which your personal rights are ignored or violated. Some examples include: consumer situations such as being short-changed, being sold defective merchandise, being served unsatisfactory food in a restaurant, receiving discourteous or inferior service, parent and family situations such as not being allowed to run your own life and make your own decisions, not having a right to your privacy, and not being allowed to raise your children in your own way; authority situations in which your right to make decisions is not respected.

The question of what one's personal rights are in a situation is not always resolved easily. However, we believe that the list of rights below is a set of guide-lines which can help people in most situations. Many situations which call for you to express your legitimate rights involve the issues raised in personal rights one and two, being fairly treated as a person of worth and making your own decisions. Rights three and four, on the other hand, relate to the more restricted, but frequent, set of situations in which you need to express your special rights as a consumer. It is our concern these rights are not followed blindly but are used with good judgment in each situation.

- You have the right to be treated fairly and as a person of worth with the same rights, privileges, and responsibilities as everyone else regardless of sex, race, religion, education, profession, social and economic status, etc.
- You have the right to make your own decisions and to live your own life as you choose (as long as you don't hurt other people or violate their rights).
- You have the right to get what you pay for, no matter how meager the price.
- You have the right to prompt and courteous service.

In general, if you are unsure of whether your rights are being violated, you may find it helpful to ask yourself two questions: "Am I being treated fairly as a person of worth regardless of sex, etc.?" "Am I being deprived of my right to make my own decisions?" Standing up for one's rights is important because it affirms oneself and one's sense of influencing one's life and circumstances.

In expressing or standing up for legitimate rights, extreme behavior should be avoided. It is exemplified by the person who is now aware and sensitive (over-sensitive?) to his/her rights and zealously crusades to stand up for every right that is violated because of the principle involved. Obviously, this behavior can be aggressive and obnoxious. The important point is to stand up for your rights where they are violated and in which it is objectionable to you that the violation has occurred.

There are risks involved when you express your legitimate rights. Be aware of these risks and weigh them before choosing your course of action. The most common risk is that, when you stand up for your legitimate rights, people, particularly those who have taken advantage of your failure to do so in the past, may not like your new behavior. We believe that it generally is more desirable to stand up for your rights in an assertive way, feel good about yourself, and take the possible risk than it is to squelch your feelings and self-esteem to avoid risking the good will of others. You will find that many people will respect you for your position.

Sometimes, standing up for your legitimate rights that have been clearly violated is inadvisable. Such situations are rare, but they include instances in which physical abuse or legal penalties are likely forthcoming. For example, if you are deliberately crowded off the sidewalk by a group of tough looking individuals, or if you are being given an unfair citation by an angry or hostile policeman, you probably will want to choose not to stand up for your rights at the time of the situation. Both are unusual, but they point out the importance of the need for brief but considered judgment before you act.

SKILL TWENTY: EXPRESSING JUSTIFIED ANGER

You have the right to express justified anger in an assertive way to other people. You have the responsibility not to demean, humiliate, or abuse them.

Many people have been taught that they should not feel anger or, at least, that they should not let other people know that they feel it, and above all, that they should not express it. It probably is impossible not to feel anger, and we believe that it often is undesirable and even damaging to an individual or a relationship not to express justified anger when felt.

A major reason people are taught not to express anger is because they are likely to become aggressive during such expressions. However, expressions of anger need not involve aggressive behavior. It is possible to raise one's voice, scowl, be intense, and show one's anger without threatening the other person, without insulting the other person, or being punitive or sarcastic. Granted this may not always be easy.

We feel it is important to express justified anger in an assertive way when it occurs. Anger is a volatile, potent emotional experience. It is difficult to bottle up and can lead to the development of psychological and psychosomatic complaints if it is felt but seldom expressed. In addition, people usually communicate their angry feelings. Many ways of expressing anger are not constructive. Some of these include revenge, impatience with the person who caused the anger or with other people, avoidance of the person who caused the anger, blowing up at the person over a trivial or minor incident, and so on. We feel you usually will feel better if you express your anger in an assertive way when it occurs, and that such expressions ordinarily will clear the air between you and the other person (s).

- Be brief. Once you've made your point, don't belabor it.
- Avoid making accusations.
- Use "I" statements.
- Be willing to listen to the other person's viewpoint. End the conversation if it may result in an argument.

CONCLUSION

Dear Reader,

As you conclude "Assert Yourself! Harnessing the Power of Assertiveness in Your Career," I hope you have embarked on a transformative journey of self-discovery, enhanced communication, and fulfilling relationships. Throughout this book, we have explored the profound impact of responsible assertive behavior and how it can empower you to achieve your career goals, build strong relationships, and lead a fulfilling life.

I want to express my gratitude for joining me on this empowering journey. Your commitment to personal growth and development is commendable, and I am confident that the insights and practical exercises shared in these pages have equipped you with the tools necessary to become more assertive in all areas of your life.

By embracing responsible assertiveness, you have learned the art of expressing your thoughts, needs, and beliefs confidently and respectfully, without denying the rights of others. This approach lets you strike a fair balance between self-advocacy and consideration for others, creating an environment where both parties feel heard and respected.

Throughout the book, we have explored the significance of assertive communication in the business world, delving into effective teamwork, conflict resolution, decision-making, leadership skills, and negotiations. By understanding the distinction between assertiveness, aggression, and passivity, you have gained valuable insights into fostering open dialogue, building trust, and collaborating effectively with colleagues and superiors.

Remember, assertiveness is not just a skill; it is a mindset that empowers you to establish meaningful connections, protect yourself from being taken advantage of, and make confident decisions aligned with your values. By focusing on self-care and self-respect, you are better equipped to nurture and support others, fostering a positive and harmonious environment in both your professional and personal relationships.

As you close the final pages of this book, I encourage you to reflect on your journey. Celebrate the small successes and milestones you have achieved along the way, for they are the building blocks of greater achievements. The practical exercises provided throughout the book are opportunities for you to practice and refine your assertiveness skills, incrementally building your self-confidence and shaping your assertive communication style.

Now, armed with the knowledge and tools you have acquired, it is time to step into the world as a more assertive and empowered individual. Embrace your true self, appreciate your strengths and weaknesses, and cultivate a deep sense of self-liking and comfort. I have full confidence in your ability to navigate any situation, express your needs and boundaries, and forge meaningful connections based on mutual respect.

Thank you for embarking on this empowering journey with me. Your commitment to personal growth is a testament to your dedication and determination. I wish you continued success as you apply the principles of assertiveness in your career and personal life. Remember, you have the power to transform every part of your life through the responsible harnessing of assertiveness.

With warmest regards,

Rae A. Stonehouse

ABOUT THE AUTHOR

Rae A. Stonehouse is a Canadian born author & speaker.

His professional career as a Registered Nurse working predominantly in psychiatry/mental health, has spanned four decades.

Rae has embraced the principal of CANI (Constant and Never-ending Improvement) as promoted by thought leaders such as Tony Robbins and brings that philosophy to each of his publications and presentations.

Rae has dedicated the latter segment of his journey through life to overcoming his personal inhibitions. As a 29+ year member of Toastmasters International he has systematically built his self-confidence and communicating ability.

He is passionate about sharing his lessons with his readers and listeners.

His publications thus far are of the self-help, self-improvement genre and systematically offer valuable sage advice on a specific topic.

His writing style can be described as being conversational. As an author Rae strives to have a one-to-one conversation with each of his readers, very much like having your own personal self-development coach.

Rae is known for having a wry sense of humor that features in his publications. To learn more about Rae A. Stonehouse, **visit The Wonderful World of Rae Stonehouse** at https://raestonehouse.com

Facebook: https://www.facebook.com/raestonehouse.aws

Twitter: https://twitter.com/raestonehouse

ALSO, BY RAE A. STONEHOUSE

Visit https://liveforexcellence.store/ for a selection of personal/professional self-development books by Rae A. Stonehouse.

If you have found this book to be helpful, please leave us a warm review wherever you purchased it.

APPENDIX:

APPENDIX ONE: ASSERTIVE PERSONAL RIGHTS

1. You have the right to judge your own behavior, thoughts, and emotions and to take the responsibility for their initiation and consequences on yourself.
2. You have the right to offer no reasons or excuses for justifying your behavior.
3. You have the right to judge if you are responsible for finding solutions to other people's problems.
4. You have the right to change your mind.
5. You have the right to make mistakes and be responsible for them.
6. You have the right to be independent of the goodwill of others before coping with them.
7. You have the right to be illogical in making decisions.
8. You have the right to say "I don't understand".
9. You have the right to say "I don't know".
10. You have the right to say "I don't care".

APPENDIX TWO: OBSTACLES TO ASSERTIVENESS

- fear of consequences
- lack of confidence
- fear of ridicule
- fear of criticism
- fear of not being liked
- fear of hurting feelings
- not feeling okay
- afraid of aggression (verbal or physical)
- shyness
- intimidation
- being passive
- lack of understanding
- feeling guilty
- wanting to please others
- anger expression in assertive way
- afraid it won't sound right
- feeling obligated
- uncertainty about one's rights
- personal beliefs
- cultural standards
- highly anxious or fearful in a situation
- lack of skills

APPENDIX THREE: MANIPULATIONS TO STOP ASSERTIVENESS

- making you feel guilty
- bringing up the past
- should messages
- conning
- threatening possible aggression
- laughing
- blaming

- disappointed
- putting you on the spot
- silent treatment
- belittling you (in front of others, causing embarrassment)
- making you feel inferior
- questioning your ability to...
- wanting return of favors
- pulling rank
- interrupting and talking over you
- comparing you with others
- crying
- putting you down
- helplessness
- emotional blackmail

APPENDIX FOUR: CHECKLIST - WHEN I MAY BE ACTING NON-ASSERTIVELY

1. **Am I aware when and if I have any of these symptoms, and whether they are related to anxiety.**

- teeth grinding
- nail biting
- finger or foot tapping
- foot jiggling
- artificial nervous laughing
- insomnia
- stomach churning
- heart beating fast
- jaw tightening
- headache
- tight neck and back muscles
- other personal ways of expressing tensions

1. **Do I do any of the following things to avoid assertion?**

- lash out, have aggressive outbursts
- procrastinate
- repress my feelings
- feel "down" or "low"
- give in to please others

www.ingramcontent.com/pod-product-compliance
Lightning Source LLC
Chambersburg PA
CBHW061137120626
46546CB00005B/1824